THE FANTASY FOOTBALL
BLACK BOOK

2020 Edition

By: Joe Pisapia

@JoePisapia17

Featuring

Adam Ronis @AdamRonis

Eliot Crist @EliotCrist

Matt Franciscovich @MattFranchise

Nate Hamilton @DomiNateFF

Derek Brown @DBro_FFB

Scott Bogman @BogmanSports

Tim Heaney @TeamHeaney

Chris Meaney @chrismeaney

Kate Magdziuk @FFballblast

Chris McConnell @CMac_FFB

Mike Randle @RandleRant

Billy Wasosky @BillyWaz88

with

Mike Tagliere @Mike TagliereNFL

Bobby Sylvester @bobbyfantasypro

Edited by Tim Heaney

Facebook: Fantasy Black Book

Instagram @fantasyblackbook

Click for link

RPV CHEAT SHEETS
NOW AVAILABLE!

Want all the RPV for every format on one easy to reference cheat sheet PDF file? Plus <u>FREE</u> updates sent in July & Aug!?

Send $5 to:

PayPal: <u>fantasyblackbook@gmail.com</u>

or

Venmo: @FantasyBlackBook

Be sure to write:

"Cheat Sheets" and add your email address in the comments!

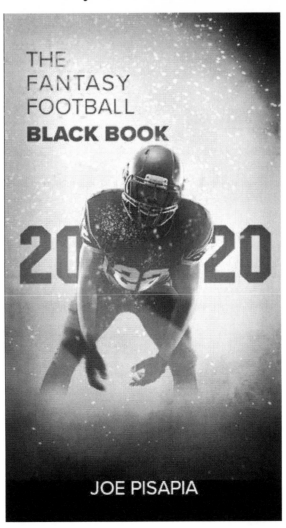

THE FANTASY FOOTBALL BLACK BOOK 2020

JOE PISAPIA

About the Authors:

Joe Pisapia *(@JoePisapia17 Twitter, @fantasyblackbook IG)*

*Joe is the author of the #1 best-selling **Fantasy Black Book Series** on Amazon and creator of the revolutionary player evaluation tool **Relative Position Value** (RPV). He currently hosts: **"Diamond Bets", "Fantasy Sports Today", "DFS Today (NFL)", "RotoExperts in the AM (NFL)"** on **SportsGridTV**, as well as "The Fantasy Black Book Podcast", "Pre-Snap NFL DFS Podcast" & "On Deck MLB DFS Podcast" (FSGA Best Fantasy Podcast Nominee '19) for **LineStarApp**. Joe is a former radio host for **Sirius/XM Fantasy Sports Radio** and won the Fantasy Sports Radio Show of The Year Award (FSGA 2016). He appears frequently on **CBS TV NY on The Sports Desk Show**, plays in **FLEX, LABR** and **Tout Wars** expert fantasy leagues. He's also worked for **Fantrax, RotoWire, The Sporting News, FanDuel** and **FantasyAlarm**. He's also the reigning Superflex champion of the **2019 Fantasy Football Expert FLEX League**.*

The Fantasy Black Book Podcast

Available on iTunes, Google, Stitcher, iHeartRadio and everywhere you listen to podcasts.

Subscribe today! Click Below on eBook version for link!

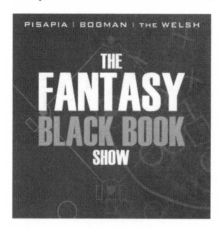

The Pre Snap NFL DFS Podcast by LineStar

Adam Ronis *has been working in the fantasy sports industry since 2008. He currently works at Fantasy Alarm covering fantasy football, baseball and basketball and sports wagering at Wager Alarm. Ronis also has been a part of Sirius XM Fantasy Sports Radio since the inception in 2010. He has worked for FullTime Fantasy, RotoExperts, FNTSY and Newsday. Ronis has been published in the New York Post, New York Daily News, Yahoo Sports, SI.com and the Associated Press.*

Eliot Crist *has been playing fantasy football for over 18 years and combines film and analytics to analyze NFL players. He has worked at Pro Football Focus, The Quant Edge, and 4for4, creating content and tools that give fantasy players the edge they need to win! You can follow Eliot on twitter @EliotCrist.*

Matt Franciscovich *currently works for EA Sports, focusing on Madden NFL competitive gaming. Previously, he spent 4 football seasons working as a fantasy analyst for NFL Media, appearing on NFL Network and as a regular voice on the NFL Fantasy Podcast in addition to writing and editing articles for NFL.com, setting weekly rankings, and developing relationships throughout the industry along the way. During his 5 years as a fantasy football analyst, Matt has also contributed to fantasy football outlets like CBS Sportsline, numberFire and FantasyPros, and is proud to be contributing to the Fantasy Football Black Book for the 2nd straight year.*

Nate Hamilton *is a regular contributor to the fantasy football industry. He has provided advice and analysis daily since joining Twitter (@DomiNateFF) in August 2013. He has produced content for some of the top fantasy sites including FantasyPros, The Fantasy Footballers, Fantasy Data, FantraxHQ, and more! He is the host of his own solo podcast, The DomiNate Fantasy Football Show, and provides live content on Periscope (@DomiNateFF)! Nate is a co-author of Amazon's #1 Best Selling "The Fantasy Football Black Book" with Joe Pisapia. He is a member of the Fantasy Sports Writers Association (FSWA).*

Derek Brown *has written for several websites, including The Quant Edge, 4for4, Player Profiler, and Fantasy Data. His DFS, redraft, and dynasty takes have been projected to the masses previously via Sirius XM, DK Sweat, and the Locked On Podcast Network. Born in Louisiana, he is a diehard Saints fan (Whodat). Derek now resides in Fort Worth, Texas, with his beautiful, football-loving wife and three kids. Follow Derek on Twitter @DBro_FFB.*

Scott Bogman *is co-owner and co-host of **InThisLeague.com**. He has been covering Fantasy Football, Baseball, Basketball and College Football for 5 years with ITL, **FNTSY Network** and **Fantrax**. He might have a bias toward players from the Pittsburgh Steelers, Texas Longhorns, Arizona Diamondbacks and Houston Rockets. You can reach Bogman through Twitter @BogmanSports or email ScottBogman@gmail.com.*

Chris Meaney *is a contributor for **The Athletic**, covering fantasy sports. Chris covered NHL, NBA, NFL and MLB as a producer, writer and host at **FNTSY Sports Network**. He was lead host of the daily live shows, **"Fantasy Sports Today"**, **"The FanDuel Show"** and **"Home Ice Advantage."** Chris has written for **The Associated Press**, the **New York Daily News**, **The Fantasy Footballers**, **Fantrax**, **The Quant Edge**, **NBA Fantasy**, **Play Picks**, **LineStarApp** and more. Follow Chris on Twitter @chrismeaney.*

Kate Magdziuk *joined the fantasy football community on Twitter back in August 2018. Prior to that, she was just an avid fantasy football player with an obsessive personality. She started the Weekly BallBlast Blog to cover fantasy news (shoutout to the 10 people who regularly read it in the 2018 NFL season), and things blossomed from there. Since then, she has also wrangled her wife Michelle into the fantasy Twitter arena, and together, they started BallBlast: A Fantasy Football Podcast. While they continue to work on the podcast together, Kate publishes her work as an NFL contributor for NBC Sports Rotoworld and RotoViz. Kate was recently accepted as a member of the Fantasy Sports Writers Association and looks forward to continuing her growth in the industry.*

Chris McConnell *is a 15-year fantasy sports veteran, and the host of the* **RotoBros Fantasy Football Podcast.** *Chris also runs the most successful fantasy sports community in the industry:* **FSA Fantasy Sports Advice & Analysis** *on Facebook, where he also hosts the weekly live show* **FSA Live.** *Self-proclaimed Chairman of the "Running Backs Don't Matter" community, Chris is a frequent guest on* **Sirius XM Fantasy Sports Radio,** *and a contributing partner at* **FleaFlicker.com.** *Residing in Georgia, Chris is a die-hard Atlanta sports fan (Rise Up!), and the biggest Preston Williams truther you'll ever find.*

Mike Randle *(@RandleRant) has covered NFL wagering for The Action Network, hosted the weekly RotoViz Fantasy Football Mailbag, and teams with Joe Pisapia on the PreSnap Wagering Podcast for LineStar. He has covered Fantasy Football for RotoUnderworld, FantasyPros, Dynasty Trade Calculator, and FanSided.*

Billy Wasosky ** YEARS PLAYING FANTASY FOOTBALL: 32 (this year will be my Rolling Rock! :) * NFFC Hall of Fame member, won over $400,000 playing fantasy football. 4 biggest wins......2019 NFFC Playoff Challenge Champions (w/Frank Mammola & Jeff Clampitt - $125,000); 2019 Diamond League winner (w/Frank Mammola) ($73,000); 2013 Football Guys Players Championship (2nd place overall - $40,000); 1995 Sporting News Fantasy Football Challenge Winner ($26,800)*

About the Editor

Tim Heaney *returns to edit his 5th Black Book after creating and managing content for the XFL. He has worked in the fantasy sports world for more than a decade, capturing industry titles (including baseball's Tout Wars) and awards for podcasting and magazine publishing. The New York native started with KFFL.com, which fused with USA TODAY Fantasy Sports, where he contributed football and baseball analysis to Sports Weekly and the web. From 2016-2019, he co-hosted podcasts and wrote/edited magazines for RotoWire; wrote ESPN columns; and offered betting tips for USA TODAY's SportsBookWire. He'll compete for the 3rd time in the Scott Fish Bowl this fall.*

The 2020 Edition is dedicated to:

My two daughters, Lu and Mic....you're the world to me!

SPECIAL THANKS TO:
Brian Alspach, Dennis Roy, Kyle Henley, Marty Smith, Jay Felicio, and the one and only Tim Heaney!
Cover Art Team by: Chad Greene

TABLE OF CONTENTS

Introduction

INTRODUCTION

10 years. A decade. 17 books.

I know many are finding the Black Book for the first time, and some of you have been here since Day 1. I'm equally grateful for you both! What started out as a project born from the frustration of trying to "carve out a niche" in the "fantasy sports industry" has become a full-fledged small business. A business that supports a single father with two daughters and now gives a platform to great fantasy minds that may not necessarily work at the "big box" fantasy shops. At least, not yet. I wrote the first Black Book while my then-infant daughter napped and during my endless train rides to teach part-time in NYC. The motivation was exactly the same now as it was a decade ago: to give people something that they can utilize to actually help them prepare and PLAY OUT their fantasy leagues.

I never started out to make Black Book a brand. I never anticipated it branching out into different sports with a staff of people working for me. I just wanted to produce the highest-quality alternative to what was out there on the market. That remains my focus and goal to this day. And I can assure you, I never, ever, thought it would be the #1 in FOOTBALL BOOKS on Amazon ahead of Tom Brady's "TB12,", let alone hold that spot every August for weeks on end year over year, for the last 3 years running.

For those of you who are new to the **Black Book, Relative Position Value** (aka **RPV**) is the one player evaluation tool that's simple, applicable to all leagues, adaptable to all formats, and friendly enough that it won't weigh you down -- the system you've been searching for your whole fantasy career. We are, and will always be, an independent alternative to what everyone else is thinking. In an age when being unique is nearly impossible, we strive to do so with RPV. We wouldn't be #1 every year in fantasy sports if our readers didn't have massive success with our product. We're not propped up by some mega site or venture capital group. We're basically me on a laptop with some help from my friends. That's what's always been so exciting about the Black Book. There's been a renegade spirit attached to it, and our readers have embraced that spirit over the years. They have made us the success we are today and have proven the theory that if you're capable of producing a passionate, high quality product, that you can still live the American Dream.

I get emotional every year, every single book, writing this introduction. I'm proud of this brand and the people who help me represent it annually. I remember the years when I wrote it solo, spending hours and hours, weeks after weeks, doing the work of an entire staff. To think of where we are now seems like a fairy tale, but it's now my "fantasy" reality. I love my team. I love my #TeamBlackBook listeners, watchers and readers.

Although I know many will skip this page jump right to the football (and that's fine by me), for those who catch these words, thank you. You've helped make a life for my daughters and I that at one time seemed impossible.

I promise you: In the next 10 years, I'll keep delivering you the goods, and we'll keep on winning together.

Joe

#TeamBlackBook 2020

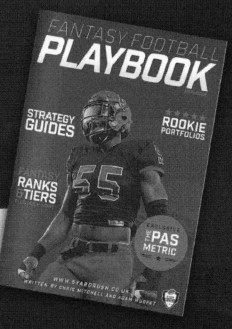

THE DOMINATE FANTASY FOOTBALL SHOW

WITH MICHAEL HAUFF
@THEFFREALIST

AND

@THEREALNFLGURU
ANTHONY CERVINO

FANTASY FOOTBALL

The FF Faceoff

PODCAST AND STREAM

W W W . F F F A C E O F F . C O M

FANTASY MEETS
REALITY WITH
THE FF FACEOFF

LIVE EVERY
TUESDAY AND
THURSDAY

@FFFACEOFF

GEOFF LAMBERT
FOUNDER & HOST
RYAN CEARFOSS
CO-HOST & WRITER
DYNASTY
REDRAFT
GERSON AGUIRRE & TIM STROBEL
DAILY FANTASY GURUS
GOINGFOR2.COM
& THE ARMCHAIR FANTASY SHOW

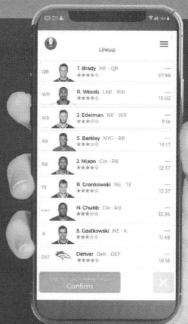

Chapter 1

RELATIVE POSITION VALUE (RPV)

Joe Pisapia

*"The format and style of your league dictates the value of a player
more than the talent of that player."*

Brace yourselves! The onslaught of everyone's "expert rankings", Top 100 lists, and other utter nonsense will be overtaking the fantasy football draft prep scene.

Obviously, well-educated and well-informed opinions are useful to an extent; otherwise, I wouldn't hire people to work with me on the Black Book. But that's just the beginning of a winning preparation process, while for most of the people you'll be playing against, it will be where their preparation ends.

NEVER mistake information and well-informed opinion for strategy. They're not, nor will it ever, be the same thing.

The sad part is that basically all that's out there is Fantasy Expert X's "Top 100," or Fantasy Expert Y's "Tiered Rankings" or Fantasy Expert Z's "Projections"? Don't get me started on those projection truthers, who never show accountability for their faulty computer software when things go awry. I don't know about you, but I don't want to live and die on hypotheticals alone. You need a cross section of these tools with an overriding, simple system, built in reality to truly understand how to approach each of your leagues.

Chances are you're playing in multiple leagues, with a myriad of different rules and scoring. That's why I created **Relative Position Value (RPV)**, the one tool to rule them all.

Rankings are what's out there, but QUANTIFIED Rankings are what RPV is all about. How much better is one player than another in a certain format? How drastic of a drop-off is there, not just player to player, but tier to tier? RPV can tell you.

RPV will automatically create player tiers -- and *define* them. It will also tell you how strong or weak a position player pool is, as a whole, entering a season. RPV is completely adaptable and adjustable to all league styles, depths and scoring systems. It's the single most useful player evaluation system available to fantasy owners and perhaps one of the easiest to grasp. I like simple and effective. RPV is both.

Year over year, this chapter won't change too much, because RPV is the foundation of the Black Book series. However, NFL players run fundamental drills in training camp, so if you're returning to RPV, consider this your return to fundamentals for the season and revisiting the basics that make you successful.

For those new to the Black Book series, RPV will have you seeing fantasy value in a whole new light. While other value-based drafting systems exist, they don't go far enough, nor do they separate the positions on a roster into subsets the way RPV does.

RB isn't a position, but RB1 is. (More to come on this later.) RPV is a more comprehensive and applicable system than any other thing you'll find out there.

STRIKING A BALANCE

Rankings are cute and wonderful debate fodder. However, it doesn't matter that Player A is ranked two slots above Player B on some "experts' board."

What REALLY matters is how much more productive Player A is than Player B -- and how much better they are than the other options at their position. Projections can be helpful, but not relied upon solely. When's the last time projectionists were held accountable (or held themselves accountable) for their many failures? The answer is hardly ever. Projections can have their place when you couple them with reality.

RPV compiles projections, previous season stats and three-year averages (when applicable) before weighing them to create a Black Book Point Total. That number is ALWAYS format-specific and is historically more reliable than projections alone, hence the success of the Black Book series. When it comes to rookies or young players, clearly we must rely more heavily on projections but use a cross-section to do so.

Now, what happens next to that Black Book Point Totals? Although I won't give away how I weigh them, I happily will give away the RPV formula: It's how we are going to proceed with a better understanding of fantasy football throughout the rest of the Black Book. RPV may challenge your perspective -- or quite possibly affirm feelings you've always had but now can see in black and white. Plus, once you have the formula, you can scale your own RPV for whatever insane scoring system you may be playing in, and you know who you are!

RPV IN THEORY

"RB isn't a position, BUT RB1 is!"

Considering a base of a 12-team league with two active RBs each week, a group of 24 running backs is a good starting point to grasp the RPV concept. However, it's NOT how we're going to truly utilize the tool.

Over 17 weeks in 2019, Christian McCaffrey led all PPR running backs with 471 pts for PPR scoring. Austin Ekeler ranked fourth with 309 pts. The 12th-best running back was Chris Carson at 236, and the 24th was David Montgomery with 170.

So, how much more valuable is each one of these guys compared to the other? Before we get ahead of ourselves, let's first see the formula in action.

The Fantasy Black Book formula is more complicated than the "basic" version I will present to you here. At the core, the way to determine the RPV -- or the percentage in which a player is better than the fantasy league average -- is:

(Individual Player Point Value – Fantasy League Average of the Position) ÷ Fantasy League Average of the Position = RPV

So, what is "Fantasy League Average?" Well, every league has a different number of teams and a varying number of active players at a given position. Some have 1RB/3WR/1FLEX, others play 2QB/2RB/3WR, and the list goes on and on.

The Fantasy League Average is a position's average production, based on the depth of your league. For example, if your league has 12 owners and starts 2RB every week, the RB pool is 24. If the top player scored 250 points and the 24th scored around 120, the fantasy league's scoring average is likely somewhere around 185 points. All players who score above this mark are "Positive RPV" players. The ones below are "Negative RPV."

Fantasy sports is a simple game of outscoring your opponents as frequently as possible from as many active positions as you can. The more your team lives in the "Positive," the greater your chances are week-to-week. It's like playing the odds in Texas hold'em. If you have a strong starting hand, the odds are in your favor. Sure, you may take some bad beats, but more often than not, the percentages will play in your favor.

Here's the trick! Even though there are 24 running backs, almost every team will likely have **one true RB1**, which means RB1 is its own unique scoring position. Rather than create a Fantasy League Average for 24 overall backs, it's more applicable to separate RB1s and RB2s into their own private groups and create an individual fantasy league average for each.

Now that we understand Fantasy League Average, let's get more specific. Last year, Christian McCaffrey scored 471 pts. The Fantasy League Average (or FLA) at RB1 (top 12) was 289 pts.

Subtract that FLA from McCaffrey's 471, then divide by that same FLA (289 pts), and you have a brilliant **Relative Position Value of +28% RPV: [471-289] ÷ 289 = 62.9%.**

That means McCaffrey was 62% more productive than the average RB1. That's substantial! That means something! For perspective, in 2018, Saquon Barkley was No. 1 with +28%. That just tells you how incredible CMC was last season.

If we took the RPV of running back as a whole over the top 24, McCaffrey's RPV would jump to a whopping +92% RPV, because the Fantasy League Average would be just 245. BUT we don't do that, because he'll be stacking up, head-to-head, against other RB1s most weeks in theoretical terms against other RB1 slots on other rosters. Calculating RB1s and RB2s as their individual positions gives a much more accurate depiction of a player's value, hence what makes RPV better than other value-based systems.

Are you in a 14-team league? Then use the top 14 to establish RB1 RPV. In a 10- team league? Adjust that way. The deeper the league, the more difficult it is to create an RPV advantage. The shallower the league, the less disparity you'll find (especially at WR). Therefore, you have more options to construct your roster in different ways. Have a wacky scoring system? Doesn't matter. RPV formula covers everything.

Below is the **Final RPV** for RB1s and RB2s from the end of 2019. You'll see not only the positive but also the negative side of RPV. The avoidance of overdrafting or overspending on players that can't really supply you "positive" production clears the path to success. You will also see as we go on how to create an RPV advantage.

2019 FINAL RB RPV for RB1 and RB2 (PPR scoring)

	Player	FPTS	RPV		Player	FPTS	RPV
1	Christian McCaffrey	471.0	63%	1	Joe Mixon	225.0	12%
2	Aaron Jones	314.0	9%	2	Todd Gurley	219.0	9%
3	Ezekiel Elliott	311.0	8%	3	Miles Sanders	218.0	9%
4	Austin Ekeler	309.0	7%	4	Le'Veon Bell	215.0	7%
5	Derrick Henry	294.0	2%	5	Kenyan Drake	214.0	7%
6	Dalvin Cook	292.0	1%	6	James White	200.0	0%
7	Leonard Fournette	259.0	-11%	7	Philip Lindsay	197.0	-2%
8	Nick Chubb	255.0	-12%	8	Devonta Freeman	197.0	-2%
9	Alvin Kamara	248.0	-14%	9	Josh Jacobs	191.0	-5%
10	Saquon Barkley	244.0	-16%	10	Marlon Mack	181.0	-10%
11	Mark Ingram	242.0	-16%	11	Melvin Gordon	180.0	-10%
12	Chris Carson	232.0	-20%	12	David Montgomery	170.0	-15%

The first obvious takeaway from last year was that McCaffrey had an all-time great fantasy season. The disparity became greater as Barkley missed extensive time, and Alvin Kamara and Dalvin Cook dealt with some injuries. Therefore, he didn't have enough challengers for the No. 1 spot to cut into that advantage.

The bottom of the tier wasn't bad; in fact, those low-end RB1s were quite productive. Chris Carson's minus-20% RPV was stark, but his 232 points were right in line with last year's 12th RB1. Basically, one player became super human (the mathematical equivalent of having a player and a half at one roster spot, and an elite one at that), which created a separation from the rest of the position.

That should return to a more normal standard in 2020, but it's striking nonetheless and something to take note of in auction leagues where you can control whom you select, as long as you're willing to pay the premium.

RB2 was much more forgiving. It only bottomed out at a -15% RPV, as opposed to the -20% RPV of RB1. It also had a lot of backs who didn't play much in the first half, like Miles Sanders, Kenyan Drake and Melvin Gordon. All three of those guys have clear RPV is not only a great tool to use in drafts but also analyzing what's happening around the league.

So, how can the fantasy player exploit RPV?

By having a high-end RB1 and then drafting ANOTHER RB1 as your RB2, you have "frontloaded" the position and created an area of strength.

The BIGGEST mistake fantasy owners make in any sports in "filling their roster for positions," instead of filling their roster with talent and strength.

When you fill your roster for positions, you get a mediocre .500 team. When you fill your roster with strength, you have an advantage over the rest of the field. As long as you can responsibly fill the other positions and avoid Negative RPV as often as possible, that roster strength can carry your season.

With more NFL teams adapting backfield committees, the true starting running backs are worth more than ever in standard formats. That especially goes for the RB1s who get goal-line carries and the bulk of touches. In PPR, you can build the same strength of front-loading WR1s as you can with RB1s, then make up ground later by buying running backs in bulk with upside. The tough sell there is the difference between definitive running back touches as opposed to expected wide receiver catches. One is frankly more reliable on a weekly basis.

The same could be said for Superflex/2QB leagues. By "frontloading" elite QB play, you simultaneously create a team RPV strength and weaken the pool for the other owners. RPV shows you how stark the value can be position-to-position. Some will bottom out at -10% while others will be -20%. With middle-tier receivers, you'll see little advantage to be gained.

RPV is the ultimate tool to truly define talent and, even more importantly, where the drop-off in talent lies. Rankings are biased. RPV is honest.

Obviously, every league will be different. Flex players and OP (offensive player) slots will change values a bit, but the RPV theory holds in **EVERY LEAGUE and EVERY FORMAT**! It just needs to be adjusted according to each league's specifications. In the Black Book, I've done much of the work for you, but you must be sure to adjust the RPV for your league(s) quirky scoring wrinkles if you are going to truly achieve ultimate success.

Now that we've outlined RPV, let's dive deeper.

RPV IN PRACTICE (Draft and Trades)

Last year, so many folks asked, "How does the Black Book determine its RPV?"

The Black Book takes a combination of 3-year averages (when applicable/available), previous season stats, and the upcoming season projections, creating a hybrid point total for each player that then gets utilized within the RPV equation.

For rookies, clearly there is no track record from which to work to create that number. Therefore, I use a composite of projected stats from a few choice entities, their college statistical profile, and their potential use in their new team system in order to create each rookie's point total for the RPV formula.

With so many new styles of fantasy football, it's crucial to understand the value of each position in your league.

For example, I prefer PPR (point per reception) setups that play a lineup consisting of QB, RB, RB/WR, WR1, WR2, WR3, TE, K, 5 IDP and an OP slot (which can be a QB) or a second mandatory QB spot.

If a quarterback is the most important skills entity in *real* football, I want my fantasy experience to mirror that truth. The RPV for this kind of league is different than a standard league. Teams play 2 QBs every week, therefore QBs become the equivalent of the RB1/RB2 RPV I just laid out in the last section.

Another big adjustment: Since I technically only have to start 1 RB, the talent pool is adjusted back into a "one large group of running backs" theory. Possession WRs and big playmakers garner attention. This is a perfect example of why a tool like RPV is so necessary. If I were to use the standard old rankings from a website or a magazine in this format, I would get crushed.

Now more than ever, there is no "one ranking system" that will be useful to you in any format. Ignore these Top 100 lists and nonsense like that -- and instead focus on the true value and weight of the player in *your* league. That's why RPV works.

The last best thing about RPV is the fact it strips away a lot of the hype and noise surrounding the athletes, as well as the fictional computer projections that can be misleading and downright destructive.

RPV is about understanding a player's value -- his ACTUAL value. Not what his value may be projected to be while you sit in last place wondering where you went wrong. The best way to evaluate a player is through a mixture of career averages, previous statistics and projections that are then weighed against the other players of the same position. NOT PROJECTIONS ALONE!

Using only last year's numbers will give you a great team ... for last season. Using just projections will give you a great team ... in theory. RPV will give you a great team in REALITY!

You can choose to be great at one spot or two, but if you are below-average at other places, your overall RPV will even out. You may find yourself managing a middle-of-the-road team. Being above-average in as many places as you can, even without a top-flight star, you will find yourself consistently out-producing your opponents. If you use RPV correctly, you may even find yourself above average in most places and great in others, which makes you the one to beat. It's the ability to adapt, adjust and understand that separates us. RPV is the difference-maker.

RPV can tell you not only how much better a player is than the average for his position, but also how much better he is than the next guy available at his position on the draft board. Understanding these RPV relationships is key in maximizing your positional advantage.

To illustrate this point and its application, let's take a draft-day example. It's your turn to pick, and you have openings to fill at WR and TE. The top available players on the board at each position look like this:

WR

- Player A: +15% RPV
- Player B: +10% RPV
- Player C: +8% RPV
- Player D: +7% RPV
- Player E: +5% RPV

TE

- Player F: +8% RPV
- Player G: -2% RPV
- Player H: -2% RPV
- Player I: -4% RPV
- Player J: -6% RPV

At first glance, you might be inclined to take Player A, who is a +15% better than the average at his position. All other things being equal, however, Player F is probably the better choice.

Even though he is only +8% better than the average, the drop-off between him and the next-best player at his position is 10 percentage points. That's a significant dip. If you take Player A now, Player F almost definitely won't be on the board when your next pick rolls around, and at best you'll be stuck with an average or below-average tight end.

If you take Player F now, however, you'll be on the right side of that 10% RPV advantage over the teams who haven't drafted a TE yet. You'll also probably lose out on Player A at WR, but you will still most likely get someone from the above list (Player C, D or E) -- all of whom are trading in the same RPV range and, more importantly, still in the positive. It may not sound like a big deal with mere percentage points, but it adds up the more you rise above or fall below the average RPV threshold.

By picking this way, you end up with a strong advantage at one position while remaining above average at the other. The alternative is to be above-average at one position and decidedly average or worse at the other. That's the reason so many fantasy owners fail. Usually they base these decisions on the **name** of the player instead of his Relative Position Value. The same can be said when evaluating trades. You must look at what advantage you're gaining and potentially losing in each deal.

The owner who does that effectively has a distinct advantage. Remember, don't marginalize your strength!

Everyone has access to opinions, but now you have access to RPV.

Chapter 2

DRAFT STRATEGY

If the Black Book is truly going to be the best tool out there, then each league format needs its own specific draft strategy section. Not a "blurb," not "general strategy", but a true look at building a roster core in different formats. This year, that includes high stakes leagues!

You'll see lots of magazines with their mock drafts, but really that's not super helpful at the end of the day. Instead, Nate and I decided to do 4 rounds of "Core Building" from each draft slot in the hopes of showing not only where we think the value lies in each format, each pick -- but to also present a cohesive voice of how to approach your draft slot.

Now, obviously every draft will be unique. What we want to do it give the reader an approach to be prepared for that inevitability. As you read on, each draft is broken down into thirds in terms of approaching draft slots. We'll also discuss each format in shallower and deeper leagues and how the draft pool affects certain positions. There will certain players who miss the first four rounds, and we'll justify why that's the case.

We want to prepare you better than everyone else does in the fantasy football industry for ALL of your drafts! Standard, PPR, Superflex, Best Ball … EVERYTHING!

Successful drafts are built with a great knowledge of the player pool, RPV and the ability of an owner to be flexible. I'm not a fan of mock drafting. I feel it sometimes leads folks into a false sense of security, and other times people are just trying out concepts, and that's not going to prepare you for a draft with money on the line.

The only thing mocks are helpful for is training your ability to be flexible and react as runs happen. The discipline of when to go with the pack and when to run the other direction is crucial, and RPV is extremely useful in those instances. Remember, it's all about building roster strength, not just filling open roster positions.

AUCTION LEAGUE STRATEGY

Most drafts are of the snake variety, which saddens me, as I am a fan of auctions. It allows for the most prepared owners to excel.

You may think, "Hey where are the dollar values?" That's not a strategy. Dollar values for players are a suggestion: You can find them on any site, and they'll all be similar.

I want to give you an **approach**. The biggest mistake people make with auction leagues is following artificial and arbitrary dollar amounts many publications will put out.

Winning leagues with salaried players is about (1) Getting proven big-time, RPV-advantage talent, and (2) finding cost-effective, low-priced talent on the back end. The "stars and scrubs" philosophy is effective because you are paying a premium for proven talent and getting premium production.

If you're a student of the fantasy game, you'll know where the values sit in single-digit-priced players. Plus, the waiver wire will be viable to make up ground in-season and fill any holes. Injuries always present new talent on a weekly basis nowadays. However, that talent is rarely STAR-LEVEL.

Therefore, you should invest heavily and without apology for the big-time RB/WR/QB talent when you can in the draft. Solidifying those guys is paramount! The worst thing you can do is let a great talent go for that one extra $1. You'll regret it later.

Also, the best in-draft strategy I can suggest is try to avoid nominating a player you really want on your team early when it's your turn early in a draft. Every time you bleed money out of the room from other owners, that's less money they have to fight you on players that you want on your team. It sounds like small potatoes, but if you do that consistently in the early going, it'll pay late dividends.

Moreover, I would avoid starting to bid on any player you truly want until the first time you hear "going twice". There's an intimidation factor at play in auctions that's equal parts football knowledge and in-draft gamesmanship. Many owners get frustrated when this happens. They go from thinking they have a player to not having them. Some can recover, but most get thrown off their game. Then they panic. Then they either back off or make a bad inflated buy. There's no reason to artificially inflate salaries of players you like by bidding on them in the early going. Wait until the bidding slows. Be patient. Then pounce. And please, forget what the websites and magazines tell you is an "appropriate salary" for a player. The "appropriate salary" is what gets you the player you believe in on your roster!

The upcoming draft sub-chapters will take you through the values, but more importantly the "Core Building". To carry this over from snake to auction is simple. You'll see in each format which team cores we prefer in each format and why. That will help you budget and attack similar strategies with dollars rather than draft picks.

PPR SCORING STRATEGY

Nate Hamilton

4-Round Draft Strategy

Tm	Round 1	Round 2	Round 3	Round 4
1	Christian McCaffrey	Todd Gurley →	Keenan Allen ↓	D.K. Metcalf
2	Michael Thomas	Clyde Edwards-Helaire	Miles Sanders	Calvin Ridley
3	Saquon Barkley	Travis Kelce	Patrick Mahomes	Deebo Samuel
4	Ezekiel Elliott	Lamar Jackson	D.J. Moore	A.J. Brown
5	Julio Jones	Amari Cooper	Melvin Gordon	Le'Veon Bell
6	Dalvin Cook	Mike Evans	Kenny Golladay	Mark Ingram
7	DeAndre Hopkins	Josh Jacobs	Adam Thielen	Devin Singletary
8	Davante Adams	Aaron Jones	George Kittle	T.Y. Hilton
9	Alvin Kamara	Kenyan Drake	Odell Beckham Jr.	Cooper Kupp
10	Derrick Henry	Tyreek Hill	JuJu Smith-Schuster	Austin Ekeler
11	Chris Godwin	Nick Chubb	Stefon Diggs	Chris Carson
12	Joe Mixon →	Leonard Fournette ↑	Allen Robinson →	Courtland Sutton ↑

In point-per-reception (PPR) leagues, your strategy should shift a bit from standard scoring. In PPR, catches earn a fantasy point (or, often, half a point). This immediately raises the value of those heavily targeted in the aerial game. Yes, this does mean that the value of wide receivers is heightened, but do not allow that to brainwash you into only thinking about that position.

Plenty of running backs (especially in today's NFL) still present tantalizing value; they not only carry the ball effectively but also have a significant role as a pass catcher. Target one of these running backs early; the WR pool is deeper, which offers you a bit more security in the fact that you can draft plenty of quality WRs in later rounds.

I'm not necessarily preaching to go RB-heavy at the beginning. Allow the draft to fall to you.

Pay attention to how your draft is going. Is everyone else drafting WR-heavy? If so, get yourself a top-tier WR early since you now know more RBs will fall to you with your next pick. If you find that your leaguemates are drafting with a nice balance of the two positions, I'd suggest grabbing that stud RB who's also involved in the passing game.

Many strategies will work to find success in fantasy football. I am simply sharing with you my personal opinion on what works best for me.

2020 Player Pool approach

Since the NFL has been evolving over the last decade to a more pass-heavy league, you'll notice the amount of running backs selected in the early rounds of PPR drafts do not drop off as much as they typically would in this format.

Each season that passes, more and more lead backs are also great pass-catching options. This is where the game is today. In the past, when wide receivers would DomiNate the early rounds, the increase of pass-catching running backs have brought balance back to draft rooms.

You'll notice the same number of running backs were taken in the first 4 rounds in this PPR mock draft as the standard mock. Joe and I do favor the running back position, but we know the value difference in PPR and remain unbiased. This confirms my thoughts on how the league is changing, especially at the running back position. Most running backs offer similar value in PPR as they do in standard scoring. The only difference: You can hold out until the late rounds to get strictly pass-catching backs who provide a safer floor than they would in standard scoring.

What's your draft slot?

Picks 1-4: The top 4 players selected in this mock are not far off from the standard mock. Michael Thomas gets a slight bump because he's an absolute PPR monster. The mindset shouldn't change much with your first pick in this range. You should highly consider the top WR with these picks, but often, you will see a 3:1 ratio between the RB and WR positions.

It's important to remember that you have many draft picks between your first 2 selections. In most cases, you'll want to grab at least 1 top-tier WR with your first 2 picks. If you don't, you may find yourself relying on younger, unproven talent at WR. This could pay off, but you may not feel amazing about that decision as your draft unfolds.

Picks 5-8: Although there were the same number of running backs selected in the first 4 rounds of PPR and standard mocks, more wide receivers were taken in the first round of this one. It makes perfect sense given the scoring format. Don't allow this to force your hand and go after a WR in these positions if you favor running back. In my experience, whenever I end up taking a WR with my first pick, I'm often tempted to take another with my second pick given the PPR emphasis.

When I start my draft with WR-WR, I find myself not happy with my RB corp. This often leads to trading (which is always fun) one of my top selected WRs for a stud RB. This negates the strategy I had in my draft and leads to me second-guessing myself throughout the season. Just be careful with Picks 5-8 and remember to think "balance."

Picks 9-12: Again, my favorite range from which to draft, regardless of scoring format. In this range, you can select 2 top-12 players at their position. Don't be afraid to go RB-RB here. As you can see in this mock draft, 2 of the 4 positions (Picks 9 and 12) used this method and still ended up with a couple of great WRs to complement and balance their teams.

The reason I love drafting from this area is because you really can't screw up your draft with these early picks. You find yourself with two picks close to one another, and because of that, you are often drafting players in the same tier each time, especially in the early rounds.

Embrace the comfort of having an uninterrupted pair of picks.

How a 10-Team league changes your approach

I could just copy and paste what I said in the "Standard Scoring Strategy" chapter, but that would be lazy writing. So, I will say the same thing but in a different way!

When you are in a shallow league, you'll notice there is less urgency with your picks. The player pool is naturally deeper since fewer teams are taking from the cookie jar. (I was hungry when I wrote this.) Just don't forget to build your roster appropriately and fill the positions of need as you move through your draft. Don't get sucked into take the best player available. Instead, take the best player available at the position you need most at that time.

Everyone is going to love their teams. Most, if not all, owners will appear to have "stacked" rosters. Just don't be too cocky about your squad. Before you begin gloating that you stole the draft, pause and look at your competition. You may quickly realize that you are around the same level as everyone else as far as roster depth goes.

How a 14-Team league changes your approach

Participating in deeper leagues presents unique challenges. You do not have the privilege of a deeper player pool as you would in smaller leagues. This should simplify your strategy.

It's critical to bring balance to your roster as early as possible. You may not love your draft picks in the middle rounds, but look around you: Everyone will have slim pickings at this point. What can separate you from most of your league is securing the elite wide receivers and running backs with your first 4 selections. Trust me, you will enjoy your draft more knowing that you've built a solid foundation to your roster before you get to the middle rounds.

Which draft slot to choose (if you can)

I know I'm repeating myself here, but I would love a pick toward then end of the first round. There is nothing more satisfying than beginning your draft with 2 players close to the top of their respective tiers. A lot of times, people are disappointed they did not get a top-4 pick, but for me, this is where you want to be drafting from.

Players who missed making the core

You will notice Tyler Lockett did not make it into the first 4 rounds of our mock draft. It really comes down to preference. I personally selected D.K. Metcalf over Lockett because I felt his upside is slightly higher than Lockett's moving forward. Although Lockett did finish ahead of Metcalf in 2020, what Metcalf produced (with 24 fewer receptions than Lockett) in his rookie season should earn him more of the target share going forward.

Another player that disappeared is James Conner. He's a versatile back in an offense that should present him with enough scoring opportunities. So why leave him out? Sometimes, you need to pay attention to the moves made by the team and allow that to have a bigger voice over a player's talent.

The Steelers drafted running back Anthony McFarland with the 124th overall pick in the 2020 NFL Draft. Sure, they could use him as a complementary piece to Conner, but a team bringing on a running back with its 1st pick of the 4th round could often lead to more of a timeshare than you'd want from one of your first fantasy picks.

How To Ruin Your Draft

I said this same thing in the 2019 Black Book: "Running backs are still a vital piece of your roster in PPR." It's even truer this year. There are more pass-catching RBs, and you should secure at least 1 or 2 with your first 4 picks.

Think of these running backs as the foundation of your roster. Not only do they provide you with stability of touches, but they add receiving value in a format that adds a reward for simply making a catch.

Do not get caught up drafting all the WRs early and missing your window to acquire running backs that could produce top fantasy points for your squad.

STANDARD SCORING

Nate Hamilton

4-Round Draft Strategy

Tm	Round 1	Round 2	Round 3	Round 4
1	Christian McCaffrey	Todd Gurley →	Patrick Mahomes ↓	DeVante Parker
2	Saquon Barkley	Miles Sanders	Odell Beckham Jr.	T.Y. Hilton
3	Michael Thomas	Kenyan Drake	Chris Carson	Courtland Sutton
4	Dalvin Cook	Amari Cooper	Clyde Edwards-Helaire	Stefon Diggs
5	Ezekiel Elliott	Tyreek Hill	Mark Ingram	Allen Robinson
6	Derrick Henry	Mike Evans	JuJu Smith-Schuster	Jonathan Taylor
7	Joe Mixon	Lamar Jackson	Devin Singletary	Adam Thielen
8	Alvin Kamara	Travis Kelce	Melvin Gordon	Cooper Kupp
9	Aaron Jones	Josh Jacobs	Kenny Golladay	Kyler Murray
10	Julio Jones	Chris Godwin	Le'Veon Bell	A.J. Brown
11	DeAndre Hopkins	Nick Chubb	D.J. Moore	Russell Wilson
12	Leonard Fournette →	Davante Adams ↑	George Kittle →	Keenan Allen ↑

As I mentioned in the 2019 Black Book, the "standard" format is what I was first introduced to in fantasy football. It will always have a special place in my heart.

Unfortunately, it appears it's no longer the "standard" format after all. There are still plenty of "old-school" standard leagues out there, though, so let's discuss!

Typically, in standard drafts, you will see the draft begin with a heavy focus on running backs. Running backs touch the ball more than wide receivers, and if you don't get extra points for catches, this automatically increases the value of all the "workhorse" backs. Obviously, the more you touch the ball, the more chances you have to register fantasy points.

You will notice, there are a few examples in which we deviated from what you would typically see in a standard draft. I'll explain those moves if you just keep reading this amazing chapter of this amazing book that helps you to be amazing in fantasy football.

2020 Player Pool Approach

Every year that passes (pun intended), we are seeing more value being placed on wide receivers position and pass-catching running backs. Though this mock is based on a standard (or what should now be called "non-PPR") league, you will notice more love given to WRs and RBs who can fetch passes. The league has become pass-happy, and these roles benefit more than they normally have in the past in standard formats.

The mindset has changed, regardless of format. Touches from your bell-cow RB are still important in standard leagues but may not be the No. 1 focus for all your league mates.

What's your draft slot?

Picks 1-4: More often than not, you will see the top 4 running backs drafted with the first 4 picks. When you have one of these top picks in drafts you are looking for volume and consistency. The top running backs will often provide you with both. Every season, there are few WRs that make the discussion for a top-4 pick. Michael Thomas is certainly on that level. There is simply no more consistent wideout in the game. So, if you find yourself picking from the 3rd or 4th spot, I'd give some thought to adding Thomas before you slam the Draft button on a running back. There should still be enough quality RBs to be had with your next few picks.

Picks 5-8: Now this is the usual area from where we see the first wide receiver go, but since the top WR was taken at 1.03, anyone possibly thinking of taking a WR reverted back to the safety of choosing from the top running backs. It may be a bit surprising to see Ezekiel Elliott fall to the 5th spot behind Dalvin Cook, but we are assuming full health for players here and believe Cook has a bit more upside should he play 16 games in 2020. Still, we're splitting hairs.

Getting back to the pick range of 5-8, you'll notice all 4 picks were running backs. Once the top 3 or 4 RBs are gone and you begin your draft with an RB, it'll often convince you to approach the rest of the draft with a balanced mindset. Each of these picks did not choose a running back with their second selection, but 3 of the 4 circled back to the RB well in the 3rd round. These can be tricky positions from which to draft, but you need to have "best player available" in mind; you will have about the same number of players taken between each of your picks. You will not have many opportunities to grab the top 2 players in your queue, so go after your guys in these positions and don't rely on hope that they will make it back to you.

Picks 9-12: This may be my personal favorite area to pick from in drafts. If you play your cards right, you are likely guaranteed 2 top-12 players at their position to start your draft. Sure, you miss out on the elite top few picks, but unlike your league mates drafting from the middle positions, you have 2 picks close to one another.

Drafting at the end of the first round while also having an early 2nd-round pick that can set you apart from the rest of the league. It's highly recommended you go with any combination of WR/RB with your first 2 picks. Whether it's RB/RB, WR/WR, or a balanced of RB/WR, you are going to feel pleased with the start of your draft. You do want to be careful here, however. Although it's tempting to take the top two WRs in this position, remember this is standard scoring, and more often than not, running backs taken this early in drafts will produce a safer floor for your team. You also want to keep in mind that your next pick will not happen until the end of the 3rd round. So, going RB/RB or a balance of RB/WR may be best in most cases.

How a 10-Team league changes your approach

In smaller leagues, everyone ends up loving their team by the end of the draft. There are fewer spots between picks, so it may feel like you're getting amazing value with each pick. There is truth to that, but it can also be misleading.

There are the same number of players in the pool but fewer league owners to take from it. This may result in you always taking the best player available and could lead to you losing sight on strategically filling your roster spots. Yes, there are more elite players to be had in a league this small, but don't forget you can't play all 10 of those WRs you stocked up. Look at which position you need to fill or add depth to and draft accordingly. Sometimes, you must pass on a higher-ranked WR to fill that 3rd RB spot and balance your roster.

How a 14-Team league changes your approach

I often preach balance when roster-building, and it's never more critical to practice this distribution than when you find yourself in a deep league. You can quickly allow your draft to get away if you're not careful. If you decide to go with the same position (for example, wide receiver on back-to-back picks, especially early on in drafts), you will find yourself watching most, if not all, running backs you didn't draft and thought 'I'll get them with my next pick' disappear from the draft board. It's important to remind yourself that you're in a deep league and that you will be waiting for quite some time before your next pick. Choose wisely.

Another thing to keep in mind in deeper leagues: Do your homework! Otherwise, you'll likely find yourself drafting players you've never heard of or old veterans you never thought you'd draft. Read up on sleepers and/or late-round players to draft. You will want to feel confident and happy with your picks toward the end. If you don't do your research, you will not enjoy the later rounds and possibly check out. This is not the recipe for deep-league success.

Which draft slot to choose (if you can)

I would love to draft toward the end of the 1st round for the reasons I mentioned in the "Picks 9-12" section. I love having picks close to one another, and it always feels great to begin your draft with possibly two top-12 players at their position. Even though I must wait a while between my pair of picks, I am often happy with selecting 2 players in the same tier.

Players who missed making the core

Joe and I originally had Marlon Mack in the first 4 rounds, but since the 2020 NFL Draft, that had to change. The Colts selected stud running back Jonathan Taylor in the 2nd round, which naturally knocked Mack's value down a bit.

Taylor was arguably the best running back coming out of the draft and finds himself behind one of the best offensive lines in football. It's a no brainer to expect he'll have immediate fantasy value in 2020 as the likely choice for majority carries at some point, if not out of the gate.

Another player who takes a hit for 2020 and falls outside of our mock draft is Chargers running back Austin Ekeler.

Philip Rivers, who heavily leaned on Ekeler in 2019, is no longer with the team. The Chargers have the likes of Tyrod Taylor at QB to likely begin the season, while grooming rookie Justin Herbert. Ekeler may not be the safety blanket with these QBs as he was for Rivers. Secondly, rookie Joshua Kelley will impact Ekeler's touches. Yes, Ekeler was still able to find success with Melvin Gordon on the field, but this offense is changing, which presents reason to fade Ekeler a bit in 2020 considering his success last season.

How You Can Ruin Your Draft

In standard leagues, it's best to go with safer options in the early rounds to give your fantasy squad a safe floor. You can ruin your draft by trying to be "too cute" with your early picks. I wouldn't reach too early on unproven rookies if you can help it. There is a time and place for everything, and although some rookie selections could pay off, it's best to save the risky plays until the later rounds in standard-scoring drafts.

SUPERFLEX/2 QB LEAGUES

Joe Pisapia

Tm	Round 1	Round 2	Round 3	Round 4
1	Christian McCaffrey	Chris Godwin →	Drew Brees ↓	Chris Carson
2	Saquon Barkley	Josh Allen	Mike Evans	Baker Mayfield
3	Lamar Jackson	Nick Chubb	Austin Ekeler	Clyde Edwards-Helaire
4	Patrick Mahomes	Leonard Fournette	Josh Jacobs	Allen Robinson
5	Ezekiel Elliott	Aaron Jones	Carson Wentz	Kirk Cousins
6	Michael Thomas	Matt Ryan	Amari Cooper	George Kittle
7	Dalvin Cook	Tyreek Hill	D.J. Moore	Philip Rivers
8	Julio Jones	Derrick Henry	Kenny Golladay	Tom Brady
9	Russell Wilson	Davante Adams	Odell Beckham Jr.	Ben Roethlisberger
10	Kyler Murray	DeAndre Hopkins	Miles Sanders	Kenyan Drake
11	Dak Prescott	Joe Mixon	Todd Gurley	Jared Goff
12	Deshaun Watson →	Alvin Kamara ↑	Travis Kelce →	Aaron Rodgers ↑

2020 Player Pool approach

As the reigning, defending, undisputed FLEX Superflex Champion, I couldn't be more excited to share this chapter with you. As my readers know, Superflex leagues are my passion, and in my opinion, they should be the industry standard!

The NFL is a quarterback league, and our fantasy experience should reflect that. As in life, timing is everything. When you take your QBs is all about gaining an advantage in RPV and making sure you are responsibly adding RB and WR talent at the same time. This can be a delicate balancing act, but hopefully I can walk you across the tightrope safely to the other side, where your trophy awaits!

The 2020 player pool for Superflex is made of some distinctive groups. You have your definitive "elite" QB tier that should fly off the board quickly. You also have a strong and deep veteran group made up of Aaron Rodgers, Drew Brees, Tom Brady, Ben Roethlisberger, Philip Rivers, Kirk Cousins, etc. I prefer to go with the elite group to start off with, but if you have a top-3 or bottom-3 pick, you can safely take top RBs/WRs and then double up on the grizzled veterans who should be safe for 2020. However, considering their mileage, you MUST draft a 3rd QB (like a Drew Lock) later on to back yourself up and prepare for a stretch in the season without them.

If it's a Superflex with full-point PPR, I suggest you can let RBs come to you. You can make up some ground with pass-catching backs and favor big-time WRs. In a half-point-PPR scenario, I would lean toward TD upside as the decision-maker. Look for guys on good offenses when building your team, and overall, don't fear the QB-WR stack. Some people avoid that, but the right pairing at the proper value, such as Patrick Mahomes in the 1st and Tyreek Hill in the 2nd, is appropriate.

The trick to building a strong roster core in Superflex is ironically being flexible. Have a plan and your targets, but then be sure to look at the board as a whole and how it's developing. Some leagues may collectively see QB as deep and devalue them. If that starts to play out, take advantage and grab those elite QBs. If QBs start flying (and some go too high), then don't be afraid to take chances on young guys like Joe Burrow and Daniel Jones. They may have plenty of developing to do, but they could end up as solid fantasy QBs regardless of that fact.

And follow @Flex_Leagues on Twitter. They're the industry leagues run by The Athletic's Jake Ciely (@allinkid), where the best of the best in fantasy football play against each other. A lot can be learned from those drafts in terms of preparing for your own!

What's your draft slot?

Picks 1-4: I'm still all for taking one of the elite RBs in the top of the draft, regardless of the Superflex format. However, if you want Mahomes or Jackson, then this is your shot. You can easily take one of them then double up on RB or WR at the Round 2-3 turn. You can also split 1 RB and 1 WR from what's best on the board. I would lean toward talent over position at that turn every time. There's plenty of depth at both.

Picks 5-8: This is the more challenging grouping, because you're at the mercy of others in the middle. I have zero qualms about taking a Kyler Murray or Russell Wilson this early, but it's safer to choosing from the elite WRs/RBs that fall here with Mahomes and Jackson pushing down the likes of Julio Jones and Dalvin Cook. However, you must monitor the QB pool carefully the next 3 rounds. You don't want to miss out and end up with two low-end QB2s. That's not the path to success in this format.

Picks 9-12: You can be very dangerous here! The 10 slot is where I won the Flex Superflex league taking Mahomes then DeAndre Hopkins last year. I would say you must leave the first two rounds at the bottom with at least one QB. You can double up with top QB's and simultaneously create a roster advantage, while dorwning the QB pool for everyone else.

How a 10-Team league changes your approach

Supply and demand changes here. EVERY 10-team league should be Superflex. Where's the challenge to starting just 10 QBs every week? The answer: none. I'm even more apt to reach for the best QBs early and often. There are plenty of RBs this year from which to pick.

How a 14-Team league changes your approach

The inverse is true with the deeper Superflex. I'm more apt to take best player available early on before imposing my will in Rounds 3-6. Taking a 3rd QB for byes is crucial. Be sure to do that, and you can always trade excess later.

Which draft slot to pick (if you can)

Give me No. 4, which guarantees me either the top 2 RBs or QBs. If not, I like 9-12. Avoid the middle. I don't like being at the mercy of the group.

Players who missed making the core: Zach Ertz, Jimmy Garoppolo, JuJu Smith-Schuster, Keenan Allen, Adam Thielen, Most Rookie RBs

It's nothing personal. These guys are all super-talented. It's just the numbers game of QB value in the format. But it's an excellent reminder of what kind of WR and RB talent could be available in Rounds 5-8. Get your QB(s)!

How To Ruin Your Draft

As I said, you have options at QB this year, but the veteran group does have real risk attached to it. If you can, stay on the younger side at QB1. You also see how many talented players can slip past the 4th round, but the QB pool can dry up very quickly. You've been warned!

BEST-BALL LEAGUES

Tim Heaney

Do you love drafting a fantasy football team but don't want to spend time tending to it? Want to get a jump on preparing for your in-person local draft by testing strategies? Try best-ball leagues.

Draft a squad without any inseason roster management: No setting lineups, making pickups or arguing with leaguemates over trades. After each week of play, the league website calculates the highest-scoring players that will fill up each starting position. Though there may be deviations with head-to-head records or other factors, generally the team with the most points at the end of the season wins.

I enjoy participating in best-ball drafts early in the offseason to start my research for my normal leagues. Working on strategy while competing for a prize will be much more educational than a mock draft.

You can still use the tips outlined in this book about player analysis and non-PPR/PPR strategy, but get to know these nuances. In best-ball, you're stuck with the players you draft. They better be players you like -- especially as a mix of stability and boom-or-bust.

GAME TYPES

As always, the 1st part of prep is to know your league's scoring and settings. The variety of best-ball formats is increasing. The one I play most frequently is the BB10 -- formerly MFL10s from MyFantasyLeague, which offer entry fees as cheap as $5. The National Fantasy Football Championship's Draft Champions games don't have pickups or trades but require inseason lineup management.

Prize payout: Your strategy and priorities should change depending on how many end-of-season places are rewarded -- sort of like DFS cash games vs. tournaments.

Does the winner take almost all, or all, of the pot? Does 2nd place merely get entry for next year or another small consolation? Go for broke; chase all the upside. Do the Top 3 all get a decent payout? Are you playing for a major overall prize on top of your league's reward? Strive for a tad more stability.

Prospective best-ball competitors have plenty to choose from as the format continues to grow. It's all about finding the settings you like.

ROSTER CONSTRUCTION

Most of the time, you're given 20+ total roster spots. BB10s have 20. They don't use a kicker, but otherwise, it's a typical lineup: 1 QB/2 RB/3 WR/1 TE/1 Flex/1 DST, with 11 bench spots. Assuming that lineup in a 12-team league, here's my typical best-ball plan:

- **3 QBs** (15% of your roster space)
- **6 RBs** (30%)
- **6 WRs** (30%)
- **2 TEs** (10%)
- **RB/WR Flex** (5%)
- **2 DTs** (10%)

I have extra coverage at the ever-important starting QB but still leave myself with upside-laden backups. Use those percentages as a guide for leagues with more than that. Playing a best-ball game with anything fewer than 20 roster spots seems like less fun. We want more players, right?

In 1-QB leagues, I make sure I have 2 RBs and 2 WRs coming out of the 1st 4 rounds -- if not 3 and 3 after the 1st 6. As long as you have one of these foundations, you can gauge the best way to attack the rest of the draft pool.

That RB/WR flex depends on how things break, though I only consider going with a 3rd tight end in leagues with deeper benches than 20. If you're in a superflex or 2-QB setup, I'd certainly use that extra RB/WR flex on a 4th quarterback.

If you still play in kicker leagues, use 1-2 spots from your combined RB-WR allotment. (I'd hate to play in any kicker best-ball leagues with fewer than 22 roster spots.)

An even better way to improve your best-ball kicker experience: Look for contests with "Team Kicker" instead of individual K's**.** The turnover is so high at the position during the season, so you shouldn't have to worry about handcuffing this, of all positions.

BEST PRACTICES

Manage bye weeks. Because you can't make inseason pickups, make sure you have enough active players to cover the starting lineup every week.

Say you finish a draft with 6 wideouts but didn't notice that 4 of them have a Week 11 bye. You're already starting at a disadvantage that week, considering that you're guaranteed to have only 2 out of 3 eligible WR starters. Enjoy the zero from WR3! Don't hurt your quest for a title *before* injuries, depth-chart changes, and other typical NFL madness has a say.

This doesn't apply to early-rounders. Seek talent with your first 6-8 picks. If you happen to have doubled up on a bye with your core names, use your remaining picks to fuse upside with schedule coverage.

Don't forget schedule quirks. While it's right to at least be mildly skeptical of preseason strength-of-schedule rankings, you can at least use some early hints to dictate preferences.

For example, try to balance your D/STs: Back up your top unit with a No. 2 who has a great matchup during No. 1's bye. Also, see who's likely to play in cold weather in December and gather alternatives accordingly. (Another point for non-kicker best-balls!)

Embrace week-to-week volatility as you build depth. RPV remains important, and you still want a foundation of consistent snap volume and opportunities for touches from RBs, WRs and TEs.

But to properly maximize your draft returns, tap into your DFS side as you move down the board. Take a stab at game-flow-dependent players who'll give you big weeks, even if they have subterranean floors:

- Pass-catching backs like the Browns' Kareem Hunt or the Patriots' James White
- Potential goal-line vultures like Packers rookie A.J. Dillon
- Wideouts who thrive on the deep ball, like the Ravens' Marquise Brown and the Texans' Will Fuller

Gone are the headaches of guessing when to start these talents. Instead, you can envision metrics-breaking +EV weeks from your value picks.

Wait for quarterbacks. Unless your format is superflex or QB-enhancing scoring, collect 3 quarterbacks after you land your "mix of 6" running backs and wide receivers. (I like 3 of each to start.) On that note:

Stack your top WR(s) with their QB(s) -- when logical. I wouldn't necessarily run to select Teddy Bridgewater over other more talented QBs because I selected D.J. Moore in the early rounds. Bridgewater doesn't excite me enough to do that.

But a Kenny Golladay-Matthew Stafford pairing could be a league-winning plan because I trust Stafford to more consistently post a weekly best-ball-worthy ceiling. Since I'm telling you to start with star wideouts, and the position is once again deep for 1-QB lineups, the timing works out.

This gets tricky when you look at the elite wideouts paired with top QBs, like Tyreek Hill-Patrick Mahomes and Amari Cooper-Dak Prescott. While it's a great plan for superflex or 2-QB contests, it puts you behind a bit with ROI in 1-QB games.

Consider RB-Defense stacks. Something like joining 49ers RB Raheem Mostert as your RB3 and San Francisco's elite defense could benefit from the Niners' often dominant game flow.

Be slightly more aggressive in grabbing your team defense. I usually just draft the D with the best Week 1 or early-season schedule, then discard them as the season flow dictates. We don't have that luxury in this format.

I typically nudge my preferred D/ST units a few rounds earlier than usual. Not before I take 5 RB/5 WR, mind you, but I might stretch a bit to get a top defense in Round 15-16 and wait to get a sleeper as my 2nd near the end. As much as I normally love to throw darts at streaming D/ST types, I don't want to be left with something like a Detroit-Cincinnati mess.

Year of the Cheap Best-Ball Tight End? This is somewhat 2020-specific but worth noting. Legit breakout candidates like Miami's Mike Gesicki, Detroit's T.J. Hockenson and Denver's Noah Fant stand out as possible bargains at tight end.

On top of that, more and more NFL squads are set to increase their use of 12 personnel (two tight ends), so even the second TE who comes onto the field could see enough looks to generate the occasional big week.

This trend opens up more profitable names to target in the middle-to-late rounds you can score as a backup or even pair in a late-rounds committee. 2 of my favorites: the Eagles' Dallas Goedert and the Vikings' Irv Smith Jr. (Vikings). Don't write off the occasional big week from the Browns' David Njoku, either, even with Austin Hooper in town.

NFFC & HIGH-STAKES STRATEGY

Billy Wasosky

When most people hear the words "high stakes," they may imagine stacks of cash or chips in a Las Vegas poker room. I used to think that as well. When hearing that now, my mind immediately goes to all the exciting high-stakes options in the fantasy football industry, and some that are actually "not-so-high-stakes", which can be affordable for all.

The National Fantasy Football Championship (NFFC) has entry fees ranging as low as $25 all the way up to their signature "Platinum League" which only cost you a measly $20,000 to enter. Although many people may feel they aren't ready to jump into their various leagues (snake drafts, draft champions, auctions, cutlines, etc.), they have to understand that people playing in those leagues started drafting in their basement, at a friend's house, in a free Yahoo league etc., were dominating the competition, and were looking for the next step up.

The focus of this chapter will be on the NFFC's 12-team "snake draft" offerings, mainly the Primetime ($1700 entry) and their Online Championship ($350 entry). These are national contests, and each has a $200,000 overall grand prize, along with ample league prizes.

The NFFC scoring is 1 point per reception (PPR), 1 for every 10 rushing or receiving yards, 1 for every 20 passing yards, and 6 points for *all touchdowns*. This includes passing TDs, so it gives QBs a little bit of a bump in this league, compared to other formats where scoring causes them to get neglected. (QBs do, however, lose 2 points for each interception thrown.) Defense/Special Teams units can earn points from sacks, turnovers, touchdowns and points allowed.

For more information on the scoring, please visit the NFFC website.

Now onto three important draft and gameplay features to know: **3rd-round reversal (3RR)**, the **Kentucky Derby System (KDS)**, and **FAAB (Free Agent Acquisition Bidding)**.

3RR (3rd-Round Reversal) and KDS (Kentucky Derby System)

"Me and Jenny go together like peas and carrots!" -- Forrest Gump

In the NFFC, the equivalent of Jenny and Forrest would be 3RR and KDS. Without one, the other would be obsolete. 3RR was conceived after LaDainian Tomlinson scored a ridiculous 28 rushing TDs and 473 fantasy points in the 2006 regular season. Before the 2007 season, the NFFC decided to incorporate "3rd Round Reversal" (3RR), so that the people drafting at the end of the draft would have an opportunity to make up ground on that No. 1 pick.

Under 3RR, the draft snakes in regular fashion from Teams 1-12 in Round 1 and 12-1 in Round 2 -- but then in Round 3, it flips back to 12-1. It then continues 1-12 in Round 4, 12-1 in Round 5, and so on, through all 20 rounds.

While 3RR would be great on its own, the NFFC decided to incorporate the Kentucky Derby System (KDS), which derives from how the jockeys/horses choose a position in the starting gate at the Kentucky Derby. Once your league is full, you then rank each spot from where you would like to draft. While you aren't always going to get the top choice that you want, I don't know anyone who wouldn't prefer to have a "say" in what pick they have, rather than, "Well, you were 7th out of the hat, so you are drafting from the 7th hole!" 3RR makes drafting from the back -- and sometimes even the middle -- more appealing.

DRAFT STRATEGY

Find those gems that others don't see.

Drafting a championship starts EARLY. While I participate in a draft that starts right after the Super Bowl ends, the majority of my preparation starts in mid-May (earlier this year, since most of us have some extra time), as free agency and the NFL Draft pretty much have players settled on their respective teams by then. So I break every team down and ask the following 4 questions:

1) Are there new coaches or coordinators in place?
2) How many passes will the team attempt?
3) How many rushing attempts will it have?
4) Are there new players, or significant players who left the team?

Once I answer those questions, I plug in the players on that team and predict what I feel they will do based on "the numbers." This gives me a foundation to find any player who I think is (or will be) undervalued on draft day.

In addition to all this, reading and listening to everything you can is helpful. This isn't the '80s (when I started playing). There's so much information out there, and everyone has access to it. Virtually every player is going to be "in the best shape of [his] career," so you have to be able to sift through the trash. Anything you can read or listen to that at least makes you think can be a valuable tool for you on draft day.

Let ADP be a guide, but don't be a slave to it, and be FLEXIBLE!

To me, fantasy football is like buying stocks and compiling that portfolio of players to make the perfect puzzle. Your goal each round of the draft should be to buy/draft a player who you feel will exceed where you are taking them at the end of the season. For example, last year I was pretty high on Austin Hooper and had him ranked as the 6th-best TE at the beginning of the season. The beauty was he was being taken in some drafts as the 9th or 10th TE, and you could get him in many drafts in the 10th round (or even later). Even though I personally had him as the 6th-best TE, I didn't need to take him as the 6th-best because "the market" or ADP (Average Draft Position) said I didn't have to.

Who out there would buy a stock for $20 when they were pretty confident they could buy it for $15, if they waited just a few days? So, while ADP is a great way to gauge where a particular player is going, I highly recommend moving someone up that you "must have" at least a round just so you get him on your team. Remember this is YOUR team, so you shouldn't take a player you don't like, just because they are "next on the list."

Again, the key to all of this is BEING FLEXIBLE! Maybe you organized a plan to start out going RB-RB, but a WR you didn't anticipate being there is sitting there in Round 2. This may be a point where you need to pivot from your plan, and start thinking how you will adjust it accordingly each round going forward. I hate when I hear people say "I'll never draft him!" or "I am taking this player at this point no matter what!" EVERY player has a price, and if that guy keeps falling for whatever reason, he then becomes a value. Conversely, there is always "that guy" (ex. Darwin Thompson, Felix Jones, etc.) who rocket up draft boards the last 2 weeks of the season, and they are pretty much taken at their peak possible value. This is fine, IF they produce at that high level, but my experience is that most times they simply don't come close to what people were expecting. In the NFFC, rookies are a HOT commodity. Be careful with this, as my experience has shown me that there are far more "misses" than "hits" when it comes to drafting rookies early. Everyone loves "the unknown" and will be looking for the next Amazon, when in reality, they could be overpaying for one of the hundreds of $2.00 stocks that never exceed their value.

AFTER THE DRAFT (FAAB)

Since there is no trading in the NFFC, the only way to improve your team after the draft is through **Free Agent Acquisition Bidding** (FAAB) each week. You start the season with $1,000 to bid blindly in $1 increments for any player you want. The best part of this is that you are trying to bid the least amount you can, so you can still get your guy. For example, if Player A bids $143 on Tyler Higbee, and the next highest bid is $8, Player A now owns Tyler Higbee for $143. So while we all want to get the best "deal" on a player, the key here is to try and nail the bid but spend as little as possible. However, if you have a dire need for a position and/or really want a player, my advice is to go get him. I speak from experience when I say there is nothing worse than lowering your bid a few minutes before the deadline, and then losing out on that player you would have won with your original bid.

There is no doubt when you manage a lot of leagues, FAAB can be a bit tedious. However, for me, it is like "Christmas morning" for 13 Wednesdays of the NFL season, as I go through each league and see my new presents underneath the tree! :)

These three features set the NFFC apart from other leagues, both local and those in the high-stakes industry. I would be completely remiss if I did not mention the camaraderie that happens at these live events. While there are options to draft online, there is NOTHING that compares to drafting LIVE in New York or Las Vegas. Since 2004, I have met some of my closest friends at these events, and I talk to many on a daily or weekly basis throughout the year. For me, it doesn't get much better than staring at a completed draft board, debating with your friends why your team is far superior to theirs, and then going out for a few drinks talking about all the great (and lousy) picks that happened in your draft. When it comes to draft day...... "Best day of the year. Better than Christmas!" - Tom Sizemore as Det. Danny Detillo

HOW DO THINGS LOOK FOR THE 2020 SEASON?

While the PPR aspect would generally lend to benefitting wide receivers and tight ends, early indications of ADP in the NFFC still have people racing to get RBs, RBs, and more RBs! A running back that catches a lot of passes AND gets a heavy workload is an invaluable asset in PPR formats.

The basic strategy of drafts this year based on early NFFC ADP seems to be simple: Get RBs, RBs, and more RBs! Many people will have their eyes on Christian McCaffrey, Saquon Barkley and Ezekiel Elliott. However, if you are fortunate enough to land one of them, there is a good possibility that you won't be able to get one of the top 14 RBs with your 2nd-round pick. So if you don't want to "reach" in Round 2 for your second RB, you might want to set your KDS at the back end of the draft and start with two of Joe Mixon, Aaron Jones, Derrick Henry, Nick Chubb and Josh Jacobs. Not bad! While these RBs might not carry the reception upside of McCaffrey or Barkley, they can be extremely beneficial as an RB1 or RB2 when building your team.

This year's NFL Draft has convoluted the RB position. Rookie studs like Clyde Edwards-Helaire, D'Andre Swift, Jonathan Taylor and J.K. Dobbins have practically slayed the value of Damien Williams, Kerryon Johnson, Marlon Mack and Mark Ingram, respectively. Again, running backs who "carry the load" , and/or catch passes in the NFFC will be in high demand, because there are so few. The need this year to get two (or three) quality running backs on your roster is going to be comparable to finding toilet paper or hand sanitizer at your grocery store, so be ready!

Wide receiver in the NFFC is a little more important, because you have to start three (and up to four) each week. While most people think WR is deep, it doesn't mean you can't build a solid squad with a WR or two in the first three picks. I have often implemented the Zero-RB strategy, with which you basically take zero or only one RB in your first five or six picks and load up at other positions. If there is ever a year to do it in a national contest, this would be it. While others are taking all the RBs, you could maybe have a start of Michael Thomas, Julio Jones, Amari Cooper, DK Metcalf and TE Mark Andrews. Sure, you are going to be behind at RB, but sometimes you have to "zig" when everyone else "zags," and if you hit on a RB or two ... no one will touch you at those positions!

I am a big believer in planning out the first 8 rounds of the draft, but you need to BE FLEXIBLE with your plan. In the NFFC for me, that generally means filling my team with a combination of RB and WR the first 7 rounds, and then taking a QB and TE in Round 8 or later. I fully understand why people will take Patrick Mahomes or Lamar Jackson in Round 2 or 3 (especially in a league like the NFFC that offers 6 points per passing TD), but I generally won't unless there is no one else at my spot that catches my eye. Drafting a team is all about roster construction, and anticipating what will happen next. Let's say I'm in Round 7 and I have six picks until my next pick. I like four WRs equally, and I planned on taking a QB in Round 8. So I'll probably take the QB that I want, and get the WR on the way back. It is always about taking VALUE if it should fall in your lap.

Unless you want Travis Kelce, George Kittle, Zach Ertz or Mark Andrews, you can afford to wait at TE. The position is sneaky deep this year. Jonnu Smith, Hayden Hurst, T.J. Hockenson and Noah Fant are looking to jump to the next level, and they come at a price from which you can build much-needed roster depth before taking them.

Defenses are all about the matchups, and I highly recommend streaming from week to week. Last year, the San Francisco 49ers D/ST weren't even chosen in standard 20-round drafts, and the Chicago Bears were the No. 1 D/ST off the board in virtually every draft. In NFFC scoring, the 49ers finished 3rd, and the Bears finished 18th. The lesson? Don't sweat over your D/ST on draft day.

Kicker? Take the best available in Round 19 or 20.

Chapter 3

QUARTERBACKS

SINGLE-QB RPV

	Player	RPV
1	Lamar Jackson	24%
2	Patrick Mahomes	21%
3	Dak Prescott	9%
4	Russell Wilson	1%
5	Josh Allen	0%
6	Deshaun Watson	-2%
7	Matt Ryan	-5%
8	Kyler Murray	-5%
9	Carson Wentz	-9%
10	Drew Brees	-10%
11	Ben Roethlisberger	-11%
12	Aaron Rodgers	-12%

SUPERFLEX/OP/2QB RPV

	Player	RPV
1	Tom Brady	7%
2	Baker Mayfield	6%
3	Daniel Jones	4%
4	Jared Goff	2%
5	Matthew Stafford	2%
6	Joe Burrow	1%
7	Ryan Taneheill	-1%
8	Kirk Cousins	-2%
9	Philip Rivers	-3%
10	Jimmy Garoppolo	-4%
11	Sam Darnold	-5%
12	Drew Lock	-7%

Player Profiles and Overview

By Joe Pisapia

Evolution is inevitable. However, habits are still hard to break, especially when past practices were best practices. Despite Superflex leagues justifiably rising in popularity, the majority of fantasy leagues still roll out that single QB every week in their lineups. There have always been transcendent seasons, such as Peyton Manning's '13, Aaron Rodgers' '11 and Tom Brady's '07 season as outliers. However, the player pool at the position was normally deep enough to find a dozen adequate QB's for a fantasy league that you'd be able to keep pace with your league mates. That time is coming to a hard and fast stop.

The cold hard fact is, the quarterback position is undergoing a revolution. Not only are we seeing a more athletic player overall at the position, we're also at a crossroads (similar to the period when the "Zero RB Strategy" took hold a few years ago, which was really just another transition between running backs aging out and the new crop yet to rise). This crossroads finds us in a position where there's a clear "elite" at the top of the position that's separating from the herd. When you then factor in a group of Hall of Famers aging out, as well as a cluster of players who underperformed and whose inconsistencies became fantasy liabilities, you have a perfect storm of change raining down upon the league.

The simplest way to address why the quarterback is becoming more worthy of early consideration is that their control of fantasy scoring on their own teams have grown exponentially. Lamar Jackson wasn't the only QB out on the loose in 2019. Josh Allen and Kyler Murray both crossed the 500 yard rushing plateau. Murray tossed in 4 rushing TD's, while Allen has 9 and Deshaun Watson had 7. The mobile quarterback is no longer the anomaly, he's quickly becoming the standard.

The rules of the game also heavily favor the QB. Opposing defenses fear penalties and fines, so the kid gloves are worn most times. The "better safe than sorry" defensive stance has allowed for the renaissance of the athletic QB to roam free and it's unlikely to change anytime soon. Another factor is specialization. Yes, the running back position has become more specialized over the last decade, but there are better overall athletes on all rosters, capable of converting points. More options, means less reliability on a single player in an offense to convert TD's. Just ask DFS players Week 12 of 2019 when a collective of second string TE's and even linemen caught touchdowns much to their dismay. However, most of these points can still be traced to, you guessed it, the quarterback.

So, just how substantial of an advantage were the elite QB's in 2019? Using Relative Position Value (RPV) from the Fantasy Black Book ™ we can answer that question. RPV compares the players at a position and tells you how much better/worse a player performed compared to the Fantasy League Average at the position.

Here's the RPV for the Top 12 QB in 2019:

	Player	PTS	RPV
1	Lamar Jackson	421.0	+34%
2	Dak Prescot	348.0	+11%
3	Jameis Winston	335.0	+7%
4	Russell Wilson	335.0	+7%
5	Deshaun Watson	332.0	+6%
6	Josh Allen	297.0	-6%
7	Kyler Murray	297.0	-6%
8	Patrick Mahomes*	291.0	-7%
9	Carson Wentz	282.0	-10%
10	Aaron Rodgers	282.0	-10%
11	Matt Ryan	281.0	-11%
12	Tom Brady	271.0	-14%

DNP Full Season

That means Lamar Jackson was 34% better than the fantasy league average QB in 2019. That's an incredible number considering how strong the fantasy QB1 field has been recently. Early projecting for 2020 RPV looks like this:

	Player	PTS	RPV
1	Lamar Jackson	400.0	24%
2	Patrick Mahomes	380.0	17%
3	Deshaun Watson	350.0	8%
4	Dak Prescott	340.0	5%
5	Russell Wilson	340.0	5%
6	Josh Allen	320.0	-1%
7	Kyler Murray	315.0	-3%
8	Ben Roethlisberger	315.0	-3%
9	Jameis Winston	290.0	-11%
10	Carson Wentz	285.0	-12%
11	Matt Ryan	280.0	-14%
12	Aaron Rodgers	270.0	-17%

There will be undeniable "haves" and "have nots" at the position. The deeper you go into the position in Superflex leagues, the more imperative this top QB advantage becomes. If you can have a Lamar Jackson or Patrick Mahomes out-producing the opposing QB you're playing by 17-24% on average, then you have a distinct edge over your competition. You must also consider the downside of waiting. Fading QB could put you woefully behind into the negative. Sure, you could double dip and play matchups with 2 QB's to maximize potential points, but that can be a dangerous game.

PPR formats make an early QB pick even more palatable when you consider 21 RB's had 191 or more PPR points in 2019. The RB position also comes with a higher injury risk. 30 WR scored over 190 PPR points last season. When you take away the transcendent seasons of Christian McCaffrey and Michael Thomas from their respective position pools, the RPV at both RB and WR tighten up considerably with less advantage to be gained.

If you're still not sold, consider the highest scoring fantasy QB's over the last few years leading up to 2017 draft class:

Andrew Luck 335 pts ('14), Cam Newton 356 pts ('15),

Aaron Rodgers 345 pts ('16), Russell Wilson 327 pts ('17)

In 2017, the Earth shifted. That class included Patrick Mahomes and Deshaun Watson, followed by the '18 class of Lamar Jackson and Josh Allen, then finally Kyler Murray in '19. The fantasy league average QB performance has risen each of the last three years thanks to Mahomes' 399 pts in '18 and Jackson's 421 pts last season. As you can also see, the previous high water marks at QB (which at times were significant over their respective peers at the time), are now more in the mid-range of scoring at the position. When you factor in the ADP of Mahomes and Jackson their respective breakout years it's no wonder they were league winners for many owners. Those discounts are long gone.

Make no mistake, I'm not lobbying to take Jackson or Mahomes as a top 5 overall pick in your run of the mill single QB format. What we must do, is be more aware that the ceiling of elite QB play has risen, while the floor has fallen out from under us simultaneously. The QB pool in 2020 is riddled with potholes, and stalwarts like Brady, Brees, Rodgers and Roethlisberger are approaching the twilight with exceeding speed. I would have personally scoffed three years ago at someone taking a QB in the second or third round of a draft. Now, you need to strongly consider the consequences of NOT doing so in 2020. We must always be evolving as fantasy owners, as the game evolves on the field.

THE ELITE

1. **Lamar Jackson, BAL:** The Black Book was higher on Jackson than most other publications in 2019. However, he exceeded those expectations with a vengeance. Let's get some perspective on just how incredible Jackson was last year. He had 5 games with at least 100 rushing yards last season. Only Nick Chubb (7), Ezekiel Elliott (7), Chris Carson (6), Derrick Henry (6) and Christian McCaffrey (6) had more. Jackson not only led his team in rushing yards but was also No. 1 in rushing yards per attempt (6.9) for the league, finishing sixth in rushing yards last year with 1,206 yards (and 7 rushing TDs). That's just half of his productivity! Jackson also led the NFL in passing TDs (36). With 27.7 fantasy PPG, Jackson was the equivalent of a No. 1 QB and a midrange RB1 combined. HC John Harbaugh and OC Greg Roman deserve a lot of credit for this massive success. Their willingness to tailor the offense to the talent, rather than the inverse, allowed the Ravens to harness Jackson's athleticism and maximize his productivity.
So, what's his 2020 value? In Superflex, it's hard to not draft him No. 1 overall. Sure, there's injury risk that one could argue is slightly higher with the "style of play." However, everyone is an injury risk, so I wouldn't let that sway me. One could also argue that after the "elite" RB/WR group is off the board, that Jackson is a middle first-rounder in standard formats with a single QB slot. In single-QB/PPR leagues, it's completely open to roster construction. The reality is, Jackson will be drafted in the first 3 rounds whether you like that truth or not. Will you be the owner to make that selection? First, check whether your league scoring rules favor QBs. Second, if you have a strong knowledge of the player pool, you'll know where to find RBs with upside and underappreciated WR/TE values. Jackson came at almost zero cost last year and won plenty of league titles for owners. The challenge now is drafting him at a premium cost and still being able to build around him. I believe it's possible to do so.

2. **Patrick Mahomes, KC:** Remember this guy? Yeah, all he did was throw 50 TDs in his first full season while winning the 2018 MVP and captured the Super Bowl the next season. He started off like gangbusters in 2019, throwing 10 TDs in his first 3 games. Then, the Chiefs hit a rough patch before a dislocated kneecap interrupted his season for two weeks. He returned with a 446-yard, 3-TD effort but had just 2 games with

2 passing TDs over his last 6 contests. Yuck. He still finished as QB6, despite it all. Was his 2019 rollercoaster season fluky? Probably. If you take his 2018 FPPG AVG of 26.1 and his 20.5 mark from 2019, I think you bid on somewhere in the middle for 2020. That's still an elite fantasy asset, however you slice it. The YAC potential of Tyreek Hill and sophomore Mecole Hardman will definitely keep Mahomes' yardage totals high. Stalwart TE Travis Kelce is still in his prime, and I love their first-round draft pick of Clyde Edwards-Helaire. He's the perfect back for this system that's been searching for a Kareem Hunt replacement for quite some time. Mahomes' peripheral stats were basically in line year over year, so it's safe to say the upside for a 40-TD season with 4,500+ yards is well within his grasp this season. He's the only other QB you can justify for an early-rounds pick based on all his surrounding factors.

TOP TALENT

1. **Russell Wilson, SEA:** Wilson finished 2019 as the QB3 overall. He was 3rd in passing TDs (31) and 6th in passing yards (4,111) while having the lowest interceptable pass percentage in the league (0.6%). It was the first time in three seasons he topped 4K yards -- but also his 3rd consecutive season with 30+ TDs. His 500-yard rushing days are behind him, but he'll still hit that 300+ mark in 2020. You may not find a more reliable QB in terms of return on investment. He has weapons and a consistent organizational philosophy. Wilson himself remains consistent, despite the fact he still plays in somewhat of a "throwback" offensive style. Don't hold your breath for that to change in 2020, but rest assured that Wilson will be a fantasy stalwart and still have plenty of keeper value left at age 31.

2. **Dak Prescott, DAL:** Prescott may have some shortcomings in real life that frustrate Cowboy fans, but so did Tony Romo! I would take both as a fantasy QB any day. Like it or not, Prescott finished as QB2 last year with 30 TDs (4th-best in the NFL), ranked 2nd with 4,901 yards passing, had 7 games with 300+ passing yards, and came in second for deep-ball completion rate (48.7%). The 1,000-yard increase in passing yardage from '18 to '19 was partially due to a full season of WR Amari Cooper, but also his confidence growing in his fourth season. He was franchised ahead of 2020, so a big payday is on the horizon. New HC Mike McCarthy has gotten great seasons out of Brett Favre and Aaron Rodgers, so there's no reason to be concerned with this transition. However, it's not realistic to think that Dak will be scratching that 5K yardage plateau again in 2020. Dak has always been a QB that limited his mistakes. As his attempts have risen over his career, the INTs haven't jumped. That's a good thing. A 30-TD season with 4.5K yards is what you should be targeting. He's not an elite fantasy asset, but he's still a top-level QB and should be valued accordingly in Superflex leagues. Oh, and he also received CeeDee Lamb in the slot role via the draft, so one could say Dak has an embarrassment of riches as he approaches a contract hoping to bring him just that.

3. **Kyler Murray, ARZ:** The buzz is real! The Cardinals didn't just add a piece to their offense; they added arguably the best WR in the league to their arsenal in DeAndre Hopkins. That's an absolutely HUGE net gain. Last season, Murray was 5th in the league in deep-ball completion rate (43.3%), and that was without a true deep-threat WR on the roster. Murray was also working as a rookie with broken-down RB David Johnson most of the season, which stressed the offense quite a bit. He now has Hopkins, Kenyan Drake (who came on strong after escaping Miami), Larry Fitzgerald and Christian Kirk. The red zone was their biggest issue (29th in conversion rate). Hopkins is one of the better red-zone targets in the game, so expect business to pick up in Arizona. Given Murray's rookie season of 3.7K yards 20 TD/12 INT with 544 rushing yards and 4 TDs, I would be targeting a sophomore season of 4K passing yards, 550 rushing yards, 28 passing TDs and 6 rushing TDs. That puts Murray near the top of any QB board. Murray is a hard worker who showed flashes of big-time upside last year. This team is much better suited for success in 2020.

4. **Deshaun Watson, HOU:** One man's gain is another man's loss. Watson will survive the loss of DeAndre Hopkins. They question: How much can he thrive without him? Will Fuller is talented but never healthy. Ditto for Keke Coutee. Kenny Stills and Randall Cobb can have moments but aren't "game-changers." Watson now has to make the guys around him better, and I think he's up for the challenge. However, Watson has yet to eclipse 30 passing TD the last two full seasons he played, topping out at 26 in back-to-back years. He does have 12 rushing TDs over that period and has averages 480 rushing yards. Watson may be drafted ahead of Dak Prescott in many drafts, but I think that's short-sighted. Though Watson may have more talent, he doesn't have the weapons around him to support him going ahead of Prescott. Also, 2019 was an all-or-nothing theme: Watson had 5 games with 3 or more passing TDs -- but he also had 7 games with 1 or 0 TD (including 4 goose eggs). Feast or famine isn't how you want to live at the fantasy QB slot. He remains a high-end QB1, but he has a few more negatives than the guy ahead of him on this list. Of course, if you end up getting a surprising discount on Watson, you should take it, especially in Superflex formats.

5. **Matt Ryan, ATL:** It was not pretty in Atlanta last season. Ryan somehow still finished as QB11 and logged 4,466 passing yards (5th-best in the league). The TDs fell from 35 to 26 year over year, but he still managed 17.8 FPPG. The good news is that Ryan still has all-world WR Julio Jones and the young, gifted Calvin Ridley, but the bad news is he lost TE Austin Hooper this offseason to the Browns via free agency. Let's not forget he opened 2019 with 6 straight 300-yard games (11 total in 2019). Plus, the Falcons did finally right the ship, going 6-2 over their final 8 games after a 1-8 start. The 48 sacks he took ßwere the biggest damper on his 2019 campaign. With more line help, Ryan should bounce back to being a steady midrange QB1.

6. **Josh Allen, BUF:** With a strong fantasy finish to 2018, Allen basically carried his FPPG AVG over into 2019. A QB7 finish was well above his ADP, but Allen continues to be a better fantasy QB than a real one. The additions of John Brown and Cole Beasley certainly helped the cause, and a full, healthy season from Devin Singletary in 2020 could also tick this offense up a notch. This offseason, the Bills acquired Stefon Diggs, who brings even more upside to this aerial game. Allen's rushing yards per game came back down to earth last year, from 7.1 to 4.7. Still, 510 rushing yards and 9 ground scores were tremendous for his fantasy value. His completion rate jumped from 52.8% to 58.8%. His 20 passing TDs and 9 INTs were a solid ratio to build upon. Allen continues to get by on his raw athletic ability, but he still has a long way to go in his development in the pocket. He had 0 300-yard games in 2019, and his highwater mark was 266 in Week 10. He also fumbled the ball 14 times (4 lost), so Allen needs to protect the football a bit better going forward. All in all, Allen is a fantasy QB1 who'll come at a decent value in 2020. With the addition of Diggs, a season-long line of 3.2K passing yards, 24 passing TDs, 500 rushing yards and 6 rushing TDs seems well within reach. As long as he doesn't fumble away drives.

POSSIBLY SOLID OPTIONS

1. **Carson Wentz, PHI:** Philly is a tough town even when everything is going well. Wentz's stats were better than the results at times, but don't get lost in that negativity. Wentz finished as fantasy QB10 last year, and that's with a wide receiver corps that underperformed. The Eagles really need to move away from the patchwork veterans and give Wentz a legit No. 1 WR. I'm not sold that rookie Jalen Reagor is that guy. Still, Wentz's 4K yards, 27:7 TD:INT, 5 300-yard games marked a strong 2019 line and a realistic 2020 expectation. Fun fact: Wentz had a passing TD in all 16 regular season games last year. Wentz's floor remains strong, and the ceiling is still viable. In fact, he may be slightly undervalued in the fantasy world right now.

2. **Jared Goff, LAR:** The "Super Bowl loser hangover" trend continued in 2019 with the Rams. Goff endured mixed results. He had 9 games with 2 or more passing touchdowns but also suffered a 3-game stretch without a TD. That slump knocked him down to QB13 overall in fantasy points. However, now that Todd

Gurley is gone, the Rams may rely even more heavily on the pass. Goff has back-to-back 4.6K passing seasons. His 32:12 TD:INT from 2018 isn't likely to return, but the 22:16 ratio from 2019 should improve. Something in between, with that steady yardage total, will make him low-end QB1 material again in 2020. Your choice will come down to Goff or one of the wily veterans in their late 30s/early 40s. I expect boy wonder Sean McVay to rebound from a disappointing 2019 and take Goff with him. If Goff can avoid making as many mistakes as he did in 2019, when he ranked 24th in interceptable passes per game, he could return a fine ROI as a high-end QB2 in Superflex.

SOLID OPTIONS (AKA OLD DUDES)

1. **Drew Brees, NO:** I said it last year, and I'll say it again: There are two versions of Brees. There's the elite one that plays in the dome -- and the pedestrian one that plays on the road. In what's been a trend in recent years with Brees, his value wanes week to week depending upon location. Even last year when he missed time, in 6 home games he averaged 332.8 passing yards per game with 17 TD. In his 5 games on the road, he averaged just 196.4 yards with 10 TDs. The good news is that Brees will win you weeks when he's at home. The bad news is that you better have some guys who can carry your offense those other 8 games. He's still a QB1, surrounded by a myriad of dangerous weapons, including arguably the best WR in the game in Michael Thomas. Continuity and stability also make Brees one of the safe investments at the position, and he should still be coveted in Superflex leagues. Be sure to pay the premium in DFS for those home games and fade him on the road. He'll average 20 FPPG in 2020 again, but be prepared for weeks of 25 and weeks of 15.

2. **Aaron Rodgers, GB:** Rodgers is still efficient. Finishing at QB9 last year, he threw for 4K+ yards with 26 TDs and just 4 picks. However, his days of being "elite" are over. Moreover, the formula of the Packers offense has changed dramatically, with Aaron Jones and the run game becoming a significant focal point. At 36, Rodgers posted the lowest full-season rushing total of his career (183 yards). That new benchmark is likely to hold. The Packers have failed time and time again to give Rodgers a secondary receiving option after Davante Adams (and no, Devin Funchess isn't the savior). That's why in back-to-back seasons he has only 4 300-yard games in each. This new version of this first-ballot Hall of Famer doesn't have as many "big games" as he used to in previous seasons. He threw for 3 or more touchdowns in a game just 3 times last year. In 9 games, he had 1 or 0 TDs. That's not the Rodgers of old; that's just the reality of this old Rodgers. In 2020, expect more of the same: a fringe top-10 QB who lacks the ability to win you a week on a consistent basis.

3. **Ben Roethlisberger, PIT:** 5K passing yards in 2018 -- let's not forget about that. Sure, Antonio Brown was still a Steeler then, but Big Ben still has some toys left to play with in Pittsburgh. The Steelers' 2019 offense disintegrated once Ben went down for the year. All signs point to a healthy return in 2020, and that probably means 4.2K yards and around 28 TDs. Sure, he's 38, and with age comes risk. I wouldn't be concerned with the undefined weapons outside of JuJu Smith-Schuster. We've been down this road before with the Steelers, and Ben has found a way to create new wide receiving stars time and time again. He boasts enough of a track record and continuity that we can look on the bright side and consider Roethlisberger a low-end QB1 at this stage in his career.

4. **Tom Brady, TB:** Brady in a Bucs uniform will be odd to see, but it wasn't surprising to see Brady and the Pats part ways after a disappointing finish to the 2019 season. Sure, the weapons were lacking last year in New England, but Brady also didn't elevate the players around him as he did in years past. At 43, he has something left in the tank, and certainly more than the 40-year-old comps we have to work on from the past. For starters, his body hasn't taken nearly the abuse of a Brett Favre or Warren Moon based on how the league protects the QB nowadays. Brady will always want to prove the doubters wrong. However, he's still a QB2 no matter how you slice it at this stage of his career. Having two Pro Bowl wide receivers in Chris Godwin and Mike Evans is a quarterback's dream, and Brady could resurrect O.J. Howard's value and

lean on old pal Rob Gronkowski. However, this is a totally new system with new verbiage, and this old dog is going to have to learn some new tricks. He'll be teaching some new tricks as well, but to overrate him based on the move is a dangerous proposition. He finished as QB12 last year, and that was with some key peers missing games. As a "double-up/QB tandem of 1A guys" in a Superflex, I think you can roll with Tom and a strong core of RBs and WRs, then take a shot on a Baker Mayfield type. Efficiency will be the biggest change to this Bucs offense. Jameis Winston threw 30 picks last year; Brady will easily cut that number in half. Expect 4.3K yards and 28 TDs as the stat line to bid on in 2020.

5. **Philip Rivers, IND:** His decision-making at the end of games was his undoing in 2019. The skillset is still there. The truth is the holes along the Chargers' offensive line forced him to check down quite a bit. In Indianapolis, the O-Line won't be an issue. It was just a 1-year deal for the veteran QB, but both HC Frank Reich and OC Nick Sirianni worked with Rivers back in the Bolts' San Diego years. That means they could very well franchise him if 2020 works out as they hope. The Colts still have T.Y. Hilton and Marlon Mack, along with intriguing youth like Jonathan Taylor, Parris Campbell and Michael Pittman Jr. Rivers has seven straight seasons of 4K passing yards and usually flirts with 30 TDs. There's every reason to believe he can repeat those stats with a more comfortable pocket with the Colts. Rivers has the potential to be one of the better QB2s in fantasy this year. He just can't throw 20 picks again.

6. **Kirk Cousins, MIN:** Cousins sandwiched 7 glorious QB1 weeks in between a dismal start and putrid finish to the season. On a brighter note, he did trim his INT from 10 to just 6 from 2018 to 2019. However, his passing yardage total dropped by 600 thanks to those terrible bookends of a season I mentioned at the top. The Vikings relied heavily on RB Dalvin Cook last year, so a bounce back to the 4K-yard passing version of Cousins is in question. This is especially true after Stefon Diggs was dealt to Buffalo. The good news is that the Vikings were able to steal Justin Jefferson in the draft to slide right into that Diggs void. When targeting a QB2, you could do much worse than Cousins. The fact is, Cousins is, and always will be, wildly inconsistent. I wish there was a metric or a split stat that I could give you clarity on when to utilize him, but you'd have a better chance understanding an Antonio Brown music video. Don't confuse Cousins' high salary with high fantasy value.

7. **Matthew Stafford, DET:** The Lions roll with a pass-first offense, which boosts Stafford's value. Before injury, Stafford threw for 2,499 yards and 19 TDs, which would have put him on pace for a career year. While I wouldn't go extrapolating that for 2020 pricing, 4.5 yards and 25+ TDs are well within reach. There have been rumblings that the Lions are open to moving on from Stafford should the situation present itself, but that seems unlikely right now. Stafford averages 17 FPPG over his career, and that makes him a fringe QB1. The back issue is behind him, and he'll be a full participant in OTAs. He's one of the more undervalued Superflex assets heading into the season. Oftentimes, steady veterans get lost in the shuffle, but I wouldn't lose sight of Stafford on your draft board. At 32, Stafford is far from "done."

SUPERFLEX QB2 CANDIDATES

1. **Baker Mayfield, CLE:** There was a camp of folks who wanted to vault Mayfield into the top-5 QB discussion last year. The Black Book was not in that camp. Still, I was willing to consider him a low-end QB1 with upside. Unfortunately, Mayfield fell well short of that moderate expectation, finishing as QB19 last year. There's no way around it: Mayfield regressed last year. The TDs went from 27 to 22, and the picks went up from 14 to 21 (with 3 more starts). He also lost 4 points off his completion percentage and was reckless with the football at times. All is not lost, however, as many a great QBs experienced similar woes, including Brett Favre and even Peyton Manning, who threw 28 picks in his first full season as a starter. I don't think Mayfield is going to necessarily end up in the HOF with those two, but what we need to understand is what to expect in 2020. Beyond all reason, Mayfield was given more weapons last year (Odell Beckham and Kareem Hunt), and things went in the opposite direction. New HC Kevin Stefanksi is

no stranger to inconsistent QBs, most recently working with Kirk Cousins in Minnesota. New TE Austin Hooper adds yet another talented asset to an already loaded arsenal. Perhaps a new voice can get Mayfield and the offense back on track. The question remains: Do you take that chance on him over the stalwart veterans who make up the low-end QB1 group in 2020? My answer is no. However, by snagging him as a QB2, you take the upside in Superflex and buy low in dynasty formats, since we all know those aging QBs are on their last legs.

2. **Jimmy Garoppolo, SF:** Turns out you can almost win a Super Bowl with Garoppolo, but can you win a fantasy league? Last year's QB19, Garoppolo threw for just under 4K yards with 27 TDs and 13 INT -- impressive considering he plays in a run-first scheme. I also believe it to be Jimmy G's ceiling. That's not a knock on him -- just an honest assessment of the 49ers' offensive identity. HC Kyle Shanahan fed Garoppolo a steady diet of slants over the middle from all sides that played into his strengths and limited his liabilities as a QB. There are some strong weapons here, including all-world TE George Kittle and emerging star Deebo Samuel (who was practically last year's Black Book mascot we loved him so much). Rookie Brandon Aiyuk should fit right into the Shanahan scheme and give Jimmy G another quick-slant monster in the making. It would nonetheless be wise to consider Garoppolo a high-end QB2, especially when you consider the trend of "Super Bowl loss hangover": Cam Newton in '16 fell off dramatically; Matt Ryan in '17 had his lowest TD total since his rookie year; Jared Goff last year fell from 32 to 22 TDs year over year … see where I'm going? Also, Garoppolo's 2019 game log featured 3 4-TD games, 6 1-TD games and 3 0-TD games. Feast-or-famine game logs tend to not create QB1s.

3. **Daniel Jones, NYG:** Look, I know Jones is far from perfect, but in 12 starts, he averaged 16.5 FPPG. That's more than Jimmy G, and one can argue Jones has a better cast of offensive weapons by a decent margin. Evan Engram is a top TE. Sterling Shepard and Golden Tate are steady. Darius Slayton showed great promise in his rookie year. When you add a healthy Saquon Barkley to the mix, you have the opportunity for a fantasy steal in the QB2 tier. When Barkley was out, Jones suffered a great deal. He threw just 3 TDs and 6 INTs while failing to top 225 yards passing in a single game (2 games under 182). Barkley's YAC not only helps Jones' totals; it also keeps defenses occupied and allows him more favorable coverages to challenge. Jones' other main issue is the fumbles: He led the league with 18! That kills drives and negates fantasy points. He must protect the football better in 2020. Luckily, the Giants had a solid draft and beefed up the offensive line, which should help Jones' turnovers a bit. All things considered, Jones is a sneaky-good second QB and will be a DFS GPP darling some weeks.

4. **Ryan Tannehill, TEN:** Magical runs happen in every sport, and 2019 was truly special for the Titans, after making the change at QB from Marcus Mariota to Tannehill. Over those 10 starts, Tannehill netted 2 or more passing TDs in 9 of 10 weeks, finishing with 22 (plus 4 rushing TDs) and just 6 INTs. The identity of the offense is without a doubt Derrick Henry, and that won't change in 2020. Still, A.J. Brown emerged as Tannehill's No. 1 receiving option in his rookie year, making the most of limited targets each week. Can this duo be as efficient as it was last year considering this is a run-first offense? Possibly. It's far more possible that the league will adjust to him, and that 70% completion rate doesn't seem sustainable. Still, we can't deny he has QB2 appeal in Superflex leagues, even with some regression built into projections.

5. **Derek Carr, LV:** Carr is steady but unspectacular. The weapons improved last year: Darren Waller emerged, and Josh Jacobs finally gave the Raiders a running game. Carr posted back-to-back 4K-passing-yard seasons under Jon Gruden, but that didn't stop them from adding Marcus Mariota as his backup. Carr has 3 years left on his contract, but he could be getting phased out as the Raiders continue to retool the organization. His lone 300-yard game came in Week 17, so Carr is a player who's about weekly floor, because he frankly doesn't have a tantalizing ceiling. One can bid on another 4K yards with 20-25 TDs. Henry Ruggs III brings an element of speed to the offense that was lacking a bit last year, but despite being taken as the first receiver in the draft, Ruggs was not the most complete wideout in this class.

6. **Sam Darnold, NYJ:** Unlucky 13? For two straight seasons, Darnold has played in 13 games, but under two different offensive schemes. What we're looking for here is progress, and there was some in 2019. His passer rating jumped from 77 to 84, the yardage total crossed the 3K mark, and the TDs went up from 17

to 19 while the INTs fell from 15 to 13. Is this earth-shattering progress? Of course not, but Year 3 offers the potential for growth, despite my many concerns over HC Adam Gase's shortcomings. Darnold's thumb ligament on his non-throwing hand did require surgery but wasn't a concern anyway; he played the final two months of 2019 with the ailment. The mono he dealt with earlier in the season, however, was no joke. A healthy Darnold should continue to grow, but he will still be limited by a subpar WR corps. Denzel Mims was a nice value where they got him, but it's asking a lot of a rookie to step in and be the No. 1 with little help from his peers.

7. **Teddy Bridgewater, CAR:** Finally, things are starting to look up for Bridgewater. In 2019, Drew Brees went down, and Teddy started 5 games for the Saints. Over that span, he averaged 16 FPPG, with some varying degrees of productivity. That's a nice way of saying it was a rollercoaster. However, it was enough to land him a starting gig with the new-look Panthers. Bridgewater will never be a great downfield passer, but Christian McCaffrey's YAC potential will pad his passing-yardage totals. D.J. Moore may be the most underrated WR in the game today, and defenses must account for Robbie Anderson as a deep threat -- something this offense has lacked in recent years. Bridgewater's ideal value is as your QB3 in Superflex. He'll be a game manager in fantasy terms, so don't get caught up too much in Teddy B's redemption tale.

8. **Drew Lock, DEN:** I know, I'm just as surprised as you are. Some may think it's a reach, but when you add Jerry Jeudy to Courtland Sutton on the receiving corps, sign Melvin Gordon to a backfield that still has Phillip Lindsay and Royce Freeman, and an emerging TE in Noah Fant, Lock's supporting cast may just be too big to fail. Lock received 5 starts last year, and outside of one clunker against eventual Super Bowl champion Chiefs, he was serviceable. The Denver offense has great potential for balance in 2020, and Lock basically has to limit his mistakes to end up as a solid QB2. In Superflex, Lock would be my ideal QB3 target -- someone with whom I'd feel comfortable starting 2-3 times in a season. He may have DFS appeal in certain matchups.

THE WILD CARDS

1. **Cam Newton, FA:** Shoulder issues are no joke, and Lisfranc injuries can be even worse to boot (see what I did there?). Puns aside, Newton's career is at a crossroads. Can a motivated Cam return to fantasy relevance? Absolutely. However, you have to keep in mind his legs are the key to that resurgence. Forget 2015; that's going to be the high point. From a passing standpoint, 3.3K yards and 24 TD/15 INT make sense in terms of what to bid on in 2020. From a rushing standpoint, he has to approach the 500-rushing-yard plateau and handful of rushing TDs to get back to QB1 status.

2. **Jameis Winston, NO:** 5K yards and 33 TDs in 2019? Wow! What a season! Oh wait, he threw 30 INTs. Yeaaahhh, not so great. Winston has always had potential. Unfortunately, no team has been able to focus that talent into steady productivity. In the offseason, he had laser eye surgery. That doesn't correct his judgement, just his eye sight. Now, it's up to us to see his future. No one saw the New Orleans signing coming, but Sean Payton and Drew Brees are about as good as it gets in terms of understanding the QB position. Can Winston soak that up and apply it someday? Maybe. There's also a good chance he sees some action this year as Drew Brees is getting up there in age and missed time in 2019. This one-year deal creates a perfect opportunity to buy Winston for pennies on the dollar in a dynasty league. With so many aging QBs in the league, he'll have value in 2021 potentially with the Saints, or another organization. That makes him possible QB1 material on your roster or potential trade bait as the aging QBs start to drop off in the next 1-2 years. Look long-term here. It won't cost you much to be wrong, but if Winston even gets a whiff of being useful again, he'll carry some value.

3. **Jarret Stidham, NE:** Well, here we are. Jarret Stidham will have to fill the shoes of the great Tom Brady. His college teammate, Giants WR Dairus Slayton, spoke in glowing terms about Stidham in the off-season, calling him a "student of the game" and "a relentless worker". His teammate Damien Harris has known him since their youth football days and is also quite complimentary of the QB. The positive PR, and vote of

confidence from the organization (not drafting a QB this year), does seem to align. However, whether that translates to on the field success is still a mystery. At Auburn, he followed up a solid 2017 season (including a win against Alabama), with a down 2018. He does have a nice touch on the deep ball, but that's not the Pats offense. He's also far more mobile than Brady ever was, so that's a positive and a new dimension to the offense, not to mention his footwork is quite strong. The Pats must have seen enough in practice and in meetings to think Stidham is ready to take over the reins in 2020. Would it surprise you in the slightest to see the Pats win 10+ games and the division yet again? It shouldn't. It's more realistic to think they're a .500 team with that defense, suffering through the growing pains of a rookie quarterback. He's a bye week Superflex QB for now.

ROOKIES

1. **Joe Burrow, CIN:** In one year, Burrow went from likely undrafted to No. 1 overall pick. The move to LSU turned out to be pure magic for Burrow as he went on to set an all-time passing TD record for TDs (60), won the National Championship and the Heisman Trophy. It's the perfect example of a player ending up in the right place at the right time. Now, Joe has landed in Cincinnati. It's certainly the right time for the Bengals to have a fresh start and a new franchise quarterback. The question remains: Are the Bengals the best team with whom Burrow can find professional success? He'll land on a team that drafted Tee Higgins, leans on WR Tyler Boyd and expects A.J Green back after he rehabs another injury. Burrow will also benefit from the presence of RB Joe Mixon, who could certainly hold out but should ultimately get paid. Burrow is more elusive than folks give him credit for and can make first downs with his legs. Watching him in 2019, it felt like watching Tom Brady with more athleticism. Like Brady, he doesn't have mind-blowing arm strength, but he's accurate and seems to have a knack for making the important completions when they matter most. That's a scary thought for the rest of the NFL. However, Tom Brady fell to the Patriots, an organization that was able to breed him into the success he became. Zac Taylor isn't Bill Belichick. Still, there's plenty of room for optimism that Burrow can live up to the billing, and from a character standpoint, all indications say he's a worthy investment for your long-term fantasy concerns. He'll start Day 1 and in 2020 is a mid-low-end QB2 depending on his supporting cast.

2. **Tua Tagovailoa, MIA:** Tua is a competitor, and that competitive streak will lead him to starting games for the Dolphins in 2020. Yeah, yeah, the general consensus is that he'll hold the clipboard all year, but I'm not buying it. My money is on 6 starts for Tua this year, with the upside of 8. It may be aggressive, but so is Tagovailoa. The Dolphins showed fight last year, almost to the chagrin of their fans, but luckily Tua fell to them regardless. In single-QB leagues, this take isn't going to make a difference. However, in Superflex formats, Tua could be useful, especially if the QBs on your roster have late byes, as he could be the starter in the second half of 2020. Long-term, it's all about health. Tua is an extraordinary talent and a winner. He also makes everyone around him better, but you can't do that from the IR. He's a risky pick, but worth the gamble in dynasty with the expected QB turnover coming in the next two years.

3. **Justin Herbert, LAC:** Herbert checks all the boxes: size, arm strength, good speed and a strong TD:INT. He's also had fumble issues and some concerns with pocket awareness. The speed of the NFL game is going to make or break his career. He'll either ramp up or get left behind, which makes Herbert a fantasy boom-or-bust. He's a clear tier behind Burrow and Tua but will likely see some playing time in December for the Chargers. We've seen mixed results for toolsy QBs at the NFL level. He has all the skills, but he's not a lock to become a fantasy QB1 anytime soon.

4. **Jordan Love, GB:** I may be in the minority, but I think Love has a lot of raw talent -- emphasis on raw. I said the same thing about Josh Allen two years ago, amidst many cynical takes, and he's worked out pretty well so far. Of all places, Love landed in Green Bay, which moved up to take him in the first round. "Shocking" doesn't begin to describe this pick. Sure, Aaron Rodgers is getting up there and has missed some time, but the Packers are a playoff team with many needs, and Rodgers' deal isn't up for a few more

years. Love will sit and learn under Rodgers, but while this situation may not be as prickly as Brett Favre and Rodgers, it's not going to be roses either. This is basically a "wait and see" situation. Depending on reports in 2020, I may try to buy Love in dynasty formats rather than waste a pick on him this year in rookie drafts, guessing he's at least 2 years from seeing the field.

RED FLAGS

1. **Gardner Minshew, JAC:** 2019 was a fun ride for the mustachioed Minshew, but the league caught up to this energetic young man, and his second act wasn't as strong as his first. Minshew could have the makings of one of those backups that has a long career in the NFL with runs of success, but nothing from his measurables or college career suggests a long-term NFL starting role is in his future. He's another guy that as a 3rd QB in Superflex for byes could be worth the roster spot. He doesn't have any challengers for his position in 2020, and his 344 rushing yards in 2019 show he could piece together a handful of fantasy-worthy performances. He also has decent supporting weapons around him, including 2019 breakout WR DJ Chark. Just don't fall into the trap confusing media attention with quality of play.

2. **Mitchell Trubisky/Nick Foles, CHI:** Regression, thy name is Trubisky. There were many inconsistencies in 2018 but still hope that 2019 would bring some stabilization. That hope died. His numbers declined across the board, and his FPPG fell from 18.8 to 13.5 year over year. Nick Foles was brought in, as Matt Nagy clings to his head coaching job by his fingernails. The truth is, neither is the answer for fantasy terms. Foles isn't as good as his SB run (which had its warts when you dig deeper), and Trubisky seems like a lost cause. All that draft capital wasted to move up for Trubisky when Patrick Mahomes and Deshaun Watson were waiting on the board. That decision will haunt the Bears for the next decade. In the immediate future, this is a QB situation to just steer clear from in 2020. Luckily, the position pool is deep enough that you can dismiss it altogether, even in Superflex.

3. **Dwayne Haskins/Kyle Allen, WAS:** New HC Ron Rivera didn't bring in Cam Newton, but he did swing for Allen, who is a real threat to start the year as the Redskins' starting QB. Haskins wasn't "Rivera's Guy" and could very well be gone completely in a year. The front office keeps saying Haskins is the starter, but he's in no position to succeed. He turned the ball over way to much last year, his run game is a mess, and Terry McLaurin is his lone weapon (and the league knows it). This is setting up to be a revolving door in 2020, and neither of these two options at QB for the Redskins are fantasy options.

Chapter 4

RUNNING BACKS

½ & FULL PPR RPV

RB1

	Player	RPV
1	Christian McCaffrey	25%
2	Saquon Barkley	14%
3	Ezekiel Elliott	11%
4	Dalvin Cook	8%
5	Alvin Kamara	5%
6	Joe Mixon	-5%
7	Derrick Henry	-7%
8	Miles Sanders	-8%
9	Austin Ekeler	-8%
10	Nick Chubb	-10%
11	Kenyan Drake	-11%
12	Aaron Jones	-12%

RB2

	Player	RPV
1	Leonard Fournette	12%
2	Clyde Edwards-Helaire	11%
3	Josh Jacobs	9%
4	Chris Carson	5%
5	Todd Gurley	2%
6	Melvin Gordon	1%
7	Le'Veon Bell	0%
8	Devin Singletary	-4%
9	Cam Akers	-5%
10	D'Andre Swift	-9%
11	James Conner	-9%
12	Jonathan Taylor	-11%

RB3

	Player	RPV
1	Kareem Hunt	20%
2	David Montgomery	17%
3	Mark Ingram	9%
4	Raheem Mostert	8%
5	James White	4%
6	Tarik Cohen	1%
7	J.K. Dobbins	-3%
8	Boston Scott	-4%
9	Damien Williams	-11%
10	K'Shawn Vaughn	-12%
11	Marlon Mack	-14%
12	Matt Brieda	-15%

STANDARD RPV

RB1

	Player	RPV
1	Christian McCaffrey	27%
2	Saquon Barkley	22%
3	Ezekiel Elliott	20%
4	Derrick Henry	8%
5	Dalvin Cook	2%
6	Alvin Kamara	-4%
7	Joe Mixon	-7%
8	Nick Chubb	-11%
9	Aaron Jones	-13%
10	Josh Jacobs	-14%
11	Miles Sanders	-15%
12	Kenyan Drake	-15%

RB2

	Player	RPV
1	Chris Carson	8%
2	Austin Ekeler	6%
3	Leonard Fournette	5%
4	Todd Gurley	5%
5	Melvin Gordon	4%
6	Clyde Edwards-Helaire	2%
7	Devin Singletary	1%
8	Le'Veon Bell	-3%
9	Mark Ingram	-4%
10	Cam Akers	-7%
11	D'Andre Swift	-8%
12	James Conner	-9%

RB3

	Player	RPV
1	Raheem Mostert	17%
2	David Montgomery	15%
3	Jonathan Taylor	13%
4	Kareem Hunt	9%
5	Sony Michel	5%
6	Jordan Howard	3%
7	Derrius Guice	-7%
8	Damien Williams	-9%
9	David Johnson	-10%
10	J.K. Dobbins	-11%
11	Marlon Mack	-12%
12	Matt Brieda	-12%

Player Profiles and Overview
By Eliot Crist

When it comes to running backs, I'm looking for snaps and weighted opportunity.

Touch share is important, but in PPR, a target is worth 2.8 times as much as a carry is, so weighting touches for value is key. Relying on snaps for player value seems so simple, but it is so important. Guys who are on the field the most, score the most points. No stat correlates to running back fantasy success more than snaps.

Once we have the guideline for the most important statistics in determining who the workhorse backs will be, I look at what team they are on. Touchdowns are the biggest weekly difference-maker, and understanding a team's scoring upside is massive to a running back's touchdown upside.

Typically, the top fantasy backs are almost always on a top-15 offense. From there, I am looking at TD equity, target share, and whether a player is one injury away from league-winning upside.

THE ELITE

1. **Christian McCaffrey, CAR:** As just mentioned, we want to know who is staying on the field, and who is getting the most valuable volume. McCaffrey led the league in both categories in 2019, playing a whopping 98.4% of his team's snaps. He logged 287 carries and led the league with 143 targets while finishing with 2,392 total yards and 19 TDs. He had only 1 game with fewer than 17 total fantasy points. He is the hands-down the best overall player in fantasy and the clear 1.01 in drafts. If you are worried about a coaching staff change, new offensive coordinator Joe Brady just fed Clyde Edwards-Helaire the most receptions for a back in the last 20 years in the SEC. If you are lucky enough to get 1.01, draft McCaffrey and enjoy his greatness.

2. **Saquon Barkley, NYG:** Barkley had a disappointing sophomore season due to a high-ankle sprain in Week 3 that kept him on the injury report for 5 weeks, and he admitted it hindered him through Week 14. Once he got past his injury, he went right back to his top-flight self. In his self-proclaimed "healthy" outings (Weeks 1-2 and 15-17), he went over 100 total yards each contest and saw fewer than 20 opportunities just once. Even in an injury-plagued season, he still finished with 1,400 yards and 8 TDs. New HC Joe Judge comes from a Patriots system that has utilized backs in the passing game as well as any team in the league. If the Giants develop his route tree and use him properly, his ceiling is the 1,000-1,000 club. 2019 was a down year for the all-world athlete, and he still finished 3rd in snap rate and 8th in targets. Look for him to be fed again this year behind an improved O-line and what should be a better coaching staff.

3. **Ezekiel Elliott, DAL:** Mr. Consistent, Elliott has been fantasy gold since he stepped foot in the NFL. He has never missed a game due to injury and has had over 300 rush attempts in every season outside of 2017, when he missed 6 games due to suspension. In 10 games that season, he still finished with 242 carries for 983 yards and 7 TDs, while adding another 269 yards and 2 TDs through the air. Zeke is locked and loaded and should play 80+% of the snaps, rank top-5 the league in carries and get as many TD chances as any back (led league in red-zone touches in 2019). Plus, he's seen his pass-game usage go up the past 2 seasons. After seeing just 77 targets in his first 25 games, he has since seen 166 in his last 31. His usage is everything we look for in a back around which to build a fantasy squad.

4. **Dalvin Cook, MIN:** Cook has one concern: injury risk. Last year, he hurt his shoulder in Week 13 and wasn't the same back, but prior to that, he was 1 of only 2 backs to average over 23 PPR points per game. The other was Christian McCaffrey. The injury concerns are real; he's missed 19 games since 2017, with multiple injury inactives in every season, but when he is healthy, he's dynamite. He is on one of the heaviest run teams in the league -- the Vikings average the 4th-most runs per game -- and is heavily featured in the passing game (63 total targets last season). While Alexander Mattison is solid, he doesn't impact Cook much and is generally regulated for mop-up duty. If the game is close, Cook is on the field and getting the ball. He has one of the highest weekly floors and ceilings as a player around whom to build a fantasy team in 2020.

TOP TALENT

5. **Alvin Kamara, NO:** One of the biggest disappointments in fantasy last year was Kamara, who scored only 6 total touchdowns after he gathered 31 across the first 2 years of his career. Kamara is due for positive TD regression, and if he gets it, it would help him finish in the elite tier. While his snap rate is lower than we would like, his pass-game usage (97+ targets in every season) is elite, and throughout his career, he has been one of the most efficient backs in NFL history. Hampered by knee and ankle injuries in 2019, Kamara still managed to average 17.8 PPR points per game, despite the lack of TDs. As mentioned above, only Cook and McCaffrey averaged 23+ points per game last year through Week 13, but with the TDs in 2018, Kamara finished the season with 23.2. He should find the end zone more frequently, and betting on one of the best players on one of the best offenses with elite pass-game usage is a good wager.

6. **Joe Mixon, CIN:** This ranking assumes Mixon won't hold out. When he's active, Mixon may be the most underappreciated back in football, in part because of how the Bengals have used him. They waited till the 2nd half of the season to start playing him over 70% of the snaps. Once that happened, he went for 100+ total yards in 5 of 8 games and saw 23+ opportunities in all but 2 of those outings. Prior to that, he had just 1 game of 100+ total yards. Per PlayerProfiler, Mixon evaded more tackles than any other back in football last season, and now he gets to play in a better offense than ever before. QB Joe Burrow is an upgrade over Andy Dalton; Cincy gets A.J. Green back; they added Tee Higgins in the draft; and they return 2019 1st-round tackle Jonah Williams, who missed all of last season. The Bengals should commit more to Mixon, whose TD equity in a potentially potent offense could push him up the ladder even more in 2020.

7. **Derrick Henry, TEN:** Snaps and weighted opportunity are king. Well, don't tell that to King Henry, who finished 14th in snap rate amongst backs a (66.9%) and had just 25 targets on the season. Those targets were 7 more than in 2018, but his snap share increased by 26%. The Titans rode Henry to the AFC Championship Game, giving him more carries than any other back in football. He was a TD machine and finished the season with 150 or more yards in 4 of his last 6 games, scoring 10 touchdowns in that span. Henry has been a slow starter, but as the season wears on, Henry wears on a defense. He will be a candidate to lead the league in carries again after the Titans gave him the franchise tag this offseason. He will live off volume and touchdowns, he but offers little pass-game upside. He is a better standard player than PPR, but he is going to put up points in bunches.

8. **Miles Sanders, PHI:** This may be the first controversial ranking, but I am willing to die on this hill. Yes, Doug Pederson hasn't typically gone with the workhorse-back approach, but talent often dictates coaching, more so than vice versa. Gone is Jordan Howard, and as of publication, Boston Scott is the main backfield competition for Sanders. Starting in Week 11, the Eagles gave the reins to the talented rookie, playing him in 80% or more of the snaps in 4 of 6 games from Weeks 11-16. He shined as a rookie pass catcher; among RBs, he finished 7th with 509 receiving yards and tied for 12th among RBs both with 50 receptions and 63 targets. He averaged the 7th -most yards per touch amongst backs, all while failing to crack 60% of the snaps in any of his 1st 9 professional games. With a bigger workload and a heavy pass-game usage, the highly efficient back could be looking at a 1,500-yard season. With no Howard to vulture him, double-digit touchdowns sit well within the range of possible outcomes.

9. **Austin Ekeler, LAC:** Gone is Melvin Gordon, and freed is Ekeler. Last year, during Gordon's holdout, Ekeler destroyed fantasy football, with only Christian McCaffrey rivaling his numbers. In those 4 games, he had 3 top-4 fantasy finishes; played 67+% of the snaps in every game; and was fed in the passing game, averaging 6 targets per game and scoring 6 touchdowns. Ekeler is used at rushing and receiving -- and may be the game's best pass-catching back. He finished 2nd in targets, receptions and receiving yards among RBs while averaging the most yards per touch of any RB. While Justin Jackson and 4th-round rookie Joshua Kelley will have a role, Ekeler is looking at 60+% of the snaps and will be used as much, if not more, than any other back in the passing game. He may feel expensive this year but will look like a steal by the end of the season.

10. **Kenyan Drake, ARI:** Give me the workhorse back in Kliff Kingsbury's scheme and let me enjoy all the fantasy points. The Cardinals traded for Drake last year after David Johnson turned to dust and Chase Edmonds got hurt. It didn't take long for him to dominate the backfield, playing 80% or more of the snaps in 5 of the 8 games he was a Cardinal. He scored 14 or more PPR points in 4 of 8 games and had 3 top-3 performances. He was also fed the ball in the passing game with 4 or more targets in all but 2 games. Prior to Drake's arrival, we saw Edmonds have 1 start in which he was fully healthy, and he finished as fantasy's top back versus the Giants that week. Even Johnson had two games in which he finished as a week's top-5 RB due to his heavy pass-game usage. If you add it all up, the Cardinals produced 6 top-5 weeks for backs across 16 games and 3 RBs, and now this is Drake's backfield. The system will give Drake plenty of light boxes and opportunities as a receiver. He's one of the offseason's biggest winners!

11. **Nick Chubb, CLE:** For Chubb's value, the biggest concern -- the reason why he isn't higher on this list -- is Kareem Hunt. In the first 9 weeks of 2019 with Hunt suspended, Chubb averaged 19.2 carries and 4 targets per game, ranking him RB6 in that time span. After Hunt was reinstated, Chubb averaged 18 carries per game and only 2.1 targets, finishing as PPR RB15. Hunt, meanwhile, averaged 5.5 targets per game as RB17 during that span. Not only did Chubb's usage suffer, but so did his snap rate. While he dominated playing time early in the season, he failed to play more than 80% of the snaps in all but 1 game alongside Hunt. While Chubb will still be a dominant runner behind a much-improved O-line, the lack of receiving usage and how frequently he comes off the field place him lower in my ranks versus the consensus.

12. **Aaron Jones, GB:** Why do coaches not let us have nice things? Jones was one of the best backs in fantasy last year after scoring a league-leading 19 touchdowns. He's due for touchdown regression in 2020, but the real concern is how much time he will spend on the field. When Jones was a workhorse back, he crushed, but the Packers liked mixing in Jamaal Williams when healthy and just drafted A.J. Dillion in the 2nd round -- another mouth to feed. Jones will be the featured pass-catcher but is looking at a drop in TDs and snaps. This doesn't mean he won't be an excellent asset, but it means fantasy drafters should tread carefully when paying up for him.

13. **Clyde Edwards-Helaire, KC:** In his previous 22 years of drafting, Andy Reid had selected zero running backs in the 1st round, until he selected Patrick Mahomes' hand-picked back in 2020. Edwards-Helaire had the most receptions in the SEC in the last 20 years and fits like a glove in the Chiefs' offense. Reid compared CEH to Brian Westbrook "but better" in his post-draft press conference. When Westbrook played under Reid, he had 4 seasons of 87+ targets, back when RBs were not featured as heavily in the pass game as they are today. Beyond his receiving usage, CEH fell into football's most explosive offense. Teams don't draft backs this high and not play them, and getting on the field in this offense puts you in fantasy superstardom in a hurry, even for a rookie. If you're wondering how valuable a back is in this offense, look no further than Damien Williams. In his two-year career with the Chiefs, when Williams has played 60% or more of the snaps, he has averaged 25 PPR points per game! Fantasy managers will be uncomfortable taking a rookie this soon, but don't be one of those people.

SOLID OPTIONS

14. **Leonard Fournette, JAX:** Fournette's uncertain situation stops him from occupying the "Top Talent" tier. He had his 5th-year option declined, and he is on the trading block. While there are likely no suitors as I am writing this, all it takes is 1 injury for a team to trade for him and possibly eliminate his workhorse role. Fournette's upside is a possible repeat of his 2019 usage, which should be categorized as elite. He played 91.7% of the Jaguars' snaps and finished 4th in targets. Unfortunately, his efficiency was bad, and he fizzled in the end zone, scoring 3 total TDs on 265 carries and 76 receptions. If he stays in Jacksonville, he jumps up a tier. The unknown factor drops him a tier.

15. **Josh Jacobs, LV:** Jacobs was awesome as a rookie, but he has the same issue as Derrick Henry and Nick Chubb: He doesn't get the pass-game usage. There were quotes from staff about how that would change this year, but after Las Vegas re-signed Jalen Richard and drafted Lynn Bowden in the 3rd round, his passing-game ceiling remains capped. As a runner, Jacobs finished with the 8th-most evaded tackles and the 6th-highest juke rate among all backs, per PlayerProfiler. In his rookie year, Jacobs played only 54.8%

of the snaps and played over 70.4% of the snaps only once all of last season, while he saw just 28 targets. If he ever gets the passing-game usage, the sky's the limit for him, but until then, his ceiling is capped.

16. **Chris Carson, SEA:** Carson continues to be a value in fantasy. The Seahawks are determined to establish the run, having posted the 3rd-highest rushing rate in the NFL last year. Last season, Carson finished with 1,231 rushing yards and 267 receiving yards, while playing 73.9% of his snaps. He will be coming off a hip fracture, which is reason to pause, but his running mate Rashaad Penny is coming off a torn ACL. (Don't worry about the Carlos Hyde signing, either.) In every game last season, he saw 15 or more carries, outside of his injury shortened Week 16, and never failed to see a target in a single game. His workload in a run-1st, high-scoring offense makes him the perfect fantasy RB2.

17. **Todd Gurley, ATL:** The "fantasy superstar" version of Gurley is likely gone forever, but that does not mean he can't be serviceable in a high-scoring offense as a lead back. The Falcons cut Devonta Freeman this offseason and gave Gurley a one-year deal, while not adding anyone else of significance, signaling that this is his backfield. The Falcons like using running backs in the passing game; last season, Freeman finished 10th in total targets among RBs with 70, despite playing just 14 games. He had 1,000 total yards and played 67% of the snaps despite being one of football's least efficient backs. With Gurley's contract, he's a safe bet to dominate the offense's TD equity, play 70% of the snaps, and see good usage in the passing game. While the production won't match the days of old, Gurley is still relevant in this fantasy tier.

18. **Le'Veon Bell, NYJ:** Adam Gase hates this man, and if it wasn't clear enough from his press conferences, the team's offseason actions have expanded on it. They signed 37-year-old Frank Gore and drafted La'Mical Perine in the 4th round to add to this RB room. While Bell is unlikely to ever see the end of his contract or live up to the hype, he is likely to continue to get elite volume. Despite running behind one of the worst offensive lines, only getting into the end zone four times, and being horribly inefficient, Bell was still relevant because of his volume, finishing as RB18 overall last year. He was 4th in snap rate, 4th in weighted opportunity, and 7th in total RB targets. Behind an improved offensive line, with a year of getting his football legs back, and due for positive touchdown regression, Bell's volume is worth betting on.

19. **Melvin Gordon, DEN:** The strangest landing spot of the offseason might be Gordon to the Broncos, but it happened, and we must adjust. Denver prioritized Gordon, making him the 7th-highest-paid RB on a per-year basis. He is looking at 65-70% of the snaps and a role in the passing game. Phillip Lindsay will move to a change-of-pace role, while Royce Freeman gets comfortable on the bench. The Broncos rebuilt their entire offense, adding 2 receivers and a tight end in the draft, along with Gordon in free agency. Look for them to improve and create more scoring opportunities for Gordon, who should dominate the backfield's TD equity.

UP & COMING

20. **Cam Akers, LAR:** Since HC Sean McVay has taken over, the Rams backfield has averaged 21.7 touchdowns per season. Yes, a huge part of that was Todd Gurley's former greatness, but the system itself is friendly to RB scores. Akers will be competing with Malcolm Brown, who is Just A Guy by all standards, and 2019 3rd-rounder Darrell Henderson, who couldn't figure out how to run behind a zone-blocking scheme. Akers has a workhorse profile, is an elite athlete, and had major college production, despite running behind the worst line in college football. Last year, the ghost of Gurley finished as RB14, so Akers' live legs have a chance to break onto the scene in a major way this year.

21. **Jonathan Taylor, IND:** Jonathan Taylor has as good of a rushing profile as any running back prospect this decade. Often compared to Ezekiel Elliott and Nick Chubb, Taylor blazed a 4.39 40-yard dash at 226 pounds and rushed for over 1,900 yards in all 3 college while scoring a ridiculous 45 touchdowns. The Colts traded up for him, which historically speaking means they plan on using him right away. Marlon Mack is in the last year of his contract, and Taylor should take over as the lead back behind one of the league's best offensive lines. The question with Taylor is his receiving game upside. Across his first 2 years, he only caught 16 total passes, and the Colts have Mack and Nyheim Hines as receivers. On top of that,

Taylor was rarely asked to pass-block and will be raw in that area. In his 1st year, he may be more of a 2-down back but will still have value, and if he ever gets that pass-game usage, he will be a league-winning player.

22. **J.K. Dobbins, BAL:** We may have to wait a year to fully unlock the stud that is Dobbins, but I am willing to be early on him. No back in this class saw more rushing attempts come from run-pass-option setups in college than Dobbins (57%), and the Ravens had the most RPO rush attempts in the NFL. The Ravens easily led the league in carries, with Mark Ingram and Gus Edwards averaging over 5.4 yards per touch in this system. Dobbins is an elite athlete boasting a dominant college profile with talent in both the run and pass game. He could easily lead the team in carries and be the starter by the end of the season. He fits like a glove into this offense. The Ravens didn't spend 2nd-round draft capital for him to not play, and the more he plays, the harder it will be to keep him off the field.

23. **D'Andre Swift, DET:** Swift top back in this class, according to many draft analysts, and got the expected draft capital. However, his landing spot with the Lions is a bit murkier than others'; Just 2 years ago, Detroit just drafted Kerryon Johnson, who has been effective when healthy – of course, he's rarely healthy. Few concerns exist regarding Swift's talent: He is an explosive, quick-twitch athlete who excels at making defenders miss and catches passes effectively. The concern is with his workload. Is he stepping into a committee in Year 1 that will have him closer to the 12-touch range per game than the desired 18-plus? Of the top rookie backs, Swift leaves me the most concerned, but he is going in the same range. The future may be bright for Swift, but letting others pay the price for Year 1 production is likely best.

24. **Devin Singletary, BUF:** People will knock Singletary, saying that Buffalo added Zach Moss and have Josh Allen around the goal line while questioning his touchdown upside. The thing that's important to note: He only scored 4 total TDs last year and only played in 12 games -- and *still* almost finished as a fantasy RB2. Singletary is a highly efficient back, finishing with the 3rd-highest breakaway-run percentage, having the 3rd-best juke rate, 5th-best average of true yards per carry, and 13th-most yards per touch, per PlayerProfiler. Buffalo's staff raved about him all offseason, and drafting a Frank Gore replacement should not have dropped Singletary's stock the way it has. Highly efficient pass-catchers are strong RB2 candidates, and if the oft-injured Moss misses time, Singletary's ceiling is sky-high.

RED FLAGS

25. **Raheem Mostert, SF:** I get the appeal with the explosive back in an offense that had the second-most carries of any team last year -- in a Kyle Shanahan system that has always produced good fantasy performances. The issue: Mostert will continue to occupy a timeshare with Tevin Coleman, but you have to pay a premium price to chase last year's production. He played over 60% of the snaps in just 2 of 16 games; he saw more than 2 targets just once; and had only 1 regular-season game of more than 15 carries. He was extremely efficient, but the volume and snap share are concerning, and once you add in the cost, you are paying full price for the ceiling.

26. **Marlon Mack, IND:** Mack was game-script-dependent and wasn't featured in the passing game during 2019. Now he is on an expiring contract, and the Colts just traded up to draft Jonathan Taylor, who does everything Mack does but better. He needs an injury to be relevant, and Taylor was extremely durable at Wisconsin. Mack is not in the Colts' current or future plans and is best left for someone else to have the headache.

27. **Mark Ingram, BAL:** You will notice a theme here amongst these backs. The Ravens selected J.K. Dobbins in the 2nd round, which leaves Ingram's role in question. He could and likely will start ahead of Dobbins to start the season, but as the season goes on, the young legs of Dobbins will likely diminish Ingram's role. Ingram will still have TD equity in an explosive offense, but even last season, he was a guessing game, playing over 60% of the snaps just twice in 16 games, and scoring 10 or fewer points in 31% of his games. Limited snaps/touches combined with touchdown variance will make him a nightmarish weekly guessing game.

28. **Kerryon Johnson, DET:** Johnson battled an ankle injury during just about his entire final season at Auburn. In his rookie year, he missed 6 games with a knee sprain, then in his sophomore NFL campaign, he missed 8 games with a meniscus tear. He has battled injuries his whole career, and the Lions seem done with it

after drafting D'Andre Swift in the top of the 2nd round. Even without Swift, Johnson has just 3 games in his career with 20+ touches. He is talented, but the Lions clearly have moved on, and so should you.

29. **Ronald Jones, TB:** Jones has struggled his entire career to get on the field, and once he is on the field, he rarely does anything. He played 37.5% of the snaps in 2019, after playing just 20.8% in his rookie season. He has offered little in the passing game dating all the way back to high school and averaged just 4.2 yards per carry last season. His calling card in college was his home-run-hitting ability, but what do you do with a home-run hitter who stops hitting home runs? In his NFL career, he has 8 total runs of 15 or more yards on 195 carries. The Bucs also drafted Ke'Shawn Vaughn, who is a serviceable back, in the 3rd round. Any competition is worrisome for Jones -- he struggled to beat out *Peyton Barber* early in his career.

30. **Zach Moss, BUF:** Moss tested poorly at the combine, but his most desirable trait does not have an athletic test: contact balance. Moss is tough to bring down, which makes him a yards-after-contact machine. He will step into the Frank Gore role but has more upside; he's currently a better all-around player. Concerns: QB Josh Allen could gobble up TDs near the goal line, and Devin Singletary could take most of the receiving work. (Gore saw just 16 targets last season.)

31. **David Johnson, HOU:** The Houston Texans traded Deandre Hopkins for a second round pick and David Johnson this offseason. Was it smart, nope, but it happened and Johnson is now the starting back for the Texans. The concern is that David Johnson is washed, he looked like a herd of snails traveling through peanut butter trying to get to the edge last year. His top ability is his work in the receiving game, but historically mobile quarterbacks have not been kind to receiving backs. Last year the Texans threw the ball to a running back only 79 total times, the fourth fewest in the league, and that was with Duke Johnson who is an extremely talented pass catching back. Johnson finished with more receiving yards (370) than rushing yards (345) in 2019, averaging just 3.7 yards per carry. This is coming off a 2018 campaign where he averaged just 3.6 yards per carry, so he has been extremely inefficient running the ball and at 28 that is not likely to change. He has some upside in the passing game and should be involved in the offense after the Texans paid a premium price to get him, but the best days are behind David Johnson

SERVICEABLE

32. **Kareem Hunt, CLE:** Hunt has serious off-the-field problems, but on the field, he's been extremely efficient. One of the best yards-after-contact guys, Hunt excelled as the Browns' pass-catcher. When he shared work with Nick Chubb late in the season, he finished as PPR RB17, compared to Chubb's RB15, while seeing 5.6 targets per game. Hunt is one of my favorite middle-rounds RBs. He has standalone fantasy value as a receiver, and if something happens to Chubb, he becomes a league-winning asset.

33. **David Montgomery, CHI:** Montgomery knows how to make people miss, but he doesn't go far once he does. Last season per PlayerProfiler, he evaded 75 tackles, which was good for 13th among RBs. However, he only had a "true yards per carry" of 3.5, ranking 56th among RBs. While he may not be efficient, he is set to have the same role as his rookie year: the primary back on 1st and 2nd downs, with minor potential to add catches. This gives him 1,000-yard, 10-TD upside on top of a median projection of a solid weekly flex play.

34. **James Conner, PIT:** Gone are the days of Conner being a fantasy star. The Steelers added another back in the draft, making that 3 straight years drafting a running back: Jaylen Samuels, Benny Snell and, in 2020, Anthony McFarland. Conner battled multiple injuries in 2019, going on the injury report 5 separate times throughout the season. When he was healthy, he had multiple big games and will still be the lead back behind a good offensive line. The Steelers like to utilize running backs in the passing game, too. The Steelers backfield under Tomlin has always been a coveted fantasy asset, and this year you get the lead back cheaper than ever before. Conner is worth taking as an RB2.

35. **Ke'Shawn Vaughn, TB:** The 3rd-rounder out of Vanderbilt will play HC Bruce Arians, who hesitated to give David Johnson any real playing time over Andre Ellington for 8 weeks, despite Johnson making a play nearly every time he touched the ball. Though Vaughn got a good landing spot, don't expect him to be the workhorse back right away. He'll come in and compete with Ronald Jones but is the superior player in the passing game. Arians has a history of building up running backs; Tampa Bay just hasn't had a good enough option. Vaughn's stock is high right now, but he'll likely be in a committee at least at the start.

36. **Jordan Howard, MIA:** Somehow, Howard continues to stay fantasy-relevant. After he signed with the Dolphins, most expected his role to be diminished to that of a backup after Dolphins would take a back high in the draft. Well, they didn't do that and only traded for Matt Breida. Howard is a one-dimensional bowling ball who barrels through defenders, hits some big runs, and finds his way into the end zone. He adds about as much as Edward Scissorhands in the passing game, but he could easily rush for 800 yards and score 8 touchdowns this season. Last year, Ryan Fitzpatrick led the Dolphins in rushing, but this is a much-improved roster, offensive line and running back group.

37. **Damien Williams, KC:** Williams was one of last year's biggest fantasy disappointments. He got hurt in camp and couldn't get right until Week 17, when he exploded and went on to have nearly 300 yards, and he 6 touchdowns in 3 playoff games. Williams has dominated when he plays over 60% of the snaps, averaging over 25 PPR points per game. While he is now the second fiddle to Clyde Edwards-Helaire, he is likely to still be involved in the passing game and is an injury away from being a league-winning player.

WATCH LIST

38. **Boston Scott, PHI:** Here's my favorite late-round sleeper. As of publication, the Eagles failed to add a notable RB behind Miles Sanders, leaving Scott in the role. He played 4 games last season in which he saw over 30% of the snaps. In those games, he scored 24.8, 13.5, 7.9, and 35.8 PPR points, seeing 6 or more targets in each. He is an electric player with elite short-area quickness who's set up to be an asset in a Eagles passing game that is missing targets on the outside. He could have a James White- or Austin Ekeler-like season and is available at the end of drafts.

39. **Matt Breida, MIA:** Fantasy players have long chanted "Free Matt Breida." He's an explosive athlete with 4.44 speed and has finished top-7 in breakaway percentage each of the last 2 years. He hasn't been asked to contribute much in the passing game, but because he's competing with just Jordan Howard, he's expected to take on that role. He's a better athlete and better talent than Howard and earn a near full-time job by season's end. A workhorse role for Breida would mean big things for the owner who drafts him.

40. **Tony Pollard, DAL:** Pollard has a lot going for him, but 1 major thing in his way: Ezekiel Elliott is not going anywhere anytime soon. Pollard should carve out a role in the passing game, but if something happens to Zeke, Pollard would become a top-10 running back. His efficiency stats were off the charts last year; he finished 9th in breakaway-run rate, 8th in yards per touch, 4th in "true yards per carry," and led RBs in "yards created per touch," per PlayerProfiler. Pollard was a dominant receiving back at Memphis and in his rookie year averaged 7.1 yards per catch. If Zeke misses anytime, you will wish you had Pollard on your roster.

41. **Justin Jackson, LAC:** Gone is Melvin Gordon, and Jackson should reap the reward. While Austin Ekeler can be considered a top-10 fantasy back in 2020, Jackson is the secondary piece in the backfield who can be had for cheap. One concern with Jackson coming out of college was that his 4-year workhorse role at Northwestern would lead to wear and tear; he then missed 9 of 16 possible games last year. The Chargers also drafted Joshua Kelley in case Jackson proves he can't stay healthy. However, if he does stay healthy, he could be looking at 10-12 touches per game. Jackson averaged 6.9 yards per carry last season. Even while sharing work with Ekeler, an active Jackson could turn into a weekly flex option.

Chapter 5

WIDE RECEIVERS

½ & FULL PPR RPV

WR1

	Player	RPV
1	Michael Thomas	26%
2	Davante Adams	15%
3	Julio Jones	14%
4	DeAndre Hopkins	11%
5	Tyreek Hill	2%
6	Cooper Kupp	-3%
7	Adam Thielen	-7%
8	Keenan Allen	-9%
9	Chris Godwin	-9%
10	Robert Woods	-11%
11	Kenny Golladay	-13%
12	Odell Beckham Jr	-14%

WR2

	Player	RPV
1	Amari Cooper	5%
2	Tyler Lockett	5%
3	JuJu Smith-Schuster	4%
4	Mike Evans	3%
5	D.J. Moore	2%
6	Allen Robinson	2%
7	Calvin Ridley	0%
8	T.Y. Hilton	0%
9	Courtland Sutton	-4%
10	Julian Edelman	-4%
11	Jarvis Landry	-5%
12	A.J. Green	-6%

WR3

	Player	RPV
1	DeVante Parker	9%
2	Deebo Samuel	8%
3	Terry McLaurin	5%
4	A.J. Brown	3%
5	D.K. Metcalf	2%
6	Stefon Diggs	-1%
7	Tyler Boyd	-2%
8	Michael Gallup	-3%
9	Marquise Brown	-4%
10	Marvin Jones	-4%
11	Dionte Johnson	-6%
12	Jamison Crowder	-7%

WR4

	Player	RPV
1	Will Fuller	7%
2	Christian Kirk	6%
3	Sterling Shepard	4%
4	D.J. Chark	2%
5	John Brown	1%
6	Darius Slayton	0%
7	Emmanuel Sanders	-1%
8	Alshon Jeffrey	-2%
9	Sammy Watkins	-4%
10	Anthony Miller	-4%
11	Jerry Jeudy	-5%
12	Brandin Cooks	-6%

STANDARD RPV

WR1

	Player	RPV
1	Michael Thomas	21%
2	Davante Adams	17%
3	Julio Jones	16%
4	Tyreek Hill	7%
5	DeAndre Hopkins	4%
6	Kenny Golladay	-5%
7	Cooper Kupp	-5%
8	Adam Thielen	-8%
9	Chris Godwin	-11%
10	Mike Evans	-11%
11	Tyler Lockett	-12%
12	Odell Beckham Jr	-13%

WR2

	Player	RPV
1	Amari Cooper	7%
2	T.Y. Hilton	5%
3	Kennan Allen	4%
4	JuJu Smith-Schuster	2%
5	Robert Woods	2%
6	D.J. Moore	1%
7	Calvin Ridley	0%
8	A.J. Brown	-2%
9	Allen Robinson	-4%
10	Courtland Sutton	-5%
11	Terry McLaurin	-5%
12	A.J. Green	-6%

WR3

	Player	RPV
1	D.K. Metcalf	7%
2	DeVante Parker	7%
3	Deebo Samuel	6%
4	Michael Gallup	2%
5	Marquise Brown	2%
6	Jarvis Landry	2%
7	Tyler Boyd	-2%
8	Marvin Jones	-2%
9	Stefon Diggs	-3%
10	Dionte Johnson	-4%
11	Mike Williams	-8%
12	Darius Slayton	-10%

WR4

	Player	RPV
1	Julian Edelman	8%
2	Will Fuller	7%
3	D.J. Chark	6%
4	Jamison Crowder	4%
5	John Brown	3%
6	Jerry Jeudy	-1%
7	Sammy Watkins	-2%
8	Anthony Miller	-3%
9	Brandon Cooks	-4%
10	Alshon Jeffrey	-4%
11	Sterling Shepard	-6%
12	Emmanuel Sanders	-7%

Player Profiles and Overview
By Adam Ronis

Wide receiver is extremely deep this season. While there are less dominant upper-tier names this season, fantasy drafters can find a lot of young, ascending talents.

Even if you don't get a wide receiver in the first 2 or 3 rounds, you can find a lot of appealing receivers in the middle-to-late rounds with winning potential. While waiting to fill out this position is a viable strategy, it could allow some top receivers to fall farther than they should. With such good depth at the position, pickers can build a successful WR strategy in a multitude of ways.

THE ELITE

1. **Michael Thomas, NO:** Thomas is money in the bank. He commands a huge target share and has a great rapport with Drew Brees. Even when Brees missed a few games due to injury, Thomas didn't disappear like some other receivers would. He had a 32% target share and led receivers in targets (185), receptions (149) and yards (1,725) last season. Thomas has at least 100 receptions in three consecutive seasons and is averaging 8.6 receptions per game the last two seasons. In 2019, Thomas, who has a career 79% catch rate, averaged almost 12 targets per game and 9 receptions and failed to reach double-digit points in PPR formats in one game. He has scored at least 9 touchdowns in 3 of his 4 seasons. Thomas has one of the highest floors to go with a high ceiling.

2. **Davante Adams, GB:** After three consecutive seasons of double-digit touchdowns, Adams fell short after missing four games with a turf toe injury that also slowed him in a few games. Adams had 127 targets, catching 83 for 997 yards and 5 touchdowns. He is clearly the No. 1 target in the offense and has a good chance to reach double-digit touchdowns. Adams got healthy as the season went on, too: Over the final 9 weeks, only Michael Thomas averaged more fantasy points per game, and Adams had a target share of 31%. Adams had at least 93 receiving yards and averaged 122 across his final 5 games, including a pair of playoff outings. The Packers didn't add any wide receivers in the draft and merely signed Devin Funchess as a complementary option, so Adams is going to be flooded with targets. He could finish as the top overall receiver.

3. **Julio Jones, ATL:** Jones continues to put up numbers year after year. He has played at least 15 games in five of the last six seasons. Jones has reached at least 1,394 yards in six straight years and has registered at least 88 receptions in five of them. The lack of TDs is a constant criticism since he's a dominant receiver. He has only reached double-digit TDs once -- back in 2012. Jones scored 6 TDs last year and 8 in 2018. He makes up for it with a lot of receptions and yards. Jones is 31 and had a career-low 8.9 yards per target last season.

4. **Chris Godwin, TB:** Godwin was a major target for me in drafts last season, and he delivered, averaging the second-most points per game for wide receivers. Godwin missed the final two games with a hamstring injury but still had 86 receptions for 1,333 yards and 9 TDs in 14 games on 121 targets. He scored more than 20 fantasy points in five games. The shift from Jameis Winston to Tom Brady won't hurt much; Godwin plays most of his time in the slot, a position Brady targets often. In '19, Godwin had a 72% catch rate, which ranked fourth.

5. **Tyreek Hill, KC:** Hill is one of the most explosive wide receivers playing in the best offense in the NFL, with Patrick Mahomes as his QB. Hill missed 4 games last season due to a clavicle injury, and Mahomes wasn't 100 percent healthy for some of the season. Hill still finished as a WR1 in points per game for PPR formats, totaling 58 receptions for 860 yards and 7 touchdowns. In the previous two seasons, Hill finished as a top-5 WR in PPR. He won't get as many receptions as the top receivers, but the yards and touchdowns put him in this group. The value increases in non-PPR, considering he has 36 touchdowns in 59 games.

6. **DeAndre Hopkins, ARI:** There's always a little concern about a wide receiver changing teams and working with a new quarterback, but Hopkins is in a good spot with an improving offense. Hopkins has at least 150 targets in 5 consecutive seasons and a target share of at least 30 percent in the last 3. That will likely decrease, but Hopkins should still be one of the top receivers for Kyler Murray, who will improve in his second season. Hopkins has recorded at least 96 receptions and been a top-5 receiver in 4 of the last 5 seasons.

7. **Allen Robinson, CHI:** Robinson is one of the NFL's most underrated wide receivers. He had 80 catches for 1,400 yards with 14 TDs in 2015 with Blake Bortles as his quarterback. Last season, he had 154 targets, which ranked third in the NFL, and caught 98 passes for 1,147 yards with seven touchdowns catching passes from the erratic Mitchell Trubisky. Robinson hasn't played with good quarterbacks and still produces, though Nick Foles should be an upgrade if he takes over under center. Robinson will continue to see a lot of targets and be one of the best wide receivers. In some drafts, he goes as a WR2.

TOP TALENT

1. **Kenny Golladay, DET:** Golladay led the NFL with 11 touchdown catches last season. He had 13 targets inside the 10 and averaged 7.8 targets per game with Matthew Stafford at quarterback in 9 games. He took a dip with Jeff Driskel and David Blough throwing him passes following Stafford's season-ending injury. Despite that, he still finished as WR9 in PPR. Golladay had 116 targets and caught 65 passes for 1,190 yards, averaging 18.3 yards per catch. His best season might still be ahead.

2. **Adam Thielen, MIN:** Physical setbacks slowed Thielen last season; he was limited to 10 games and often battled a hamstring injury when active. He looked good in the postseason with 7 catches for 129 yards against the Saints and 5 receptions for 50 yards against the 49ers. He played in all 16 games his first 5 seasons. In 2017, he had 142 targets, and the next year he had 153 targets, finishing as a top-10 WR in both years. The departure of Stefon Diggs will increase the target share to the 26-28% range, and he could get back to the 140-to-150-target window. He should be among the league leaders in targets. Volume is important in fantasy. Thielen will be 30 when the season starts, but even in a run-centric offense, he doesn't have much competition to take away targets. He has a high floor.

3. **D.J. Moore, CAR:** Moore finished as WR16 in PPR catching passes from Cam Newton, Kyle Allen and Will Grier last year. He caught 87 passes for 1,175 yards and four touchdowns in his second season on 135 targets in 15 games. After averaging 9.6 yards per target as a rookie, he averaged 8.7 last season. He'll be a good fit for Teddy Bridgewater, who likes to check down and not take chances deep. When Bridgewater did take downfield shots last season, he was more accurate than Allen. Moore thrives after the catch, averaging 5.7 yards for his career, and will be one of the top receiving options along with Christian McCaffrey. Carolina's defense shapes up to be bad, the club could pass more to play catchup. The only knock on Moore is a lack of TDs, with six in his first two seasons. Moore has a high PPR floor, and more end-zone trips could vault him into the top 10 WRs at season's end.

4. **Odell Beckham Jr., CLE:** Beckham played with a core muscle injury in 2019, and Baker Mayfield struggled behind a bad offensive line. It led to Beckham finishing as WR25. He still had 133 targets and caught 74 passes for 1,035 yards, but only 4 touchdowns. He also had 13 end-zone targets, but he finished as a top-10 WR in only one week. Those who had Beckham last season will likely move on, but he could be a bargain depending on the room. The Browns bolstered the offensive line, and the offense should improve, and Beckham still has upside in his age-27 season.

5. **JuJu Smith-Schuster, PIT:** After Smith-Schuster had 2,344 receiving yards in his first 2 seasons, he crashed last year. A lot of it was due to Ben Roethlisberger suffering a season-ending injury in Week 2 and the offense falling apart with bad QB play from Mason Rudolph and Devlin Hodges. Smith-Schuster also got hurt and played in 12 games. Expect a bounce back with Roethlisberger healthy. Smith-Schuster, only 23 years old, had 166 targets, 111 catches for 1,426 yards and 7 touchdowns 2 years ago playing alongside Antonio Brown.

6. **Amari Cooper, DAL:** Cooper has been good since coming over to the Cowboys. He has 14 touchdowns in 25 games and was a top-10 WR through the 1st half of last season, before slowing down by playing through injuries. He finished with 79 catches for 1,189 yards with 8 touchdowns on 119 targets and averaged a career-high 15.1 yards per reception. In 8 of his first 9 games, he had at least 9 points in PPR formats. In the final 7 games, Cooper had 7 points or fewer in 4 games with 1 touchdown. Copper had a career-best 10 yards per target in 2019. Cooper has at least 7 TDs in 4 straight seasons and has developed a good rapport with Dak Prescott.

7. **Calvin Ridley, ATL:** Ridley should see a lot more time in the slot with the departures of Mohamed Sanu, who was traded last year to the Patriots, and Austin Hooper, now in Cleveland. Ridley saw almost 2 more targets per game after Sanu left. Ridley had a 16.8% target share last season and tied for 20th in targets. In 13 games, Ridley had 93 targets and caught 63 passes for 866 yards and 7 touchdowns; in his final 6 games, he averaged 17.1 PPR points per game. He was a top-15 wideout in points per game before missing the final 3. In 29 career games, Ridley has scored 17 TDs. Atlanta didn't add receivers in the draft, setting up Ridley to explode. He has a good chance to finish as a fantasy WR1.

8. **Cooper Kupp, LAR:** Kupp was one of the best wide receivers for more than half the season coming off an ACL injury. In the first 12 weeks, he played 87% of the snaps. Over the final 5 weeks of 2019, he played only 63% of the snaps with a 15% target share. That coincides with the emergence of tight end Tyler Higbee. Kupp finished 2nd among wide receivers with 10 touchdowns. Kupp caught 94 passes for 1,164 yards on 134 targets. The departure of Brandin Cooks should help Kupp, but a lot will come down to the personnel the Rams employ. They could run more 2-TE sets and shift away from the 11 personnel they have run often. Still, Kupp has

produced in his first 3 seasons, and Jared Goff tends to look for him in the red zone. Kupp has 16 touchdowns in his past 24 games.

9. **A.J. Brown, TEN:** Brown is tricky to project. He's clearly an excellent receiver but plays in a run-1st offense that doesn't pass often; when they did last season, they were extremely efficient. From Weeks 12-17, Brown was the WR1. The floor is low for Brown due to the lack of aerial volume, but the ceiling is high if Brown gets busier. Brown had 6.1 targets per game with Ryan Tannehill at quarterback, and for the season, he caught 52 passes on 84 targets for 1,051 yards with 8 touchdowns. He averaged 20.2 yards per catch and 12.5 yards per target, while dropping 1 pass. The volume increase should somewhat negate the decline in efficiency with Brown as the top receiving option.

10. **Tyler Lockett, SEA:** Lockett was on a torrid pace before coming down with a bad case of the flu down the stretch. Lockett likely would have had 100 catches, but he only had 23 catches for 290 yards with 2 touchdowns over the final 7 games. He still had a career-high 110 targets and caught 82 passes for 1,057 yards with 8 touchdowns. He has 18 scores over the last 2 seasons and will get a good amount of the targets from Russell Wilson. Lockett had 13 end zone looks last season, and he's one of the most efficient receivers in the NFL with a catch rate of 81.4% in 2018 and 74.5% last season.

11. **Robert Woods, LAR:** Woods has finished as a top-15 WR in each of the last 2 seasons with 130 targets in 16 games in 2018 and 139 in 15 games last season. Woods led the team with a 23% target share last year. He had 86 catches for 1,219 yards with 6 touchdowns in 2018 and had 90 catches for 1,134 yards with 2 touchdowns last year. Woods has a rushing touchdown in each of the last 2 seasons, but he doesn't get many targets in the end zone, which limits his scoring chances. Woods had at least 7 targets in 12 of 15 games last season, though, and has a high floor in PPR formats. He had 560 yards after the catch, which ranked 2nd among wide receivers.

12. **D.J. Chark, JAC:** Chark had a breakout season in his 2nd year after 14 receptions in 11 games as a rookie. He led the Jaguars in targets, receiving yards and touchdowns. Chark had 73 catches for 1,008 yards and 8 touchdowns in 15 games and only dropped 2 passes. Much of the success for Chark came with Gardner Minshew II at quarterback, and he will enter the season as the starter. Chark had 12 end-zone targets, and with his size and speed, he will produce another good season.

13. **D.K. Metcalf, SEA:** Metcalf was a physical freak in his rookie campaign. He played all 16 games and caught 58 passes for 900 yards with 7 touchdowns on 100 targets. He averaged 15.5 yards per grab and is tied to Russell Wilson, one of the best quarterbacks in the NFL. If the Seahawks open up the passing game more, Metcalf could be even better. Metcalf averaged 9 yards per target and 72 yards per game over the last 10 games. He had 19 end-zone targets to lead the NFL and 11 outings of double-digit points in PPR formats.

14. **Terry McLaurin, WAS:** McLaurin was an excellent value last season and a great waiver-wire pickup in leagues, too. 11 wide receivers were drafted before him in 2019. He would have had a 1,000-yard season if he didn't miss 2 games due to injuries. He did well, though, with 93 targets, 58 catches, 919 yards and 7 touchdowns. He did this in a bad offense that endured a midseason coaching change. McLaurin should continue to get a sizable target share, and he's a game-breaking moment waiting to happen. He had 15 plays of 20-plus yards, 10 end-zone targets, and an average of 9.9 yards per target.

15. **Courtland Sutton, DEN:** Sutton took a big leap in his 2nd season in the NFL despite catching passes from Joe Flacco, Drew Lock and Brandon Allen. Sutton was targeted 124 times and caught 72 passes for 1,112 yards with 6 touchdowns. He's the top target for the Broncos, and as long as Lock can progress, Sutton can continue his ascension. Sutton is a big target with 23 end-zone targets in 2 seasons.

SOLID OPTIONS

1. **DeVante Parker, MIA:** Parker finally had his breakout in season 5. After teasing for years and dealing with injuries, he caught 72 passes for 1,202 yards with 9 touchdowns on 128 targets. In his final 8 games, Parker averaged 9.5 targets per game. From Week 11 until the end of the season, he led the NFL with 733 receiving yards. He had 9 touchdowns in his first 4 seasons and then, last year, averaged 16.7 yards per catch and finished top-5 in yards and touchdowns. Parker, a 1st-round pick in 2015, is still just 27, and it wouldn't be surprising to see him post another good season, although he has a schedule full of top cornerbacks.

2. **T.Y. Hilton, IND:** Hilton has been durable throughout his career but missed 6 games last year and turns 31 in November. Hilton scored 5 touchdowns in the first fi5ve games last season before injuries slowed him down the rest of the way. Hilton hasn't topped 6 touchdowns in four straight seasons, so he needs the receptions and yardage to be high. Hilton should bounce back with Philip Rivers as his quarterback.

3. **Jarvis Landry, CLE:** Landry provides a steady floor. The target share has been consistent for him whether he's been with the Dolphins or Browns. Landry had targets shares of 29% in 2015 and 2016. Including the past two with the Browns, Landry had 27% in each of his past 3 seasons, including 139 in '19. Landry had a career-high 14.1 yards per reception and 8.5 yards per target last year to complement 83 catches for 1,174 yards and 6 touchdowns. He has finished as a top-20 fantasy WR in 5 straight seasons. Landry is coming off hip surgery but hasn't missed a game in his 6-year career.

4. **Tyler Boyd, CIN:** Boyd played well in an offense that struggled most of the season in 2019; he caught passes from Andy Dalton and Ryan Finley behind a bad offensive line. Boyd showed he could be a No. 1 receiver in the offense, and with Joe Burrow at quarterback, there's potential for this to be an excellent unit. Boyd had 148 targets last season, catching 90 for 1,046 yards with 5 touchdowns. While the return of a healthy A.J. Green and the addition of rookie Tee Higgins could cut into Boyd's workload, Boyd has averaged 14.6 fantasy points in games played with Green. The offense should be more efficient if Burrow lives up to expectations, which should help offset the target decrease.

5. **Michael Gallup, DAL:** Gallup was going to be one of my favorite undervalued targets, but the draft pick of CeeDee Lamb will slightly cut into Gallup's potential. Gallup averaged 79.07 yards per game last season, which was almost 5 yards more than Amari Cooper. Gallup averaged 8.1 targets per game; Copper was at 7.4. Gallup is a big-play threat that took a big leap in his sophomore season with 66 catches, 1,106 yards, 16.8 yards per catch and 6 touchdowns in 14 games. The Cowboys will have one of the best offenses in the NFL, but the Gallup's ceiling dips with a more crowded receiving corps. This may cause Gallup's price to drop more than it should in fantasy drafts, though, which will mitigate some of his risk.

6. **A.J. Green, CIN:** Green was given the franchise tag instead of a long-term contract. It's all about health for Green, who missed all of 2019 with an ankle injury. In his first 5 seasons, Green never played fewer than 13 games. Green has missed 23 of the last 32 games. He will be 32 when the season begins; that's an age at which many receivers start to decline. Green carries a lot of risk, but if he stays healthy, he possesses big upside.

7. **Marvin Jones Jr., DET:** Jones will get overlooked due to being 30 years old and ending last season with an injury. Jones played 9 games in 2018 and 13 last season, but he's still good when Matthew Stafford is throwing him the ball. In 8 games with Stafford last season, Jones had 42 catches for 535 yards and 6 touchdowns. Jones has scored 9 touchdowns in 2 of the last 3 seasons and was on pace for 9 last year before the injury. Jones has been a top-30 WR in points per game for wide receivers the last 3 years. He's undervalued.

8. **Jamison Crowder, NYJ:** Crowder has a high floor and should be the most targeted player in the offense. He's not going to have huge games, but the slot wideout can provide points in PPR formats. Crowder averaged 8.2 targets and a 24.2% target share when Sam Darnold was QB. Crowder had 78 catches for 833 yards with 6 touchdowns last season, which was WR26 in PPR. He had 122 targets and averaged 7.6 per game, which ranked 24th among receivers.

9. **Brandin Cooks, HOU:** Cooks was traded for the 3rd time in his career. Cooks has produced a 1,000-yard season with the Saints, Patriots and Rams, but he's coming off a bad year due to a concussion. He has had 5 documented concussions in his career. Cooks should get a good amount of targets with the Texans, though; the departure of DeAndre Hopkins opens up 150 targets. Cooks is a big-play threat with 54 receptions of 20+ yards the 5 five seasons. Deshaun Watson will find him; he led the NFL in completion rate on deep passing attempts (42%). Cooks is at best a fantasy WR3, though, given his boom-or-bust weekly performance.

RED FLAGS

1. **Mike Evans, TB:** There is some concern for Evans going from Jameis Winston, who wasn't afraid to take shots down the field, to Tom Brady, who won't take as many chances. Evans depends on big plays and touchdowns. He averaged 17.7 and 17.3 yards per reception the past 2 seasons. Brady averaged 6.6 yards per attempt last season, and while that should improve with better talent in Tampa Bay compared to the Patriots last season,

Evans might disappoint: He's still being drafted as a top-10 receiver in early drafts. Evans has only had a catch rate of more than 60% once, so he may top that with better efficiency with Brady. Evans has reached 1,000 yards in all 6 seasons. However, with an improved defense and a QB who won't turn it over as often as Winston, the volume and big plays probably will dip.

2. **Keenan Allen, LAC:** Allen relies on burst, quickness, and catching passes in short areas to pile up receptions. The pace of the offense and the fit with Tyrod Taylor or rookie Justin Herbert are concerns. The floor for Allen is lower than it has been. He's still the top target on the team, but matching numbers from the last few seasons is going to be difficult. Allen has at least 97 receptions and at least 1,196 yards in the last 3 campaigns. Allen is 5th in the NFL in targets and has been a top-12 fantasy receiver in the last 3 seasons, but that will end this season without Philip Rivers throwing him the football.

3. **Stefon Diggs, BUF:** Diggs has never played 16 games in his 5 seasons. He did play in 15 in each of the last 2 seasons, but a move to Buffalo isn't great for his fantasy value. The Bills were 21st in pass attempts per game last season and bottom-5 in passing yards percentage. While Diggs is one of the best route-runners and will hit some big plays with the strong arm of Josh Allen, he will be inconsistent in an offense that will be run-heavy. Allen had a 58.2% completion rate last season. There's also the concern of bad weather late in the season in Buffalo. John Brown led the team with 115 targets last season, and if Diggs can get in that range, he won't be as bad. Diggs has shown the ability to excel on limited targets. Diggs had 94 targets in 15 games and caught 63 passes for 1,130 yards with 6 touchdowns.

4. **Will Fuller, HOU:** Fuller is an interesting case. Those who have rostered Fuller over the last few seasons have been burned and are likely to stay away. It makes sense, considering he's had a difficult time staying on the field. Fuller has played 14, 10, 7 and 11 games, respectively, in his 4 years, missing 20 over the past 3 seasons. Fuller has seen target shares over 20% with DeAndre Hopkins on the field, and Hopkins is now in Arizona. Hopkins had 150 targets last season, averaging 10.1 per game. Still, the Texans added Brandin Cooks and Randall Cobb, which complicates his potential weekly attention. Fuller has shown a good rapport with Deshaun Watson and averaged 6.5 targets last season; he has a good chance to explode if he stays healthy. Fullers has definite risk -- but also a high ceiling.

5. **Julian Edelman, NE:** The Patriots offense won't be the same without Tom Brady, who always looked for Edelman. On one hand, there's a lack of competition for targets for Edelman, but the Patriots' offense will take a step back and won't move the ball as much or be as efficient. They likely will rely more on the rushing attack and defense to keep them in games. Edelman will be 34 at the start of the season and has always battled injuries, playing 16 in just 3 of 10 seasons. Edelman has at least 153 targets in 2 of the last 3 seasons, and that's likely to decrease. An aging receiver in a descending offense isn't appealing.

6. **John Brown, BUF:** Brown was an excellent 20th in PPR scoring last season, notching double-digit points 13 times in those formats. In 15 games, he caught 72 passes for 1,060 yards with 6 TDs on 115 targets. The Bills didn't pass often, though, and Stefon Diggs will take away targets. Brown will play a secondary role to Diggs and is more appealing in best-ball formats.

UP & COMING

1. **Deebo Samuel, SF:** Samuel took long to get involved in the offense in his rookie season, but once he did, he posted great numbers. From Week 9 onward, he finished as a top-10 fantasy receiver, and from Week 10 until the end of the season, Samuel averaged 4.4 receptions and 72 yards per game. Samuel caught 57 of 81 targets for 802 yards and 3 TDs while adding 14 carries for 159 yards and 3 rushing TDs. The 49ers do a good job of designing plays to get the ball in Samuel's hands and let him be a playmaker. He averaged 9.9 yards per target and 8.1 yards after the catch. Samuel had 3 100-yard games in the final 8, and he should take some of the targets vacated by the departure of Emmanuel Sanders.

2. **Marquise Brown, BAL:** Brown was inconsistent last season due to health, a lack of targets, and limited snaps as he was coming off Lisfranc surgery. The Ravens also had many blowouts that allowed them to rest Brown late in games. Brown played in 14 contests, catching 46 passes for 584 yards with 7 touchdowns. He opened the season with 5 catches for 147 yards, followed by 2 touchdowns and 8 catches for 86 yards in Week 2, but he had a lot of bad outings and was limited in practice. Brown underwent an offseason procedure to remove the screws put into his foot from his 2018 Lisfranc injury, so that may ease concerns. The Ravens only passed 439

times last season, so they will need to pass more for Brown to break out, but he's worth drafting as a WR3/4 for his high ceiling.

3. Diontae Johnson, PIT: He played well in a terrible situation last season with Mason Rudolph and Devlin Hodges at quarterback. The Steelers' offense ran the 4th-most plays in 2018 with Ben Roethlisberger, and Big Ben is back. Johnson gains a lot of separation and had 59 catches for 680 yards with 5 touchdowns last season on 92 targets. Johnson is an excellent middle-rounds target with big breakout potential.

4. Anthony Miller, CHI: It took a while for Miller to emerge last season, and that should depress his price. Miller wasn't a full-time player in the 1st half but averaged 7.9 targets per game over the final 7. From Weeks 11-15, Miller had at least 13 PPR points each game. Miller had 7 TDs as a rookie 2 years ago and has managed to be productive with Mitchell Trubisky throwing him passes, and Miller could improve if Nick Foles starts. Outside of Allen Robinson, Miller doesn't have a lot of competition for targets.

5. Justin Jefferson, MIN: The rookie landed in a good spot for targets with the trade of Stefon Diggs. The Vikings are a run-centered offense, but Jefferson could absorb a lot of the 94 looks that've opened up from 2019. The 1st-round pick runs great routes, has good hands and has the makeup of a playmaker (6'1", 202 lbs., 4.43 40-yard dash). Outside of Adam Thielen, Jefferson has little competition for attention among wideouts. He collected 111 catches for 1,540 yards and 18 touchdowns for LSU last season.

6. CeeDee Lamb, DAL: Clearly, this wasn't Lamb's ideal landing spot for immediate work; he fell to Pick 17 in the NFL Draft to the Cowboys, who took the best player on the board. Lamb still could become undervalued in fantasy, thanks to the worry that Dallas also has to feed Amari Cooper, Michael Gallup, Blake Jarwin and Ezekiel Elliott. Still, Randall Cobb was Dallas' 3rd receiver last season and caught 55 passes for 828 yards and 3 touchdowns on 83 looks. The Cowboys have 190 vacated targets, making Lamb a solid fantasy WR4 with upside.

7. Jerry Jeudy, DEN: The Broncos were rumored to trade up to acquire Jeudy but didn't need to; he fell to them with the 15th overall pick. Jeudy is a great route-runner and has a penchant for getting open. He will have Courtland Sutton on the other side to take away some defensive attention. Jeudy should get a target share around 15-18%, but his value will depend on the development of 2nd-year quarterback Drew Lock.

8. Henry Ruggs, LV: The rookie was selected as the 1st wide receiver off the board in the draft. While he wasn't the draft's best receiver, he goes to a team that needed WR help. He's not going to command a huge target share, but he'll be involved and could play every down. The explosive 5'11", 188-pounder ran a 4.27 40-yard dash. He's not only a deep-route receiver, though, and the Raiders will find ways to manufacture ways to get the ball in his hands.

9. Parris Campbell, IND: The Colts don't have a lot of depth at wide receiver, and Campbell could get a major opportunity in 2020. He only played 7 games in his rookie season due to injuries and caught 18 passes for 127 yards on 24 targets, but showed he can do a lot after the catch. He has great athleticism and ran a 4.31 40-yard dash.

MATCHUP PLAYS

1. Mike Williams, LAC: Williams is an excellent receiver but doesn't get the volume he needs to help every week. Williams is 6'4", 220 lbs., yet somehow only scored 2 TDs last season despite averaging 20.4 yards per catch. On 12 end-zone targets, he scored once. He had 90 targets and caught 49 passes for 1,001 yards. 2 years ago, Williams had 10 touchdowns on 66 targets. Williams will see positive TD regression, making him more appealing in non-PPR, but Tyrod Taylor tends to play it safe and not take many chances. Rookie Justin Herbert could play at some point later in the season, which could help Williams.

2. Robby Anderson, CAR: Anderson will be the vertical threat in the Panthers offense. He didn't have much competition for targets in his years with the Jets, but Anderson has to vie with D.J. Moore, Curtis Samuel, Ian Thomas and Christian McCaffrey for the ball. Anderson is familiar with Panthers coach Matt Rhule, playing under him at Temple. The Panthers defense looks to be one of the worst, so they could play from behind often and pass more. Still, Anderson will be inconsistent week-to-week.

3. Mecole Hardman, KC: The explosive Hardman didn't have a big role in this excellent offense as a rookie. He played 45% of the snaps and only had a 7% target share. But he did plenty with his 41 looks (26 receptions, 538 yards, 6 TDs) while averaging an absurd 20.7 yards per reception. He could become a big factor if an injury opens a pathway for more targets and, at minimum, remains a solid best-ball pick in the middle-to-late rounds.

4. DeSean Jackson, PHI: Jackson is the epitome of a best-ball play. He can have huge weeks and then some when he crushes your lineup. He's riskier this season than usual; he turns 34 in December and played just 3 games last season. If he shows early in the season that he still can burn defensive backs, he can be used in the right matchup. He had 8 catches for 154 yards with 2 touchdowns in the first game of the season in 2019. Jackson has missed 27 games over the last 6 seasons, though.

WATCH LIST

1. Darius Slayton, NYG: Slayton played well in his rookie season last year. The 5th-round pick had 48 catches for 740 yards with 8 TDs on 84 targets in 14 games. He averaged 8.8 yards per target. Slayton has a lot of competition for looks but is a vertical threat who could emerge to lead the team in targets. Slayton had a 57.1% catch rate due to the inconsistency of QB Daniel Jones. The Giants didn't play a game with Slayton, Sterling Shepard, Golden Tate and Saquon Barkley on the field together. Still, Slayton has the most speed of the receivers; Shepard has battled injuries; and Tate will be 32 when the season starts.

2. Sterling Shepard, NYG: Shepard has been inconsistent in his NFL career. He has missed 11 games in the last 3 seasons, including 6 in '19. He averaged 8.3 targets per game and had 57 catches for 576 yards with 3 touchdowns. He has a lot of competition for targets, but based on last season when he played, it shows he could lead the Giants. He's a decent late flier.

3. Breshad Perriman, NYJ: Perriman has talent, but injuries stunted his growth early in his career. He was a 1st-round pick by the Ravens in 2015 and is now on his 5th team in 5 years. Perriman has done well with the limited chances he has been given the last 2 seasons. On 95 targets, he averaged 18.9 yards per catch and 10.5 yards per target with the Browns and Buccaneers. In the final 4 games last season with the Buccaneers, Perriman took advantage of injuries to Mike Evans and Chris Godwin and had at least 1 touchdown and/or 100 yards in each game. In his last 5 outings, Perriman had 25 receptions for 506 yards and 5 touchdowns. Perriman will vie with Denzel Mims and Jamison Crowder for targets, but he could see 90-100 as the deep threat for the potentially emerging Sam Darnold.

4. Preston Williams, MIA: Williams impressed as a rookie. Though DeVante Parker finished with a flourish, Williams led Miami in targets, receptions and yards before his season-ending knee injury. In 8 games, he had 60 targets (21% share) for 32 catches, 428 yards and 3 TDs. Williams had at least 9 PPR points in all 8 games he played. Parker will draw the top cornerbacks, opening things up for Williams. He has been extremely cheap in early drafts.

5. Christian Kirk, ARI: Kirk had a 24% target share last season, which will likely decrease with the addition of DeAndre Hopkins. Larry Fitzgerald will get his attention, but Kirk could still be Kyler Murray's 2nd look in this ascending offense. He played in 13 games last year, catching 68 passes for 709 yards on 108 targets with 3 TDs. Hopkins will draw the top CBs, which will help Kirk. While the target total will likely decline, the efficiency could increase. Kirk scored all 3 TDs in 1 game and only had 4 end-zone targets, so his value takes a hit in non-PPR.

6. N'Keal Harry, NE: The 2019 1st-round pick battled injuries and played a limited role when he returned for 7 games. Harry has little competition for targets outside of Julian Edelman. Rookie WRs rarely produce for the Patriots, and last season shouldn't be held against him.

7. Allen Lazard, GB: The Packers did nothing to improve their wide receivers in the draft, giving Lazard a shot to be the No. 2 receiver opposite Davante Adams. He will compete with Marquez-Valdes Scantling, Devin Funchess and Equanimeous St. Brown. Lazard got more playing time as the season went on and had 17 targets over the final 2 games. Aaron Rodgers also has given some praise for Lazard recently.

Chapter 6

TIGHT ENDS

½ & FULL PPR RPV

TE1

	Player	RPV
1	Travis Kelce	41%
2	George Kittle	31%
3	Zach Ertz	25%
4	Darren Waller	-1%
5	Mark Andrews	-4%
6	Evan Engram	-6%
7	Jared Cook	-9%
8	Austin Hooper	-11%
9	Hunter Henry	-13%
10	Tyler Higbee	-16%
11	Hayden Hurst	-18%
12	Noah Fant	-19%

TE2

	Player	RPV
1	Rob Gronkowski	17%
2	Jonnu Smith	15%
3	Jack Doyle	14%
4	Ian Thomas	12%
5	Eric Ebron	4%
6	T.J. Hockenson	1%
7	Chris Herndon	-3%
8	Dallas Goedert	-5%
9	Mike Gesicki	-11%
10	Blake Jarwin	-12%
11	Kyle Rudolph	-14%
12	Greg Olsen	-17%

STANDARD RPV

TE1

	Player	RPV
1	Travis Kelce	48%
2	George Kittle	34%
3	Zach Ertz	17%
4	Mark Andrews	10%
5	Evan Engram	2%
6	Darren Waller	-7%
7	Jared Cook	-11%
8	Austin Hooper	-12%
9	Hunter Henry	-16%
10	Noah Fant	-19%
11	Rob Gronkowski	-22%
12	Hayden Hurst	-24%

TE2

	Player	RPV
1	Tyler Higbee	18%
2	Jonnu Smith	12%
3	Eric Ebron	8%
4	Dallas Goedert	6%
5	Chris Herndon	3%
6	Jack Doyle	1%
7	Blake Jarwin	0%
8	T.J. Hockenson	-3%
9	Mike Gesicki	-6%
10	Kyle Rudolph	-10%
11	Ian Thomas	-11%
12	Greg Olsen	-17%

Player Profiles and Overview
By Kate Magdziuk

The tight end position has been tough to navigate for some time now. We continue to see top tier, consistent performers, and then the rest fall off the fantasy cliff. That doesn't mean it's over, though. The 2019 rookie tight end class showed promise, but as time moves on, we continue to lose productive veterans. We have to fill the gap somehow, right? Derek Brown touched on it last year, but I'm gonna say it again. The only way to navigate the tight end position is to draft elite tight ends early or punt the position to take late-round value with upside.

Time and time again, middle-tier tight ends have been death to your fantasy rosters. Liken them to a Jeff Fischer-led team, forever bound to go 8-8; always performs "fine," doesn't win you anything, and doesn't do anything to bolster the long-term (or season-long) value of your team. Some middle-tier tight ends drafted in 2019 included Evan Engram, Hunter Henry, O.J. Howard, Vance McDonald, David Njoku; they finished as the TE18, TE9, TE29, TE30, and TE85 in PPR leagues, respectively. The worst part? You probably drafted each of these before the seventh round.

Though there is an inherent risk to fantasy assets at all positions, the volatility of the tight end position makes it much harder to invest mid-round draft capital given the range of outcomes. The top-five ranked tight ends in 2019 averaged 224.12 fantasy points. Those ranked 6-10 averaged 162. It's a huge discrepancy, and one that only highlights the fact that you don't have to have a stud to win at the position; you can just be *good enough*. I may have just segwayed into a discussion regarding the merits of 2-TE league formats; I digress.

Finding the late-round values doesn't have to be that difficult. When identifying a tight end breakout, I'm looking for those tight ends who ran lots of routes (like a Mike Gesicki), those who could benefit from an increased target share (like an Ian Thomas), or tight ends entering their second or third year, who have had another season to acclimate to the role of an NFL tight end (like an Irv Smith Jr.). Now, let's dig in.

THE ELITE

1. **George Kittle, SF**: Kittle has led tight ends in yards after the catch and yards per route run for two consecutive seasons. Simply put, he's a monster. At 6'4", 249 pounds, Kittle ran a 4.52 out of the University of Iowa. After his 2018 breakout, there was some concern regarding whether the target volume would be safe, considering his role in a run-first offense. It turns out, yes, his role seems quite safe. The 49es continue to emphasize the run under head coach Kyle Shanahan, which is great for the efficiency in the passing game and the ability to scheme large humans like Kittle open. He's cleared 1,000 receiving yards for two consecutive seasons, and he's showing no signs of slowing down anytime soon. His youth, athleticism and integration in the San Francisco offense have brought him to the surface of the leagues' best at the position.

2. **Travis Kelce, KC**: All of Patrick Mahomes' main weapons are in high demand for fantasy rosters. Kelce has been the centerpiece of the Chiefs' offense since 2013 and surges toward another top-end year. The Chiefs made it clear that they'd like to avoid any significant offensive changes in 2020, and Kelce's involvement should be no different. He's had no fewer than 103 targets since 2015 and no fewer than 1,000 receiving yards since 2016. Kelce is elite, and he's at the beck and call of a quarterback who has already defined elite for the next NFL generation.

3. **Mark Andrews, BAL**: Andrews was one of the most pleasant surprises at the tight end position in 2019. He was featured in last year's "Up & Coming" section by Derek Brown, and Andrews did not disappoint. After being drafted on average as the TE15 in redraft leagues, Andrews finished as the TE5 and first among tight ends in fantasy points per snap. Andrews' biggest fault in 2019 was his constant appearance

on the Ravens' injury report, between back and foot injuries. Though he missed just 1 game on the season, he was consistently limited in practices and never surpassed 55% of Baltimore's offensive snaps. His health will determine if he can improve there, but with the rapport he has developed with Lamar Jackson, it's hard to imagine him finishing as anything but a top-3 TE.

TOP TALENT

1. **Zach Ertz, PHI**: This section is looking ... bare. Ertz's move down from "Elite" was a doozy, but one most saw coming with the growth of Dallas Goedert within the Eagles offense in 2019. Ertz has been a dynamic, top-tier tight end. He has been a tremendous beneficiary of a voluptuous target share over the past two years. But with the new weapons they've installed into the offense, we might not be set for more of the same. Though the skill set remains, the organization kept Alshon Jeffrey on staff while drafting Jalen Reagor and Quez Watkins and trading for veteran Marquise Goodwin. More bodies not named Nelson Agholor is always bound to be a good thing for a passing game. In 2019, Ertz saw his lowest target share and fewest yards after the catch since 2015. Ertz's contract will keep him in Philly for at least one more season, but with a diluted target share, we may be seeing the first glimpse of Ertz's fantasy decline.

SOLID OPTIONS

1. **Hunter Henry, LAC:** We've waited long enough for the Henry breakout, and if all goes well, we should see it in 2020. Henry has yet to play a full 16-game season *or* top 652 receiving yards, but circumstances are different now, right? He's fully healthy, sure, but this offense now has questions now that QB Philip Rivers has left. Still, whether it's Tyrod Taylor or Justin Herbert under center, the Chargers present a tight-end-friendly scheme and a world of opportunity. When he's on the field, he's a reliable option; QBs targeting him had a passer rating of 117.6 in 2019, the second-best figure among TEs with 50-plus targets. He finished as TE9 in 2019, despite missing four games, which shows you both Henry's potential and the lack of fantasy depth at this position. When in doubt, target the 6'5", 250-pound monster running out of the slot.

2. **Evan Engram, NYG:** Engram might have found himself among those in the "Top Talent" category, but alas, he cannot stay healthy. He absorbed an astounding 115 targets in his rookie season and finished as the TE5. Engram's pass-catching ability exceeds his blocking skills by a mile, and that's great news for fantasy owners, since we unfortunately don't get credit for outstanding blocks. Engram is as athletic as tight ends come, running a 4.42 out of college with explosivity and fluidity as a route runner. There might not be hesitation in drafting him at cost in fantasy leagues if we didn't need to consider how many games you can expect from him in 2020. Rumors have circulated that the Giants questioned Engram's ability to stay healthy after the 2019 season, and it's not unfounded; he's missed 13 games over the last two seasons. He'll return in 2020 to more competition over targets in the presence of Golden Tate, Darius Slayton, Sterling Shepard, and of course, Saquon Barkley. He has tremendous upside when healthy and is certainly bound to finish as a top-10 TE in 2020.

3. **Noah Fant, DEN:** Compared to fellow rookie tight end T.J. Hockenson, Fant got off to a slow start in 2019. He did finish strong, though, leading all 1st-year tight ends in routes run and, for those with at least 15 targets, in yards per route run. His performance was a bit up and down; he had several single-digit-yardage games alternate with 2 100-yard receiving outings. Inconsistency aside, he showcased his upside in the final half of the season. Surrounding him with WRs Courtland Sutton, Jerry Jeudy and K.J. Hamler can only help his development.

4. **T.J. Hockenson, DET:** Hockenson (6'5", 247 lbs) was an elite prospect out of Iowa State in the 2019 draft and gave us every indication that he could be more than productive for fantasy football. He managed 2.21 yards per route run in college, ranking fourth in the FBS and boding well for his production as an NFL pass-catcher. He did get off to the hottest start possible in 2019, posting six receptions for 131 yards and a score in his first NFL game. The only issue? That game was against Arizona, 2019's best TE streaming

opponent. Hockenson was placed on IR to finish the season, but in Weeks 1-13, he saw the 10-most targets of any tight end in that span. With Matthew Stafford under center, Hockenson's upside is unreal.

5. **Tyler Higbee, LAR:** Higbee finished as the TE8 in 2019 and didn't even break out until Week 13. Before we acknowledge the breakout, let's acknowledge what led to it. Higbee had been laying in the shadows of Gerald Everett but blossomed almost immediately into one of the Rams' most productive playmakers to close out the season. As a starter in Week 10, Higbee immediately went on a 4-game streak of 100-plus receiving yards and capped off the season going 8-84-1 in Week 17. Everett returned to the active lineup in Week 16, and though he was cleared from the injury report, he saw just four offensive snaps over those next two games. Higbee tied Travis Kelce, Noah Fant and Zach Ertz with eight red-zone targets -- opportunity galore. Though the Rams drafted wide out Van Jefferson, the departures of Brandin Cooks and Todd Gurley have vacated 112 targets, providing more opportunities for Higbee in 2020.

6. **Darren Waller, LV:** Waller was the steal of 2019 leagues after breaking out on a second opportunity in the NFL with the Raiders. It became clear that Jon Gruden liked what he saw through training camp and that rookie Foster Moreau might not see the spotlight so soon. Gruden involved Waller early; he saw 115 targets in 2019, the third-most in the NFL, and he was paid for it. The biggest question mark with Waller is what his target share will look like moving forward after Las Vegas drafted wide outs Henry Ruggs III, Lynn Bowden and Bryan Edwards across the first 3 rounds of 2020. They'll probably get involved immediately given the lack of weapons ahead of them and WR Hunter Renfrow.

UP AND COMING

1. **Mike Gesicki, MIA:** Gesicki is probably the one up-and-coming tight end on this list that you're going to have a harder time buying in dynasty leagues. He was drafted in 2018 by the Dolphins as a 6'6", 250-pound beast out of Penn State. Though his 2019 stat line (51-570-5) doesn't exactly jump off the page, his usage does: Out of Gesicki's 701 total offensive snaps on the season, he ran a route on 521 of them. This was the third-highest total by any tight end, and the fantasy opportunity remains ripe. Incredibly for his potential, the Dolphins escaped the early rounds without a receiver at the top end of this historic draft class. The usage is there. The targets should be. We just have to see this combo turn into fantasy points.

2. **Irv Smith Jr., MIN:** Kyle Rudolph's contract will likely keep him in Minnesota through 2021; his contract carries $12 million in dead cap through then. Fret not, though; the Vikings have another guy to turn to. Smith was drafted 50th overall last year and saw offensive snaps immediately as a blocker and route runner. He fell 1 target short of matching Rudolph's 48 for the season and saw just 3 fewer end-zone looks. It's encouraging to see that kind of usage, particularly in his 1st season. Tight ends often show a big jump in development in Year 2 and beyond, and Smith looks set for one in 2020. He is a prime buy-low candidate in a tight-end friendly scheme.

3. **Jonnu Smith, TEN:** Smith has been a hot buy in dynasty leagues this offseason. He didn't exactly make a splash in fantasy leagues last year, posting his best line of 6/78/1. Regardless, Smith is a tremendous athlete with speed, strength and agility -- a lethal combination in an efficient offense like the Titans'. The team also cut Delanie Walker this offseason, eliminating veteran competition in the TE room (at least for now). Smith's athleticism makes him a pick with tremendous upside, but when we consider his late-round value and likely increase in offensive attention, Smith is a prospect that could outperform his ADP in the seasons to come.

4. **Ian Thomas, CAR:** The departure of Greg Olsen has left a giant 6'5" hole in the Panthers' offense. Thomas will (hopefully) step into that role, under a new coaching staff, with a new checkdown-friendly quarterback in Teddy Bridgewater. Thomas is big-bodied, but his explosiveness, wingspan and big hands provide him with major pass-catching fantasy upside. Thomas has shown us flashes that provide hope for his future as a featured tight end within an NFL offense. After Olsen went down in Week 13 of 2018, Thomas averaged nearly 10 PPR points per game, and if he can keep that pace up, we'll have a TE1 on our hands for the 2020 season.

5. **Hayden Hurst, ATL:** Hurst was a former first-round pick by the Ravens, drafted just 7 picks ahead of league MVP Lamar Jackson. It's wild to think about his draft capital now, considering the elite prospects that came in the class to follow. Hurst is on the older side at 26, but he has limited miles on the tires, entering just his third NFL season in 2020. If Hurst had been traded to virtually any other team, his presence probably wouldn't hold as much weight. Atlanta's scheme favors the tight end, though, and they've produced a top-6 tight end in back-to-back seasons. QB Matt Ryan utilizes his TEs, and Atlanta was extremely successful in scheming Austin Hooper over the past few seasons. We should only expect to see more of it with Hurst in the mix.

MATCHUP PLAYS

1. **Rob Gronkowski, TB:** Gronkowski, aka your WWE 24/7 champion, once again laces up the cleats to rejoin former teammate and quarterback Tom Brady. Together, they embark on a new adventure in the Sunshine State. After a year in retirement, Gronk reports that he is fully healthy and ready to return to the game. Though word and pictures were widely circulated that Gronk had lost his football form, agent Drew Rosenhaus says he is back up to his playing weight of 260 pounds. Even so, we have to temper expectations for his performance after a year spent outside of football. Now he returns to a brand-new offensive scheme. The myriad of weapons available to Brady is overwhelming, and even if Gronkowski is his favorite, the competition for targets will make Gronk less reliable than desired on a week-to-week basis.

2. **Greg Olsen, SEA:** One of the greatest tight ends in the last decade teams up with one of the best quarterbacks … who happens to utilize the tight end position? Yes, please. The Seahawks have a myriad of receivers ready to catch balls for Russell Wilson, but Olsen is just … *different*. He had his pick of the lot in free agency, having no shortage of team visits, including those with the Redskins and Bills. Though his upside is likely curbed given his age, his injury history, and (if healthy) Will Dissly, he's now tied to an accurate quarterback that likes to target the tight end … when he has one. Olsen finished as PPR TE13 in 2019 at the ripe age of 35. If nothing else, he should be utilized heavily in the red zone to provide massive upside in an efficient offense.

3. **Jack Doyle, IND:** Yes, I conscientiously left Trey Burton out of the mix here. Doyle is the only Colts tight end that I predict to have any fantasy relevance, even on a streaming basis. Doyle had a bad run of luck when it came to injuries in 2018, but came back to play a full 16-game season last year alongside Eric Ebron. Ebron has moved on to sign with the Steelers, leaving Doyle behind to be Philip Rivers' right-hand man. Though the Colts drafted Michael Pittman and have a top-end veteran presence in T.Y. Hilton, Indy still has plenty of room for another receiving asset to flourish. Rivers was accustomed to utilizing his tight ends with the Chargers, and now the Colts are likely looking at Doyle as their TE1. Doyle's age and lack of premier performance in fantasy through his first seven seasons highlight his limited upside, but the tendencies of his QB and efficient offensive line could make him a streamable option

WATCH LIST

1. **Chris Herndon, NYJ:** Let's call 2019 a write-off for Herndon and, for that matter, the Jets. Herndon was a late-round fantasy favorite until news came of his three-game suspension. After that? It was a hamstring. Up next, a broken rib to polish off the season and land him on injured reserve. After showing a rapport with quarterback Sam Darnold in his rookie season, he fell hard and fast. However, the Jets offense still has plenty of room for another pass-catcher, even after drafting Denzel Mims in the second round. This offseason, the team lost free-agent Robby Anderson to help the cause. If he can manage to string together a complete season, Herndon could carve out a significant role. He's a late-round flier with more upside than most in his tier.

2. **O.J. Howard, TB:** Howard is an interesting candidate to monitor, but not because he's bound for production in this crowded offense. Rumors have been swirling for some time that Howard may be on his way out of Tampa Bay, and we could see him start for another team in 2020. The Bucs have now signed a healthy Rob Gronkowski, who yearned for a reunion with Tom Brady after he signed his contract with Tampa. They also have Cameron Brate, who has proven more than capable as a blocker and red-zone target. Howard's athleticism is off the charts, and we got a taste of in the first 10 games of 2018, during which he was the TE7. There are lots of what-ifs with Howard, but while his dynasty value is in the tank, he's worth more than a glance.

3. **Kaden Smith, NYG:** Smith is an inexpensive dynasty prospect to acquire, and every Evan Engram owner should be making moves to get him. As a rookie, Smith stepped into a starting role in Week 12, as the oft-injured Engram went down with a foot injury. In that span, he posted 20/267/3, averaging a healthy 8.5 points per game in PPR formats. For the record, Noah Fant averaged 6.9 points per game. T.J. Hockenson averaged 6.7. In Engram's absence Weeks 10 through 17, Smith ranked 5th among all tight ends with 239 routes run, demonstrating just how quickly he gained the trust of his coaching staff with a key offensive player down. It's not often that I will give advice to handcuff your tight end, but given Engram's health history, I'll concede.

RED FLAGS

1. **Austin Hooper & David Njoku, CLE:** Kevin Stefanski likes to utilize a 2-tight-end set, you say? Hooper and Njoku are talented athletes and reliable receivers. More isn't always better, though, particularly considering a coaching staff geared toward the run. Njoku seemed to fall out of favor in 2019. As of May, Hooper is still being drafted as the TE7 or better, but drafters should be wary of his consistency in a new offensive scheme with an unfamiliar quarterback at the helm in Baker Mayfield. Njoku may present more true value in fantasy leagues given that he is being drafted late, but he's likely only viable in best-ball formats unless Jarvis Landry's season start is delayed as he recovers from hip surgery.

2. **Jared Cook, NOS:** At 33 years old, Cook finished 2019 as the TE7 in PPR formats and shocked plenty with his athleticism. He led all tight ends in fantasy points per touch and average depth of target; he was the picture of efficiency for Drew Brees. Though Cook had the best season we could have asked of him, he's yet another year older, and the Saints have finally found their WR2. Barring an injury to Emmanuel Sanders, regression will almost certainly strike for Cook.

3. **Vance McDonald, PIT:** Since being drafted in 2013 by the 49ers, McDonald has yet to play a full 16-game season. 2019 was supposed to be his year, after an uptick in involvement in Pittsburgh that amounted to 50 receptions for 610 yards in 2018. It seemed promising, but his health has been a detriment. Though they got a discount, the Steelers made a statement by signing Eric Ebron; they needed help. Though McDonald has shown flashes, his health has betrayed him, and he is a goner in all fantasy formats.

4. **Jimmy Graham, CHI:** Graham signed a surprisingly decent deal with Chicago, coming in strong at 2 years for $16 million and a no-trade clause. Though he's certainly not the "young buck" he once was, Graham has a certain veteran presence that could benefit Mitchell Trubisky in a contract year (or Nick Foles if he takes over). The excitement surrounding the signing didn't last long, however, as the Bears were quick to fill out the depth chart. The Bears currently have nine active tight ends on their roster and have just drafted heir apparent Cole Kmet, who was widely regarded as the TE1 in a barren 2020 class. Graham may have some late-round value in best-ball leagues, but outside of that, he's a touchdown-or-bust option that's better left undrafted.

5. **Kyle Rudolph, MIN:** Rudolph finished as a top-10 tight end for three consecutive seasons … until Irv Smith Jr. arrived in 2019. Rudolph has proved himself a reliable asset as both a receiver and a blocker, but he did lose snaps once Smith began to emerge. According to Pro Football Focus, Smith also earned higher blocking scores -- the true key to keeping any tight end on the field for every down. Though Rudolph is a well-rounded team asset, he will eventually lose out to youth on a rookie deal.

Chapter 7

Kickers

Kate Magdziuk

Kickers are people, too. It's the official hashtag of every single one of your home leagues, desperate to keep the kicker to emulate real NFL football. It's true though, right? Kickers in fantasy are annoying, sure, but they're annoying for any NFL team. To play a strong defensive game and/or produce points on offense -- then lose the game because your kicker misses a field goal? It hurts; it doesn't matter if it's NFL or fantasy football.

Some in the industry will never approve of the kicker position in fantasy. To the rest, here's my advice:

Take your kicker in the last rounds of your draft. Kicker is a "streamable" position in most leagues as long as you don't have a transaction limit. An elite kicker with accuracy certainly *helps* your fantasy roster, but kicker performance can sometimes be random. Was the offense efficient that week and only kicked extra points because they obliterated the defense with touchdowns? It's a bummer for your kicker and the fantasy points he *could have* scored, regardless of how accurate he is. Don't waste an early pick on a position determined by many outside variables.

When drafting your kicker, consider his home environment: Pending the lack of global warming, what kickers are most likely to be influenced by external factors, like wind, rain, or snow? No matter how accurate your kicker is, the fewer external detriments, the better. Look for kickers whose home turf includes a dome or retractable roof to relieve weather impact. Find the list of stadiums below.

Stream the position (if your format allows it): I noted it briefly above, but take note once again. A fantasy kicker can sometimes perform randomly, but it doesn't mean the position isn't streamable. Consider factors that can impact kickers week to week. Sure, you'll always want an *accurate* kicker, but then what? It's difficult to note in the beginning of the season, but look for "the bend-but-don't-break" defenses. What offense makes its way to the end zone but struggles to convert?

Weather-Proof & Weather-Proof-ish Stadiums:
- **Fixed-roof dome:** Lions, Falcons, Saints, Vikings, Raiders
- **Retractable roof:** Cowboys, Texans, Colts, Cardinals, Rams/Chargers

Tier 1		Tier 3		Tier 4	
1.	Wil Lutz, NO			16.	Chris Boswell, PIT
2.	Justin Tucker, BAL	9.	Robbie Gould, SF	17.	Brett Maher, NYJ
3.	Harrison Butker, KC	10.	Matt Prater, DET	18.	Jason Myers, SEA
		11.	Michael Badgley, LAC	19.	Jake Elliott, PHI
Tier 2		12.	Josh Lambo, JAC	20.	Ka'imi Fairbairn, HOU
4.	Matt Gay, TB	13.	Chase McLaughlin, IND		
5.	Younghoe Koo, ATL	14.	Dan Bailey, MIN	Tier 5	
6.	Zane Gonzalez, ARI	15.	Brandon McManus, DEN	21.	Justin Rohrwasser, NE
7.	Joey Slye, CAR			22.	Jason Sanders, MIA
8.	Greg Zuerlein, DAL			23.	Austin Seibert, CLE
				24.	Randy Bullock, CIN

Chapter 8

INDIVIDUAL DEFENSIVE PLAYERS (IDP)

RANKINGS & PROFILES

Scott Bogman

I never understood why IDP wasn't more standard in fantasy football.

Let's face it. No one likes drafting a team defense. We take a defense dead-last and then dump them on their bye week because we can't let that one backup running back go because he has so much upside.

Fantasy Baseball doesn't just draft a pitching staff; that's not fun. Those players take individual pitchers because it makes sense!

Team Defenses are for casual fans, and you -- yes, you, reading this paid for this book -- you are beyond the casual fan! There are questions that interested IDP rookies need answered, and I'm going to try to help you out here.

Standard IDP scoring

This is probably the biggest issue in standardizing IDP in most leagues. There isn't really a standard:

"Standard" formats:
- Solo Tackle: 1.5 pts
- Assisted Tackle: 0.75
- Sack: 4
- INT: 4
- Forced Fumble: 2
- Fumble Recovery: 2
- Pass Defense/Deflected: 1
- TD: 6

*Yahoo! has its own standard scoring
- Solo Tackle: 1
- Assisted Tackle: 0.5
- Sack: 2
- INT: 3
- Forced Fumble: 2
- Fumble Recovery: 2
- Pass Defense/Deflected: 1
- TD: 6

ESPN really doesn't help out for IDP scoring settings. They just keep what they have from team defenses (INTs and Sacks), and then you have to fill in the rest. Some leagues like to beef up big plays so that the seemingly more impactful plays are worth more. It brings the offensive and defensive sides a bit closer together.

KNOW HOW YOUR LEAGUE SCORES. This isn't just for IDP, of course. I've been guilty of this, and anyone who likes to pile on as many leagues as they can probably has fallen victim to this a bit. None of these sites help really in a draft room. Yes. they all have projections which will help people that are going in blind, but none of them have a proper ranking system that leads to answering the 2nd-biggest question for this unique game:

When should I take IDPs in my draft?

This goes to the 'know your league scoring' bit, of course, but it also depends on how many IDPs your league is going to use. On a per-game basis in the standard scoring I listed above, Colts linebacker Darius Leonard averaged 15.46 points per game last year, and that was 61st overall or the 1st pick in the 6th round of a 12-teamer. The next-highest was Jordan Hicks at 13.27, which was 95th overall. Budda Baker was the highest defensive back at 12.52 (109th) and Danielle Hunter was the best defensive lineman at 9.84 (189th).

Format matters for this conundrum, too. What does your required IDP lineup look like?

Beginners: 3 total -- 1 defensive lineman, 1 linebacker, 1 defensive back
Just get a taste. IDPs won't make or break your entire team, and there's more than enough on the wire to add free agents if the guys you drafted aren't great. You can wait until the end of the draft and still get great production.

Veterans: 7 total -- 2 DL, 2 LB, 2 DB, 1 Utility (any position)
This is the standard for most IDP leagues. Obviously, you are going to need to do a little bit of preseason research as you just can't pick up upper-echelon players every week, although there will still be more than enough to play weekly matchups.

Advanced: 7 Total -- 1 defensive end, 1 defensive tackle, 1 EDGE rusher, 1 LB, 1 cornerback, 1 safety, 1 UTIL
We're getting a little complicated here, specifically because Yahoo! doesn't offer a separator in the LB category. ESPN and Fantrax both offer EDGE as a position, but nobody offers OLB or ILB anymore. The added degree of difficulty mainly comes from the positions that can give you a donut in DT, EDGE and CB.

Expert: 11 Total -- 2 DE, 1 DT, 2 EDGE, 2 ILB, 2 CB, 2 S
We are way out into the weeds now. This is actually more starters than we have on offense in a standard league, and we really need to know each position well. EDGE rushers are a little bit liberal on Fantrax, but CBs are tough enough with 1 -- and the difference between Leonard and the 36th LB (3 per team in a 12 team) is about 1 TD.

I can't convince my league mates to make the switch.

If you're the commish, tell them just to try it for a season and pull the trigger with a low amount of IDPs, and I guarantee you everyone will like it WAY more than D/ST. It's way more fun to flip on a game and watch a player you picked make plays than an entire defense. You'll probably have them asking to add more players the next season. If not, you can always say you gave it a try, and it just wasn't for you.

Why do some of the best players score so little?

Cornerbacks are the most volatile. It's often wiser to draft CBs who don't cover well because they'll have more opportunities to record tackles. There's nothing we can really do about that at this point, but if IDP gets some more steam, a change will be made sooner rather than later. The CB translation between "good in real life" and "good in fantasy" is by far the worst.

The second big complaint is big time EDGE rushers not averaging more and putting up the occasional donut. The simple way to fix that is make sacks worth a little more and add tackles for loss into the scoring; these decisions will bring some of those guys back toward the pack.

Defensive tackle is also the subject of frequent complaints; the position isn't going to score a lot. Pittsburgh's Cameron Heyward led at the position and scored 1.5 more points per game than 2nd-place DeForest Buckner. We don't have to go far down the list to find a donut: Highly ranked Grady Jarrett had a 0 during the season. Only 3 of the top 12 had one last season, though, so the scoring has improved dramatically since I started playing IDP.

My league is a keeper league. How would I add IDPs?

The fewer keepers you have, the easier it is. With only a few keepers and regular IDP scoring, you can just get rid of team defenses in favor of IDPs. If you have a deeper league, you can add them slowly or have an IDP draft with a randomized draft order. Adding IDPs in a dynasty league makes the rookie draft way more fun, which in turn makes the NFL Draft way more interesting every year moving forward as well.

Here's a recommendation on how to build IDPs into your existing league:

Defensive end/EDGE rusher: They're boom-or-bust, infrequent tacklers -- but big plays are the ticket for EDGE players. 2 Sacks in one game would put them over the highest average score at their position.

Defensive tackle: The position overall is better than it ever has been, but it's still limited by an overall lack of tackles. Position labeling is getting more liberal, so that should benefit the spot overall.

Linebacker: This is where we make the money. Inside LBs make a lot of tackles, and that is what we want. Tackles are more consistent than splash plays like takeaways (interceptions and fumble recoveries) and defensive TDs. The issue is knowing who the MLB is. I'll have them listed on the cheat sheet, but be sure to check out a depth chart. A lot of Edge Rushers are listed at LB when only DL, LB and DB are the labeled positions.

Cornerback: This can be pretty frustrating. The upper-tier players aren't challenged by QBs most games, so they don't get tackles and have way fewer INT opportunities. For now, we want a bad corner on a good offensive team. Last year, Logan Ryan was the top-scoring fantasy CB -- and he ranked 62nd out of 112 qualified CBs in Pro Football Focus' grading system.

Safety: The last line of defense gets a lot of tackles! Some safeties get just as many or more tackles than linebackers, so this would be the 2nd big position for IDP scoring. They are plentiful, though, as the 10th overall safety all the way to the 33rd-ranked option averaged between 8 and 10 points last season. Baker was the highest at 12.5.

2020 IDP RANKINGS

1. **Darius Leonard, LB, IND:** Leonard has led all IDPs in points per game across in his first 2 NFL seasons. He's the obvious choice to be the No. 1 overall IDP pick in any draft. Not only does he rack up tackles (284 total in the last 2 years), but he also gets takeaways (7 interceptions, 6 forced fumbles and 2 fumble recoveries over the past 2 years) and sacks (12).
2. **Bobby Wagner, LB, SEA:** I'm a bit worried about how Seattle will use 1st-round pick Jordyn Brooks, who racked up tackles at Texas Tech, but Wagner hasn't averaged fewer than 11 fantasy points per game in any pro season. He'll also get the occasional pick and sack.
3. **Blake Martinez, LB, NYG:** Big free-agent get for the Giants! Martinez has been a tackle-compiling machine the past 3 seasons (144, 144 and 155 combined, respectively), and that shouldn't change with the Giants. He's not going to come away with too many big plays, but the tackle totals are so consistent that he only scored fewer than 10 fantasy points 4 times and never lower than 6.
4. **Cory Littleton, LB, LV:** Another good FA landing spot! Littleton has been great over the last 2 seasons, compiling 259 tackles, 5 picks and 7.5 sacks. The Raiders have been desperate for some speed in the middle of the defense, and they got their guy here.
5. **Jaylon Smith, LB, DAL:** Normally I don't like to put a middle LB with a great teammate in the upper tier, but we already have them in Indianapolis and Seattle, so Smith works fine despite the presence of Leighton Vander Esch. LVE only ended up playing 9 games last season, and Smith outscored him in all but 2, so I think we know who the leading scorer between the 2 will be.
6. **Joe Schobert, LB, JAX:** Another stud on the move, Schobert has been a stalwart over the last 3 season, finishing 5th in 2017, 17th in 2018 and back up to 5th in 2019 for fantasy PPG. He's moving to Jacksonville after getting paid, and the Jags need someone in the middle of that defense; Myles Jack hasn't cut it. Expect Schobert to continue his torrid tackling pace.
7. **Zach Cunningham, LB, HOU:** Cunningham was 2nd in the league in solo tackles last year, and I think he still has room to grow going into his 4th season. He doesn't have a great track record of making big plays (3.5 sacks, 3 FF, 3 FR and 1 INT over 3 seasons), but he gets so many snaps that he's just out there piling up tackles every game.

8. **Roquan Smith, LB, CHI:** Smith heads into his 3rd season, and I think this is when he really breaks out! Danny Trevathan is a great presence next to him, but he has only played 16 games in 1 of the past 6 seasons. Smith's season ended with a torn pectoral, but he should be ready to rock by the time camp rolls around.

9. **Jordan Hicks, LB, ARI:** Hicks was the No. 1 overall scorer last year and only behind Darius Leonard on a per-game basis. The Cardinals have a rough DL and drafted Isaiah Simmons in the 1st round, so I bumped Hicks down a little bit, but he should still be a top producer.

10. **Budda Baker, S, ARI:** Baker has been on the steady incline since entering the league. He has improved his combined tackle totals for 2 straight seasons (74, 102, 147, respectively). Last season, he led DBs in fantasy points after finishing 9th in 2018. Even if the tackles tick down because of the new talent in Arizona in front of him, he should have even more opportunities for tackles and INTs. The Cardinals have added WR DeAndre Hopkins, and QB Kyler Murray is primed for growth in his 2nd season. Opponents are going to have to throw frequently to keep pace, and this could breed more takeaway chances.

11. **Demario Davis, LB, NO:** I don't really get why I see Davis listed much lower than this in other spots. A lot of us thought the Saints were going to spend their 1st-round pick on a LB, which would have hurt him, but they waited until the 3rd; Zack Baun will compete with Alex Anzalone more for snaps than Davis. Davis was 2019's top-graded LB, according to PFF; has played all 16 games every single season of his 8-year career; and has had at least 90 tackles every year but his rookie campaign.

12. **Danielle Hunter, DL, MIN:** Hunter was the top-scoring DL last season and 3rd in 2018; if there's one thing we want at DL, it's a little stability. With most DLs' value being more tied to sacks, it's nice to get some decent tackle upside with them, and that is exactly what Hunter offers. With the last 2 seasons being almost identical (72 tackles in 18, 70 tackles in 19 and 14.5 sacks in both), Hunter doesn't offer much upside, but he offers stability.

13. **Jamal Adams, DB, NYJ:** Adams and the Jets' organization have fought over his future, but when it comes to gametime, we don't have to worry about him performing. Adams was 1st in DB scoring in 2018 and 5th in 2019. He's consistent, and I can't imagine he lets a contractual dispute affect him with 3 years left on his deal.

14. **Devin White, LB, TB:** If White didn't have Lavonte David next to him, I would have him ranked higher, but they will eat into each other's production a bit. White not only put up great tackle numbers in his rookie season (91 total), but he also made splash plays with 2.5 sacks, 3 FFs, 4 FR, 1 INT and 2 TDs! He'll get more rest on the sidelines with about 20 fewer INTs from his offense, too!

15. **Devin Bush, LB, PIT:** Bush had a similar statistical season to fellow rookie Devin White, but Bush hit a bit of a wall midseason and lost snaps, while White played 90% of the Bucs' defensive snaps from the 8th game onward. Bush shouldn't have that problem this season; Mark Barron, who was taking some of his snaps, is now gone, and Bush might even be afforded more big-play opportunities with a properly moving offense this season.

16. **Myles Garrett, DL, CLE:** Barring any unforeseen circumstances, Garrett probably won't stay suspended to open the 2020 season. As I'm typing this, nothing has been said either way, but the thought process is the final 6 games of 2019 were enough, though Roger Goodell has been known to make a surprise decision. Assuming he plays from Week 1 onward, Garrett has the most upside among defensive linemen. He had 10 sacks in his 10 games and was on pace for close to 50 tackles. He has gotten better 3 straight years and could be among the best this year.

17. **C.J. Mosley, LB, NYJ:** I want to rank him so much higher. In his 6 seasons, he has finished as a top-5 scorer twice, and he is in a perfect situation playing with inexperienced LBs around him. He only got in 2 games last year with a torn pectoral, and the last update we got, he was expecting to be back for camp but still not 100%. I'm optimistic about him returning and taking advantage of the situation, but I would back him up quickly in a deeper league.

18. **Shaq Thompson, LB, CAR:** I wanted to make Shaq a top-10 player this year; the tackle opportunities are going to be there following Luke Kuechly's abrupt retirement. 2019 was the first year Thompson passed 100 tackles in a season and averaged over 10 FPPG. The arrival of Tahir Whitehead took a little light off the shine of this season, however, and the fact that Thompson has missed 2 games a year for all 5 seasons he's played is a weird trend.

19. **Joey Bosa, DL, LAC:** Bosa stayed healthy all season in 2019, so this should be his down year as he's gone 12 games, 16, 7 and then 16 again over his 4 seasons. I worry a little bit about the health, but the production is strong! The 67.5 tackles last year signal more consistency than many other top DLs, though he did dip lower than 5 FP in 5 games last year. Bosa has room to improve, though; he was already the 5th-highest-scoring DL last year.

20. **Lavonte David, LB, TB:** I wanted to rank David higher, but seeing that he but up his 2nd-lowest per-game production, which was still an impressive 11 PPG and finished 17th among LBs, he is turning 30 this year. So he's on the wrong side of 30 with a 1st-round pick stud going into his 2nd year next to him. David will still play almost all the snaps and be productive, but I think a little comes off his stat line.

21. **Leighton Vander Esch, LB, DAL:** This is a bit of a middling rank for LVE, but that's how I feel about him. He is obviously going to put up points when he's out there. He's averaged over 10 points per game in his 2 seasons. Still, I'm nervous about the neck injury. Vander Esch missed the last 6 games of the season with a neck injury, on which he underwent an operation in January. He is expected to be back for camp but hasn't been fully cleared yet. This is why I'm so high on Jaylon Smith.

22. **Landon Collins, DB, WAS:** Talk about consistency: Collins has averaged over 10 points a game in each of his 5 seasons, and only once has he not had 100 tackles. Sean Davis coming over from Pittsburgh is a better tackler than Montae Nicholson, but I don't see him eating into Collins' opportunities too deeply.

23. **Harrison Smith, DB, MIN:** Smith is as consistent as it gets: He has averaged between 8.6-11.5 points every season since entering the NFL in 2012. He has averaged almost 6 total tackles a game, though he has almost no upside, so he's fairly boring. Of course, midrange stability doesn't hurt in some fantasy situations.

24. **Tracy Walker, DB, DET:** Walker could be ranked a little bit higher on this list; in his 1st season starting (2019), he was the 4th-best DB in per-game scoring, averaging 11.8 fantasy points. He isn't higher because he took a beating starting every contest and missed 3 games in the middle of the season with a knee injury. He recovered and played 90% of the snaps in the final 4 games, and he shouldn't have a lingering issue.

25. **Sam Hubbard, DL, CIN:** I was hesitant to buy into Hubbard putting up bigger numbers from '18 to '19, but he proved me wrong! He averaged 8.7 PPG, coming in as the 4th-best DL after his snap percentage spiked. His 3rd year could be big; he should see more pass-rush opportunities as opponents look to keep up with Cincinnati's capable offense.

26. **Jayon Brown, LB, TEN:** Brown and Rashaan Evans eat into each other's tackle productivity, but they were both over 100 wrap-ups last season. I rank Brown first. As shown by his 8 pass deflections and 1 INT last year, he is around the ball a little more than Evans, who has 1 PD in 2 seasons. This gives Brown more chances to make a big play.

27. **Nick Bosa, DL, SF:** This is an all-upside pick for me. Bosa doesn't have the stats from last year to merit going this high, but he improved every year in college, and I expect him to do the same in the pros. Just take a look at his output in 3 playoff games the 49ers: 11 solo tackles, 4 assists, 4 sacks, 2 pass deflections and a forced fumble, for an IDP scoring average of 13.1 points. That would have beat DL leader Danielle Hunter by over 3 points per game.

28. **Derwin James, DB, LAC:** James didn't even play in a game until Week 12 last season because of a Jones foot fracture he suffered in the preseason, and he wasn't the same player he was as a rookie. He dipped from 10.9 PPG in 2018 to 8.8 last year dropping him from the 8th-highest DB to the 26th. This is a lot like the Nick Bosa ranking: I expect some improvement. An entire offseason of rest should bring James back to 100%, and his 3rd year should be his best yet.

29. **Aaron Donald, DL, LAR:** Donald may have regressed down to the mean last year, averaging only 7.2 PPG and dropping to the 14th-ranked fantasy DL, but there was a good reason. Donald suffered a back injury in Week 2 against the Saints and never took a week off, and while he looked dominant at times, it seemed to wear on him at the end of the season: He averaged fewer than 6 points the last 4 weeks. He still led the league in hurries by a DT with 55 (2nd behind only T.J. Watt with 59) and beat Cameron Heyward by 22.

30. **Cameron Heyward, DL, PIT:** Speaking of Heyward, he flipped a switch last season and went into a new mode. He has been in the league since 2011 and never averaged more than 7.6 PPG, but last year he averaged 9.2; his tackle total was a career-high 83. Heyward didn't do it all with splash plays, but he did have 9 sacks -- the 2nd-best total in his career -- and finished second among DTs with 33 QB pressures, behind Donald's 55.

31. **Kenneth Murray, LB, LAC (R):** Our first rookie shows up! The Chargers made a move 1 spot in front of the Saints to take Murray, so he will probably get a long leash to perform immediately. Murray was all over the

field at Oklahoma with 325 tackles over 3 seasons. The Chargers have been without a great MLB for a while now, so Murray should have room to feast.

32. T.J. Watt, LB, PIT: Watt led the league in QB pressures, tied for 4th in sacks with 14.5, and finished 3rd in Defensive Player of the Year voting behind Stephon Gilmore and Chandler Jones. Watt had career highs in everything except tackles last year, and while he has improved his play every year, he has to improve his tackling to move up IDP lists. The splash plays are pretty good, though (8 FFs, 2 FRs, 8 PDs and 2 INTs last year).

33. J.J Watt, DL, HOU: We have seen *this* Watt come back from some bad injuries in his career, so there is no doubt he could be a top-10 player this season, but the fact is he suffered another injury that forced him to miss 8 games. He did come back in the playoffs and played the last 2 games for the Texans, but he wasn't the same. This is an upside pick, mainly because there's a group of DLs that are all in the same area, and we've seen Watt put up No. 1-overall IDP numbers.

34. Eric Kendricks, LB, MIN: Kendricks is amazingly consistent, averaging between 9.7 and 11.2 PPG every season for 5 straight years. He doesn't offer much splash-play upside (9 sacks, 6 FFs, 4 FRs and 4 INTs over 5 years), but he did have 12 PDs last season with 0 INTs. Shaquill Griffin was the only player with more passes defensed and 0 picks.

35. Jordan Poyer, DB, BUF: Poyer has been consistent over the last 3 seasons, averaging at least 10 fantasy PPG over that time and he has only missed one game in 3 years. While I have him next to DBs, Poyer signifies the end of the top tier of IDPs.

36. Jabrill Peppers, DB, NYG

37. John Johnson, DB, LAR

Peppers is coming off a transverse back fracture, and Johnson went on the IR with a shoulder injury after 6 games. Those injuries keep them lower than they should probably be. Johnson and Peppers finished 7th and 8th, respectively, in PPG last year among DBs.

38. Justin Simmons, DB, DEN: Simmons has never averaged over 10 PPG in a season, but the Broncos should be putting up more points, which will give Simmons more shots at big plays when opponents try to respond on offense. He showed potential last year with 4 INTs and 15 PDs (tied for 6th in the NFL).

39. Cameron Jordan, DL, NO

40. DeForest Buckner, DL, IND

We are getting to the end of a tier of DL here with Jordan and Buckner. These guys should provide pretty good value at DL which is way deeper and clumped together at the top than I ever remember it being. Jordan had a career high in Sacks and still didn't average 10 PPG and Buckner is moving away from the comfort of Nick Bosa and Arik Armstead playing on the same line.

41. Tremaine Edmunds, LB, BUF

42. Chandler Jones, LB, ARI

43. Deion Jones, LB, ATL

These will not be popular rankings, but I just don't see Edmunds climbing much higher than this after averaging just under 10 PPG last year. He and Matt Milano eat into each other's tackle total (115 for Edmunds last year, Milano 101), and the Bills added A.J. Klein, who had a nice 69 tackles last season. Chandler Jones has had 49 sacks in the last 3 years, but that just keeps him at pace with the high-tackle total guys in points. Last but not least, Deion Jones probably isn't going to ever get back to the high finishes in PPG (12th, 8th and 2nd between 2016-18), but he can do better than 55th from last season, especially with De'Vondre Campbell and his massive amount of tackles leaving for Arizona.

44. Anthony Walker, LB, IND

45. Todd Davis, LB, DEN

46. Patrick Queen, LB, BAL (R)

A nice little tier of LBs here. Walker had 124 tackles last year with few splash plays next to Darius Leonard. Davis had 134 tackles with literally no big plays last year, and if the Broncos offense scores some point,s he could lose coverage snaps late as teammate A.J. Johnson is much better in coverage. Queen is the 2nd-ranked rookie on this list; he could be playing next to fellow rookie Malik Harrison this year fighting for tackles.

47. Jessie Bates, DB, CIN

48. Taylor Rapp, DB, LAR

49. Kareem Jackson, DB, DEN

50. **Malcolm Jenkins, DB, NO**

4 high-tackle safeties from 2019 here in Bates (100), Rapp (100), Jackson (71, in 13 games) and Jenkins (81). Bates, Jackson and Jenkins will be afforded more opportunities for big plays with their respective offenses being better. Rapp didn't start getting serious snaps until Week 8 in his rookie year, but that was when John Johnson went down, and they'll be playing together in the D-backfield this year.

51. **Chase Young, DL, WAS (R)**
52. **Justin Houston, DL, IND**
53. **Carlos Dunlap, DL, CIN**
54. **Maxx Crosby, DL, LVR**
55. **Arik Armstead, DL, SF**
56. **Jadeveon Clowney, DL, FA**

These DLs have ample upside. Young was the No. 2 pick in April's draft and had 16.5 sacks with 46 tackles in 12 college games. Houston is getting long in the tooth but welcomes DeForest Buckner to that Indy DL to take up blockers. Dunlap is coming off a career year in his 10th season. Crosby started his rookie campaign with a broken hand but ended with 11 sacks. Armstead loses Buckner, though San Fran added a solid rookie in Javon Kinlaw. Clowney still hasn't signed, but he has to improve off a 3-sack '19 wherever he lands.

57. **Fred Warner, LB, SF**
58. **Jamie Collins, LB, DET**
59. **K.J. Wright, LB, SEA**
60. **Isaiah Simmons, LB, ARI (R)**
61. **Jerome Baker, LB, MIA**
62. **Benardrick McKinney, LB, HOU**
63. **Rashaan Evans, LB, TEN**
64. **Shaquil Barrett, LB, TB**
65. **Kwon Alexander, LB, SF**
66. **Danny Trevathan, LB, CHI**

This is the spot where IDPs really hit a break. The LBs are all going to offer so many more points on a consistent basis than the other positions that we hit this big LB wall of guys with upside, though we're talking limited upside compared to the LBs ahead of them. Barrett is in this section because I just flat-out don't buy that he can reproduce something close to the 19 sacks he had last season. Warner had an amazing 2019, but his average dropped from 12 PPG to only 8.3 in the 8 games Alexander played next to him, which would have dropped Warner from 12th to 99th in PPG. Conversely, Aleander had never averaged fewer than 11.5 PPG in Tampa Bay and only scored 6.8 PPG in San Fran last year. Collins is getting a new address but has always been consistent. Wright, McKinney, Evans and Trevathan are all the 2nd-best fantasy LB on their team but will still have high tackle numbers. Baker is the best on his team but will have value in this same range. Simmons is an impressive rookie that had over 100 tackles, 8 sacks and 3 INTs for Clemson last season, but he goes to a defense with tackle vacuum Jordan Hicks and De'Vondre Campbell, who had 129 last season.

67. **DeMarcus Lawrence, DL, DAL**
68. **Yannick Ngakoue, DL, JAX**
69. **Melvin Ingram, DL, LAC**
70. **Robert Quinn, DL, CHI**
71. **Frank Clark, DL, KC**
72. **Josh Allen, DL, JAX**
73. **Brandon Graham, DL, PHI**

Ugh, I don't like picking from this tier of DLs, but they all have a decent amount of upside. We have seen Lawrence play much better, but he was banged up for a majority of the 2019 season and played through it. The Cowboys added Gerald McCoy and Dontari Poe on the interior, and they should get him more chances at the QB. Ngakoue just has to show up to be the best of this group, although he and teammate Allen lost the presence of Calais Campbell, who's now in Baltimore. Ingram will probably lose shots at the QB with the offense losing Philip Rivers and Melvin Gordon. Quinn and Clark have both had much better seasons than they did in 2019 and get a little benefit of the doubt. So does Graham, who is making too much money not to be given every chance to make plays.

74. **Matt Milano, LB, BUF**
75. **Cole Holcomb, LB, WAS**

76. **Tahir Whitehead, LB, CAR**
77. **A.J. Johnson, LB, DEN**
78. **Logan Wilson, LB, CIN**
79. **Jason Pierre-Paul, LB, TB**
80. **Za'Darius Smith, LB, GB**
81. **Myles Jack, LB, JAX**
82. **De'Vondre Campbell, LB, AZ**
83. **Christian Kirksey, LB, GB**

Two of these things are not like the others: JPP and Smith are the big-time pass rushers. JPP only ended up playing in 10 games last season; a car accident last May left him with a fractured neck and a start on the PUP. He came back with 8.5 sacks but a tackle total so low he had his lowest average PPG since the firecracker year of 2015. Smith tied for the lead league in QB Hits with 37 and still only averaged 8 PPG. Milano, Holcomb, Whitehead and Campbell all had 100 tackles last season, so the upside is capped; they will be steady, though.

Johnson should be in line for more snaps as he was ranked way higher than teammate Todd Davis, according to PFF, and was much better in coverage. Jack didn't get any help with the Jags bringing in Joe Schobert, and he was actually lower than this per game last year. Wilson is going to have to earn that starting job for Cincy, but the Bengals have been so desperate for speed from the LB position that it shouldn't take much. Kirksey just needs to hold up; during his last 2 full years (in '16 and '17), he averaged over 12 PPG, but he's only played in 9 games since then.

84. **Kenny Moore, DB, IND**
85. **Tyrann Mathieu, DB, KC**
86. **Vonn Bell, DB, CIN**
87. **Bradley McDougald, DB, SEA**
88. **Kevin Byard, DB, TEN**
89. **Justin Reid, DB, HOU**
90. **Patrick Peterson, DB, ARI**
91. **Tre'Davious White, DB, BUF**
92. **Carlton Davis III, DB, TB**
93. **Logan Ryan, DB, NYJ**
94. **Johnathan Abram, DB, LV**
95. **Minkah Fitzpatrick, DB, PIT**

We get our first real CBs in this section of DBs. (Kareem Jackson mainly plays safety but qualifies). Moore has averaged over 9 PPG the last 2 straight seasons, so he has to be fantasy's No. 2 CB. While Peterson and White hit career highs in PPG, I don't expect them to repeat that; QBs will look to throw away from them. Bell was the 5th-best DB in PPG last year, but he had a career-high 5 fumble recoveries, which is just too much luck for me to bank on moving forward. Mathieu actually has some upside if he gets to stick at safety a little more this season.

Even with his 5 INTs and decent tackle total, Byard has still only cracked 10 PPG in '17, when he had 8 INTs. Reid has averaged 83 tackles in his first 2 games, and McDougald has fallen to around that range over the last 3 seasons. Davis was thrown at a lot and had 60 tackles at CB last year with only 3 splash plays. Abram was put on IR after his first game of his rookie season last year, but expect him to come up big in his 2nd season with a high tackle total. I know I'll look like a bad fan with Fitzpatrick this low, but he had 8 TOs after only 2 in his rookie season and 2 TDs -- just not sustainable.

96. **Jonathan Allen, DL, WAS**
97. **Grady Jarrett, DL, ATL**
98. **Calais Campbell, DL, BAL**
99. **Emmanuel Ogbah, DL, MIA**
100. **Stephon Tuitt, DL, PIT**
101. **Chris Jones, DL, KC**
102. **Trey Flowers, DL, DET**

Allen was the highest scorer out of this group last year (7.5 PPG), and he might actually have the highest upside of the bunch when considering Washington added Chase Young to the line. The other guys are mainly interior presences and can have a big game followed up by a dud. Everyone on this list had at least one game of 2 points or fewer last year.

The rest of the Top 150

103.	Thomas Davis Sr., LB, WAS	127.	Khalil Mack, LB, CHI
104.	Bud Dupree, LB, PIT	128.	Harold Landry, LB, TEN
105.	Nathan Gerry, LB, PHI	129.	Anthony Hitchens, LB, KC
106.	Mack Wilson, LB, CLE	130.	Chuck Clark, DB, BAL
107.	Avery Williamson, LB, NYJ	131.	Justin Evans, DB, TB
108.	Dont'a Hightower, LB, NE	132.	L.J. Collier, DL, SEA
109.	Damarious Randall, DB, LV	133.	Yetur Gross-Matos, DL, CAR (R)
110.	Kyle Fuller, DB, CHI	134.	Von Miller, LB, DEN
111.	Janoris Jenkins, DB, NO	135.	Dante Fowler Jr., LB, ATL
112.	Karl Joseph, DB, CLE	136.	Stephon Gilmore, DB, NE
113.	Ha Ha Clinton-Dix, DB, DAL	137.	Adrian Amos, DB, GB
114.	Xavier McKinney, DB, NYG (R)	138.	Ronnie Harrison, DB, JAX
115.	Terrell Edmunds, DB, PIT	139.	Anthony Harris, DB, MIN
116.	Chase Winovich, DL, NE	140.	Jeremy Chinn, DB, CAR (R)
117.	Clelin Ferrell, DL, LV	141.	Jimmie Ward, DB, SF
118.	Derek Wolfe, DL, BAL	142.	Bradley Chubb, LB, DEN
119.	Kenny Clark, DL, GB	143.	Preston Smith, LB, GB
120.	K'Lavon Chaisson, LB, JAX (R)	144.	Kiko Alonso, LB, NO
121.	Anthony Barr, LB, MIN	145.	Vince Williams, LB, PIT
122.	Kyle Van Noy, LB, MIA	146.	T.J. Edwards, LB, PHI
123.	Micah Kiser, LB, LAR	147.	Sione Takitaki, LB, CLE
124.	Dre Greenlaw, LB, SF	148.	A.J. Klein, LB, BUF
125.	Raekwon McMillan, LB, MIA	149.	Nick Vigil, LB, LAC
126.	Nick Kwiatkoski, LB, LV	150.	Matt Judon, LB, BAL

Chapter 9

TEAM DEFENSE/SPECIAL TEAMS

Derek Brown

The debate rages on every year: Does defense matter? For fantasy football and filling our starting lineups with a team's defense and special teams (D/ST) units, the answer is no. It doesn't. Over the last four years, the top-ranked D/ST in fantasy versus the 12th-ranked is only separated by 4.77 points per game, on average. Also, over that same span, 45.8% of defenses that have finished the season as a top-12 unit have been undrafted in fantasy football leagues.

2 important rules to follow concerning fantasy defenses:

1. Do not draft a defense unless required by your league rules.
2. Stream defenses.

With such a narrow margin of scoring separating the top defense to the last "startable" defense, players have no reason to spend draft capital there. The sharp move is to instead draft a player that is one injury away from fantasy prominence. This holds for all drafts regardless of timing, as injuries are a yearly occurrence. Diamonds in the rough do exist in fantasy and can be mined during the draft.

The question remains: What indicators should you look for in a defense that can be a top-12 unit or a multi-week streamer? The answer is simple. Because the NFL is a passing league, target defenses that excel at defending the pass.

Looking at the last four years of top 12 fantasy defenses compared to the top 12 leaders in various metrics for rushing defense (rush defense DVOA, rushing yards per game allowed, and yards per carry allowed) and passing defense (pass defense DVOA, pressure rates, and quarterback rating allowed), the lean to pass defense is distinct.

Over the last four years, pass-defense metrics held between a 56.2-70.8% rate of hitting a top-12 defense. QB rating allowed had an extremely high hit rate with 75% of the top 12 fantasy defenses in 3 of the last 4 years, allowing the 12 lowest quarterback ratings.

Rush metrics were spotty at best, only managing a 37.5 to 45.8% hit rate. Look for teams that excel at pass defense, and if picking one high-level metric as a means to spot a streamer, it's quarterback rating allowed.

With this in mind, here's my rankings list for 2020 D/STs.

FANTASY DEFENSE/SPECIAL TEAMS RANKINGS

1. **Baltimore Ravens:** After the arrival of CB Marcus Peters in Week 7 last season, the Ravens were the top-ranked defense in fantasy. With Jimmy Smith re-signing, Baltimore returns a nasty starting secondary of Smith, Peters and Marlon Humphrey. The pass rush will be fearsome with the team retaining sack leader Matt Judon (franchise tag), signing Derek Wolfe, trading for Calais Campbell, and drafting Patrick Queen.

2. **Pittsburgh Steelers:** The Steelers' trade for Minkah Fitzpatrick was transformative. Pittsburgh was the second-ranked defense in fantasy after Fitzpatrick arrived in the Steel City. Bud Dupree returns under the franchise tag to terrorize opposing quarterbacks with T.J. Watt. The Steelers return mostly the same cast that allowed the third-lowest quarterback rating in 2019.

3. **New England Patriots:** Over the last eight years, no team has repeated as the top fantasy defense. While the Patriots will return a formidable unit led by shutdown corner Stephon Gilmore, history and variance will make it the ninth year of crowning a new king of the D/ST mountain top. Drafting Josh Uche will help soften the blow of losing Kyle Van Noy and Jamie Collins in the offseason, though.

4. **San Francisco 49ers:** The 49ers got their DeForest Buckner replacement in Javon Kinlaw during the draft. Arik Armstead, Nick Bosa and Dee Ford will continue to bring the heat up front. Ahkello Witherspoon was playing at a shutdown-corner level opposite Richard Sherman before missing time with a sprained foot. If Sherman can avoid Father Time another year and Witherspoon can flash last year's early-season form, the 49ers will again be a defense to be reckoned with.

5. **Cleveland Browns:** The return of Myles Garrett can't be understated. Garrett has racked up 23.5 sacks over the last two seasons (26 games). The Browns have an emerging young tandem of corners on the outside. Denzel Ward has teased shutdown-corner potential over his first two years. Greedy Williams held his own in his rookie season while performing well in man and press coverage. With the addition of safety Grant Delpit in the draft, this defense can take a huge leap forward this year.

6. **New Orleans Saints:** Cameron Jordan showed no signs of slowing down at age 30 last year, tallying a career-best 15.5 sacks. The Saints were among the leagues' best at pressuring the passer last year. If Marcus Davenport continues to mature, the Saints will be among the top again in 2020. Extending Janoris Jenkins was a must after Eli Apple hit free agency. The Saints have the makings of a top-tier defense against both the run and the pass.

7. **Minnesota Vikings:** The Vikings cleaned house in their cornerback room, jettisoning Xavier Rhodes, Trae Waynes, and Mackensie Alexander. Outside of Alexander, the Minnesota corner play was dreadful last year, so it's hard to fault the front office for the majority of these moves. Retaining Anthony Harris was needed so he could again team with Harrison Smith to form the backbone of this pass defense. Rookie corners Jeff Gladney and Cameron Dantzler will dictate this defense's 2020 ceiling.

8. **Los Angeles Chargers:** The Chargers spent the offseason attempting to address a bottom-10 rush defense, drafting Kenneth Murray and signing Nick Vigil and Linval Joseph. Melvin Ingram is getting longer in the tooth, but he and Joey Bosa still form a formidable sack-stacking duo. A full 16-game effort by Derwin James, a bounce-back season by Desmond King and the arrival of Chris Harris could vault this defense to the league's upper echelon.

9. **Buffalo Bills:** The Bills had to address their pass rush in the draft and did so by taking A.J. Epenesa in the second round. Epenesa is going to have to hit the ground running after Buffalo lost its top two sack leaders from last season: Jordan Phillips and Shaq Lawson. While the Bills' ability to collapse the pocket is in question, their secondary is not. Tre'Davious White is a premier shutdown corner. Recently re-signed

safety Jordan Poyer and his partner in crime Micah Hyde remain among the leagues' best at their positions.

10. **Kansas City Chiefs:** The Chiefs are the only defense to turn in a top 12 finish in fantasy in each of the last four years. Despite their consistency, Kansas City's defense has been undrafted in 12 team leagues in two of the last four years. The Chiefs still possess a talented defense with the likes of Chris Jones, Frank Clark, and Tyrann Mathieu. With Bashaud Breeland possibly missing time with off-field incidents, look for the Chiefs to potentially address the corner position further before Week 1.

11. **Philadelphia Eagles:** The Eagles were a top-5 defense against the run last season. Philly succeeded this offseason in making significant upgrades in pass coverage with the additions of Darius Slay and Nickell Robey-Coleman. The signing of Will Parks softened the blow of losing steady safety Malcolm Jenkins, just in case Jalen Mills isn't ready to assume the mantle. Mills played safety some at LSU and is familiar with Jim Schwartz's scheme. Even with an unconventional offseason program, there is optimism with Mills' positional switch from corner.

12. **New York Jets:** The Jets might be a yearly mess on paper behind Adam Gase, but the defense was quite good last year as the seventh overall fantasy group. The Jets return a run-stopping group that was top-3 against the rush in 2019. The secondary was questionable in 2019, and that remains this season as well. The Jets replace Darryl Roberts with Pierre Desir on the outside. The hope is Desir bounces back to his 2018 form and that he finds a Brian Poole-esque rejuvenation moving to the Jets' man and press scheme. In 2018, Desir allowed a 47% catch rate in man and press coverage. Poole was retained wisely after thriving last season under the Jets' defensive design. If their secondary plays above expectations, this D possesses some upside.

13. **Chicago Bears:** Losing a trio of productive starters in Leonard Floyd, Ha-Ha Clinton-Dix and Prince Amukamara is going to hurt. The Bears are expecting Artie Burns or rookie Jaylon Johnson to step into Amukamara's starting role without a drop-off, which is asking a lot. The new influx of talent has a tall order to fill for this defense to remain a top-10 group.

14. **Denver Broncos:** The Broncos are going to have to avoid the injury bug if this defense is to excel under Vic Fangio. After combining for four games played last year, Bryce Callahan and Bradley Chubb are going to need better health as linchpins of this year's defense. New arrival A.J. Bouye is a wild card after struggling in the No. 1 corner role last year in Jacksonville after Jalen Ramsey's trade. This defense could be top-10 if all the moving parts gel and Von Miller's play doesn't decline.

15. **Tampa Bay Buccaneers:** Last year, the Bucs fielded an elite run-stopping unit in their first season under Todd Bowles. Tampa returned Shaquil Barrett on the franchise tag after his massive breakout season of 19.5 sacks. After shuffling around the secondary week—to-week last year, the Buccaneers received some standout play from Carlton Davis and Sean Murphy-Bunting. On talent alone, this defense should be ranked higher, but considering the gauntlet of NFC South offenses, they are outside the top 12.

16. **Atlanta Falcons:** Last season's defensive turnaround was impressive. After their Week 9 bye, the Falcons transformed from a zone defense into heavy man and press coverage. The results were eye-popping amd transforming from a defense that had allowed 31.25 points per game across Weeks 1-8, to allowing only 18.6 points per game for the rest of the season; in that second window, Atlanta was the fourth-ranked defense in fantasy. If the Falcons build off last season's momentum, they could make for a high-end streamer.

17. **Tennessee Titans:** The Titans fielded a top-10 rush defense in 2019, but their secondary was suspect week-to-week. Adoree' Jackson dealt with injuries all season. The tandem of Logan Ryan and Malcolm Butler took turns losing foot races on deep routes. The Titans have one of the most talented linebacker groups in the league with the addition of Vic Beasley to Harold Landry, Jayon Brown and Rashaan Evans. Second-round pick Kristian Fulton has to step up opposite Jackson. If not, the Titans will be Jekyll and

Hyde as secondary receivers take turns burning Butler and the newly signed fossil known as Johnathan Joseph.

18. **Green Bay Packers:** The Packers return the heart of their defense with Za'Darius Smith and Preston Smith ready to rack up the sacks. Kevin King and Jaire Alexander have been erratic players with moments of lockdown capability while also lapsing into burnt-toast territory. The Packers are a streaming option only against weaker rushing teams. Mike Pettine has a long enough track record of ceding rushing production to opposing clubs that thrive on the ground (hello, Kyle Shanahan's 49ers).

19. **Seattle Seahawks:** The Seahawks were a middle-of-the-road defense last year versus both the run and pass while ranking 22nd in points per game allowed. The trade for Quinton Dunbar, who was playing at an elite level for the Redskins in 2019, could pay huge dividends, depending on his pending legal troubles as of publication. Overall, though, even if the Seahawks re-sign Jadeveon Clowney, they are still probably no better than an average defense again.

20. **Dallas Cowboys:** The Cowboys' star-studded cast of characters on defense has never amounted to an overall productive fantasy defense. Dallas has never finished higher than 15th (2017) in fantasy defensive scoring. Even with the Cowboys drafting Trevon Diggs, the loss of Byron Jones is huge. Jones' ability to take away half of the field can't be emphasized enough. A starting trio of Diggs, Anthony Brown and Chidobe Awuzie isn't going to strike fear in any OC's heart.

21. **New York Giants:** This defense has the talent to take a step forward this season. New York fielded a top-10 rush defense in 2019 and upgraded massively in the secondary with the signing of James Bradberry. DeAndre Baker's play picked up immensely during the second half of the season. Teaming Baker and Bradberry on the outside has the chance to be the best cover duo in the NFC East – depending on the result of Baker's legal troubles present as of publication. The signing of tackling machine Blake Martinez was another solid move by Dave Gettleman.

22. **Los Angeles Rams:** The Rams still have a handful of the league's elite with Aaron Donald and Jalen Ramsey leading this roster. The Rams lost many names in the offseason, though, with Dante Fowler, Eric Weddle, Clay Matthews, Cory Littleton and Nickell Robey-Coleman all out the door. A'Shawn Robinson and Leonard Floyd will help mitigate these departures, but this defense is going to be hard-pressed to match last year's top-5 fantasy finish.

23. **Arizona Cardinals:** The Cardinals have invested in the defensive side of the ball this offseason. The Cards drafted do-it-all dynamo Isaiah Simmons in the first round. Arizona followed that up by taking two defensive tackles (Leki Fotu and Rashard Lawrence) out of their next three picks. They also upgraded their front 3 by signing nose tackle Jordan Phillips from the Bills.

24. **Miami Dolphins:** If Xavien Howard can bounce back, the Dolphins can be one of the better sleeper defenses in fantasy. New South Beach hire Byron Jones is at the height of his powers with the ability to wipe an opposition's top receiver off the map. Shaq Lawson and Kyle Van Noy are low-key signings that could pay off handsomely in 2020.

25. **Indianapolis Colts:** Trading for DeForest Buckner is a massive upgrade for this D-line. Darius Leonard and Justin Houston remain standout players in their right, but the Colts' secondary is filled with age and questions. The signings of T.J. Carrie and a washed version of Xavier Rhodes are middling starters at best. The Colts pass defense could be treading water even at its best.

26. **Jacksonville Jaguars:** With 6 of their first 8 picks in the draft going to the defense, the Jaguars' front office is well aware of its depth chart needs. Losing Calais Campbell will sting even more if Yannick Ngakoue is dealt before Week 1. D.J. Hayden and Tre Herndon played exceptionally well last year. With C.J. Henderson replacing A.J. Bouye, these corners are a talented and underrated group. Taven Bryan continuing his top-end play and third-rounder DaVon Hamilton stepping up will be critical to this team stopping the run in 2020.

27. **Washington Redskins:** Adding a stud like Chase Young to an already stout defensive line is a boon. The Redskins are likely to improve upon their bottom-5 pressure rate of last season. The secondary could be better than advertised with the additions of Kendall Fuller and Ronald Darby. Washington's biggest hindrance is the top-level passing attacks they are set to face for six games in the Cowboys, Eagles and (yes) the Giants.

28. **Cincinnati Bengals:** The Bengals transplanted two-thirds of the Vikings starting secondary from 2019 by signing Trae Waynes and Mackensie Alexander. If Waynes can resemble his 2017-2018 play and not last year's abysmal showing, this secondary could improve. The push upfront is aging and uninspiring, with Cincy still leaning on Carlos Dunlap and Geno Atkins to be major cogs alongside Sam Hubbard.

29. **Detroit Lions:** Subtracting Darius Slay to add Jeff Okudah is a puzzling move at best. Darryl Roberts and Justin Coleman form the remainder of a burnable secondary. Losing Mike Daniels and Damon Harrison along the defensive line only to replace them with Danny Shelton and Nick Williams is probably best viewed as a push. Hard to see the Lions carrying a ton of value even in the deepest of leagues.

30. **Las Vegas Raiders:** The Raiders upgraded their LBs, adding Carl Nassib and Cory Littleton. 1st-round pick Damon Arnette and signee Prince Amukamara offer hope for the secondary. Maxx Crosby netted an impressive 10 sacks as a rookie, but he can't carry the load alone.

31. **Carolina Panthers:** The Panthers devoted their entire draft to the defense with all 7 picks addressing needs on that side of the ball. Derrick Brown, Yetur Gross-Matos, and Jeremy Chinn are all talented, but when Donte Jackson is your top corner, you're in big trouble.

32. **Houston Texans:** When your head coach and general manager piles up a long list of head-scratching moves, this is what you're left with. Unless Deshaun Watson becomes a two-way player lining up at corner, the Texans are short on hope for defense.

Chapter 10

2020 Rookies + 2021 Preview

Scott Bogman

2020: QB | RB | WR | TE | UDFA • 2021: QB | RB | WR | TE

2020 Rookies

QUARTERBACKS

Joe Burrow, CIN (LSU -- Round 1, Pick 1 Overall): With Burrow, we probably saw the strangest rise to the top for any QB that I can remember. Burrow had 3,181 yards, 18 TDs and 5 INTs in 23 career games going into 2019. 5,671 yards, 60 TDs, a 76.3% completion percentage (highest collegiate rate EVER), a Heisman trophy and a National Championship later, Burrow is the No. 1 pick! He has almost no holes in his game, and with Andy Dalton gone, he will start Day 1 for Cincinnati.

- **2020 Value:** Burrow will walk into a great fantasy situation with weapons all over the place: RB Joe Mixon and pass-catchers A.J. Green, Tyler Boyd, John Ross, and fellow rookie Tee Higgins. Tons of upside even for Year 1, but I don't usually take rookies as a QB1. If you need/want a QB2 with a ton of upside, take Burrow. For a Superflex league, pair Burrow with a top-tier QB.
- **Dynasty Value**: Top-10 QB in fantasy, especially with so many starting QBs on the verge of aging out of the league. Cincinnati's offensive line needs to improve, but he already has great skill-position players. As they advertised by picking Higgins, the Bengals are committed to surrounding him with help.

Tua Tagovailoa, MIA (Alabama -- Round 1, Pick 5): The Dolphins probably have been obsessed with him for 2 years and were able to stick at 5 to get him. Tua was the clear No. 1 overall pick going into the 2019 season, and if Joe Burrow wouldn't have had the best college football season in history, he probably still would have been, even with his hip injury. Tua didn't have enough pass attempts to qualify, but he would have been tied for 7th all-time in CFB completion% if he qualified. The biggest knock on Tua is the "injury-prone" tag since he had 2 ankle surgeries and an extensively invasive hip surgery. The hip was cleared a while ago, and he is not at risk for further injury, according to his doctors. This dude is accurate, has great poise and rarely makes mistakes. The floor and ceiling are high.

- **2020:** In a perfect world, Tua would get to sit for the entire 2020 season and learn behind Ryan Fitzpatrick and Josh Rosen. Most QBs that are drafted in the first round start at least 1 game their rookie season. (In 2013, EJ Manuel was the last first-round QB not to in 2013.) I think they'll give Tua the last month of starts. If Fitz is hurt, I imagine Miami will go with Rosen to showcase him for a potential trade next year. An expectation of 4 starts/games makes sense; Tua's coming off the hip surgery and won't have a normal camp/preseason in the pandemic.
- **Dynasty:** Just a shade below Burrow, in my opinion. Burrow would beat him out because of the weapons he gets walking in the door, but as far as skill, I have them pretty close. The Dolphins focused on building the OL in this draft (Austin Jackson in the first, Robert Hunt in the second and Solomon Kindley in the fourth), so the weapons will probably be the focus of next year's draft. DeVante Parker, Preston Williams and Mike Gesicki doesn't make up a bad start for Tua.

Justin Herbert, LAC (Oregon -- Round 1, Pick 6): Herbert has all the physical tools scouts look for in a QB. He has a big arm, a big frame (6'6", 230 lbs), and great wheels (13 rushing TDs in his collegiate career). He does lack some polish, though. He can get stuck on the first read and then either throw it into traffic or take off running if Option 1 isn't open. My biggest complaint is that he doesn't like to throw the ball deep: Hebert's averages of yards per attempt and air yards per attempt were well below Burrow and Tua's. To be fair, Herbert didn't have the surrounding cast that Burrow and Tua enjoyed. I still think he gave up some big plays by taking a short route or running; this can be fixed, of course, because he has a monster arm and the ability to make any throw on the field.

- **2020:** The Chargers have repeatedly said that they really like Tyrod Taylor. That could have been a draft smokescreen bit, though. I think Herbert will start a handful of games at the end of the season, but I would like to see him sit as long as possible. The Chargers have a shaky OL and didn't draft anyone to improve it in the draft.
- **Dynasty:** I'm not the biggest Herbert fan in a dynasty league. He was a high pick, so he will get a longer leash than others. However, the OL is subpar; WR Keenan Allen is a UFA next year; and Hunter Henry is playing on the franchise tag, so we don't know if he'll be surrounded by talent or scrubs next season when he's really ready to go.

Jordan Love, GB (Utah State -- Round 1, Pick 26): Love represents a tale of two seasons. In 2018 with HC Matt Wells, Love was spectacular; he improved his completion rate by 10% from 2017, threw for 3,500+ yards and had a 32:6 TD:INT. In 2019, Wells left for Texas Tech, and Love regressed, with the most notable stat being a 20:17 TD:INT. Scouts were torn on Love. Some saw him as a 3rd-round project, but some saw the "Patrick Mahomes upside" with his mobility and arm. I love him landing in Green Bay; he'll be polished while learning behind Aaron Rodgers for a while before he sees real game action. Very high ceiling with a very low floor.

- **2020:** Pretty much none. It would take an injury to get him onto the field, but unless that happens late in the season, I'm not even 100% sure the Packers would go to Love first.
- **Dynasty:** He's a project, so you would have to have the roster space and need for a QB (2QB league, Superflex or 16-plus-team league) to grab and wait. Love is a long-term lottery ticket.

Jalen Hurts, PHI (Oklahoma -- Round 2, Pick 53): I really liked this pick. I was surprised by the hate from Eagles fans; they of all people should know that having a good backup QB can save your season. Philly has are other big-time needs, but Carson Wentz is fairly injury-prone. In 2019, Wentz finally started all 16 games for the first time since his 2016 rookie season, but he still ended the season leaving the Wild Card game with a concussion. Hurts made the move from Alabama to Oklahoma for 2019, and he was awesome. He brought his completion rate up from his starting season's at 'Bama (69.7%), and he threw for over 3800 yards, 32:8 TD:INT and he ran for damn near 1,300 yards with 20 TDs! Hurts has the opposite problem of Herbert: He throws downfield to covered WRs too often and doesn't quite have a feel for the pocket quite yet. A little bit of a project, but he can pay off if he gets the chance.

- **2020:** Well, Wentz has missed games in his past, so Hurts could see starts sooner rather than later, but I think they'll have packages like Wildcat, other goal-line packages and trick plays set up for him. Still, I only consider him a Wentz handcuff for this year.
- **Dynasty:** Pretty high upside, especially if you are the Wentz owner. If he is given enough time to get comfortable in an NFL pocket to combine with his wheels, he has the ability to be a high-end QB. The floor is low, but it is for any NFL QB.

Jacob Eason, IND (Washington -- Round 4, Pick 122): I have never really been a fan. He was benched his sophomore season at Georgia (2017) in favor of Jake Fromm (who took the Bulldogs to the National Championship Game) and ended up sitting out 2018 after transferring to Washington. Eason struggled to win the starting gig over Jake Haener going into 2019 and was only announced as starter a week before kickoff. Eason has a cannon of an arm, but he doesn't have great touch and too often tries to muscle throws into spots he shouldn't. He could get plenty of time to develop behind Philip Rivers and Jacoby Brissett, but both could be gone at the end of 2020, which would thrust Eason into a starting role. Physical tools are there, but he needs a lot of work on progressions and pocket manipulation.

- **2020:** He shouldn't see the field this year. Rivers is the starter, and Brissett will back him up.
- **Dynasty:** He seems to be in a decent spot to sit and learn in Indy. Frank Reich is a great teacher, but I would slot in Eason as a career backup.

James Morgan, NYJ (Florida International -- Round 4, Pick 125): Morgan and Eason mirror themselves on many levels. Eason gets hype because he was a 5-star Georgia recruit that transferred to Washington, while Morgan transferred from Ball State to FIU. Morgan has a big arm and lack of touch but showed high-level flashes last year. He can put some throws on the money when given time, but his footwork is awful. He looks clunky on a deeper dropback, and the longer he holds the ball, the worse the throw probably will get. He'll be a nice backup behind Sam Darnold, but don't expect much more.

- **2020:** Morgan will only see the field if Darnold gets hurt.
- **Dynasty:** Darnold handcuff for the foreseeable future

Jake Fromm, BUF (Georgia -- Round 5, Pick 167): Fromm is the opposite of a lot of this class. His questionable arm strength likely dropped him to the 5th round (his prop bet was drafted O/U 60.5 overall). His penchant to attempt mostly shorter throws may reflect a lack of confidence going downfield. He won't turn the ball over (78:18 TD:INT in college), but he won't make any spectacular plays downfield. Fromm is exactly what a team should want out of a backup QB: a guy who won't try to do too much but is accurate and has way better decision-making skills than most QBs at any level.

- **2020:** Josh Allen does play a reckless brand of football, but Matt Barkley might still be the immediate backup to him anyway.
- **Dynasty:** Starting can't be off the table yet, but I would be surprised if he isn't a career backup.

Jake Luton, JAX (Oregon State -- Round 6, Pick 189): Luton is another physical specimen from this class; at 6'6", 225 lbs, he looks like a perfect rendering of an NFL QB. Despite Luton's size, his arm is just OK by NFL standards. Luton also almost always throws to his first look or an underneath route instead of moving his eyes downfield. He does look natural in the pocket and even when getting flushed out, but his mechanics are wonky, which leads to a lot of one-hop throws that he's leaving on the table.

- **2020:** I don't think that Luton will even be 2nd on the depth chart; the Jags traded for Joshua Dobbs right before the season started last year, and he'll probably back up Minshew. Luton has a better shot than Eason, Morgan or Fromm, but that's only because Minshew isn't fantastic and Dobbs has never started a game in the NFL.
- **Dynasty:** Like any QB taken after the 3rd round, Luton is probably too much of a project to be a long-term asset.

Cole McDonald, TEN (Hawaii -- Round 7, Pick 224): It was easy to see where the excitement and questions come with McDonald if you just watch one game he's in. He has a big arm and can run, which is something to behold in the Run N' Shoot offense from Nick Rolovich. McDonald's INTs came in bunches: 4 in the opener against Arizona in which he was benched, and 3 against Washington. Still, he had about 1,000 close calls that would make me super-nervous if I were counting on him. I think he's behind the QB that can teach him the most in Ryan Tannehill because they are athletically similar.

- **2020:** If the Titans don't bring any a vet to compete for the backup job it'll be between McDonald and Logan Woodside for the backup role, and I would take McDonald in that one.
- **Dynasty:** This is a flier pick for Tennessee. They almost never work, so don't waste your time.

Ben DiNucci, DAL (James Madison -- Round 7, Pick 231): I like the fit for Dallas: an RPO QB with great wheels fits as a Dak Prescott backup. The Cowboys did bring in Andy Dalton for the "real" insurance if Prescott doesn't end up signing his franchise tender. A lot of scouts were making the comparison of DiNucci to Jake Delhomme, which is some high praise. DiNucci started his college career at Pittsburgh and then ended up transferring to James

Madison to finish off his career. He fit much better at James Madison with a little more of an RPO offense that allowed him to use his legs more frequently.

- **2020:** Doubtful he gets any playing time being 3rd string, if he even makes the roster.
- **Dynasty:** Meh, he fits behind Dak, but he has an uphill battle to make the roster this year, so the future is a big question.

Tommy Stevens, NO (Mississippi State -- Round 7, Pick 240): The story behind this pick is pretty funny. Apparently, Stevens had promised the Panthers that he would sign with them as a UDFA. Sean Payton got wind of that and traded back into the 7th round to get him -- after they traded the rest of their picks to move up for another pick. This is an eventual replacement for Taysom Hill; I can't imagine they want to pay Hill $16 million again. The guy never played in more than 49% of the snaps in any one game.

- **2020:** Probably won't get much playing time. I assume he'll live on the practice squad.
- **Dynasty:** Not much here; he isn't really a QB -- just more of a superutility player like Hill.

Nate Stanley, MIN (Iowa -- Round 7, Pick 244): I actually like this fit. Stanley ran pro sets at Iowa -- often with 2 TEs -- so he shouldn't have much trouble picking up Minnesota's offense. The real difficulty is that he will be behind Sean Mannion and Jake Browning to back up Kirk Cousins, so he might be a longshot to break camp. No rookie camp/minicamp won't help his odds for this year, either.

- **2020:** If he does make the roster, he'll most likely be the 3rd QB and a practice squad player.
- **Dynasty:** Not much here; he's going to be a roster bubble guy in his rookie season, so becoming a full-time backup is the immediate goal.

RUNNING BACKS

Clyde Edwards-Helaire, KC (LSU -- Round 1, Pick 32): CEH swiftly moved up dynasty boards when he became a HUGE piece of the Tigers' National Championship roster. Edwards-Helaire was the 2nd-biggest riser in the nation, after his QB Joe Burrow. I wasn't sure that he was going to be more than a 3rd-down back going into the year, but he turned into a complete 3-down player and was the 1st RB off the NFL Draft board. He's a bit smaller (5'7") but packs a punch at 207 lbs. He improved his YPC from 3.4 in '17, to 4.5 in '18, all the way to 6.6 last season. CEH only had 14 catches going into last season' and he was 2nd in the nation among RBs last year with 55. The best part about him is the landing spot. Andy Reid describes him as 'better than Brian Westbrook,' so CEH will quickly become a big part of the offense.

- **2020:** RB2 with a ton of upside this year. Damien Williams is still on the roster, and we know that the Chiefs still like Darwin Thompson, so I can't really justify taking him over some proven backs. But I still like Edwards-Helaire a lot.
- **Dynasty:** CEH is a for sure long-term RB1. He's going to go 1.1 in most rookie drafts, which makes sense. He's a 3-down back playing for the best offense in the league, so all of the stars are aligned for him to be a top back for a long time.

D'Andre Swift, DET (Georgia -- Round 2, Pick 35): Swift is my favorite back from this class. He's a smaller rumbler, like many in this class (5'8", 212 lbs), but he is for sure a 3-down grinder just like CEH. The thing that stuck out to me the most about Swift is his vision: He takes the proper cut almost every time he can make people miss in the open field. Swift can catch the ball out of the backfield, too; he was the checkdown recipient on a ton of those Jake Fromm passes. Lions GM Bob Quinn mentioned Swift is a 3-down back who faced the toughest defenses in college football while playing in the SEC. Georgia usually deploys a backfield committee, so Swift still has plenty of tread on his tires; he only had 220 touches for Georgia last year, 41 fewer than the next closest back in the first 2 rounds.

- **2020:** Borderline RB2 for this year, but I would only draft him as an RB3 at best. I imagine his rookie season mirroring Miles Sanders' from last year. Sanders had 568 total yards and 2 TDs in his first 8 games and finished with 759 yards and 4 TDs during the final 8.
- **Dynasty:** I really like him as an RB2 in the future. The Lions have only had 1 1,000-yard rusher in the last 10 years (Reggie Bush with 1,006 in 2013), and it's been awhile since they have properly used an RB. If

Swift sticks, he'll be around longer than Stafford and might become the focal point of the offense when he leaves.

Jonathan Taylor, IND (Wisconsin -- Round 2, Pick 41): I really like this landing spot. He's a big 'bellcow' back, and he's going to be running behind one of the best OLs in the NFL. Taylor isn't going to juke a lot of defenders out of their shoes, but he has a nice power-speed blend to give the Colts a real home-run threat. Taylor ran for 6,174 yards and 40 TDs over his 3 seasons with the Badgers. I know that's a lot of carries, but the Badgers RB is always the main focus of the offense, and he won't be needed for the Colts nearly as much as he was for Wisconsin. Taylor didn't catch a ton of balls at Wisconsin, but he did have 26 receptions in 2019 after only eight in each of the previous two seasons. The only real struggle Taylor had in college was when he would occasionally fumble; he put the ball on the ground 18 times in his 3 years with 6 coming last year. Even with the fumbles, Taylor was most evaluators' No. 1 RB going into this draft and landed in an almost perfect spot.

- **2020:** He will compete early with Marlon Mack for touches and might be behind the 8-Ball with the possibility of little ramp-up time in an abridged offseason. Taylor should usurp most carries from Mack midway through the season; he's just a faster and more complete back. This probably puts him in the RB2/RB3 tier for single-year formats.
- **Dynasty:** Taylor is a long-term fantasy RB1. This guy has proven in college that he can more than handle 300 carries, and he'll be running behind on the top OLs in the league. Super-high ceiling.

Cam Akers, LAR (Florida State -- Round 2, Pick 52): Akers is tough to evaluate. FSU had issues on the OL the entire time he was there; Jimbo Fisher left after his Freshman year; and Willie Taggart was fired before he left. Akers was a 5-star prospect going into Florida State and was by far the best weapon the Seminoles had while he was there. Akers can do it all athletically; he's fast and shifty. But the big question mark is his vision. Akers had to create his own lanes a lot because of poor run blocking, so we know he can be creative, but we haven't really seen him run behind an effective line. Akers probably won't be getting 3rd downs in his rookie season -- he's not great in pass protection -- but he had 69 catches in college, so he can be effective as a receiver.

- **2020:** This season could go a long way in deciding his future. He could earn a lot of carries, but Darrell Henderson (a Round 3 pick last year) stands in his way.
- **Dynasty:** I think he's just too far ahead of Henderson not to win the job at some point this year; it'll depend on how quickly he picks up Sean McVay's offense and improves in pass protection. Todd Gurley had one of the best fantasy seasons ever in this offense, so Akers has a high ceiling.

J.K. Dobbins, BAL (Ohio State -- Round 2, Pick 55): I was very surprised Dobbins fell this far and hated it because the Ravens seemed to get all the breaks in this draft. Dobbins is an explosive back with great vision, and he's going to thrive in this run game next to Lamar Jackson. The question really is when will that happen; Mark Ingram remains under contract through the 2021 season (though he has a potential out in his deal). This situation should be very familiar to Ingram; it's exactly what happened with him in New Orleans when the Saints drafted Alvin Kamara. I don't think it will happen this year, but Dobbins should be impressive enough to outproduce Ingram as soon as next season.

- **2020:** Not as much as any of the RBs taken ahead of him, but I highly doubt that he averages fewer than 10 touches per game this year.
- **Dynasty:** Being next to Lamar Jackson is an RB's dream! Ingram is good enough to still hold off Dobbins for the most carries this season, but next year, Dobbins should be the primary back in Baltimore and hopefully for the foreseeable future.

AJ Dillon, GB (Boston College -- Round 2, Pick 62): Dillon came into the combine with a lot of comparisons to Derrick Henry (6'0", 250 lbs). While he's the same type of back, and as much as I like his overall game, I wouldn't say he has the same upside. Dillon was a true workhorse at BC with 845 carries over 3 seasons for an average of just over 24 carries a game. Even with defenses knowing what was coming, Dillon still averaged over 5 YPC over those 3 seasons and piled up 40 total TDs.

- **2020:** Obviously, Aaron Jones will be Green Bay's main back this season, but I would not be surprised if Dillon gets goal-line duties. That lines him up as a frequent flex play.

- **Dynasty:** If Green Bay lets Jones walk after his contract expires at the end of the 2020 season, Dillon will probably get first and second downs next year. Dillon could develop into a 3-down back, but most other backs are going to be better than him as a receiver.

Antonio Gibson, WAS (Memphis -- Round 3, Pick 66): Gibson is more of a weapon than he is a true running back. Ron Rivera said Gibson has a Christian McCaffrey skill set. I would have said more like Curtis Samuel if I were comparing him to a Carolina player, though he was not as successful collegiately as Samuel. Gibson only had 77 touches over 2 seasons at Memphis after transferring from East Central Community College, but in those 77 touches, he scored 14 TDs. The math works out to scoring every 5.5 times he touches the ball, or scoring on 18% of his touches. Gibson will also most likely be tasked with returning kicks as he averaged 28 yards per return last season and scored a TD on one of them.
- **2020:** The Redskins see Gibson as more of a WR than RB, which is nice for his potential playing time as they already have Derrius Guice and Adrian Peterson at RB. I wouldn't expect more than 5 touches per contest unless he scores at a similar pace as his college days.
- **Dynasty:** There is a lot of competition for touches in Washington, but luckily Gibson is going to see snaps at WR and RB. He's a nice dart throw a little bit later in drafts; he has tremendous upside if he can earn a decent amount of snaps and touches early in his career.

Ke'Shawn Vaughn, TB (Vanderbilt -- Round 3, Pick 76): I was not the biggest fan of Vaughn coming into the draft, but he did land in a RB-desperate situation. Vaughn has really good vision and balance, but he's not great in pass protection, and he's not overly explosive. Vaughn does more with effort than with speed and shiftiness. Vaughn was productive at Vanderbilt after transferring in from Illinois his junior season, even though Vandy failed to make a bowl and went 9-16 in his 2 seasons there. Vaughn put up back-to-back 1,000-yard rushing campaigns while totaling 24 TDs, even with defenses keying in on him.
- **2020:** It's safe to say the Ronald Jones era in Tampa Bay is done. Vaughn is definitely going to get a chance to lead this backfield in touches this year. He's a great flex and a decent RB2.
- **Dynasty:** The leg up he has over Ronald Jones or anyone in this backfield is that he's Bruce Arians guy. I'm not the biggest fan of Vaughn's skill set, but he's the most talented back on roster. If he produces this year, he'll get to be the primary back for a few more.

Zack Moss, BUF (Utah -- Round 3, Pick 86): I like this pick! Moss is a punishing runner, a team leader and a hard worker. The Bills have a complete running game; Moss and Devin Singletary complement each other well, and Josh Allen is the 2nd-best running QB behind Lamar Jackson. The biggest concern about Moss is the knee injury that ended his 2018 season. He was obviously cleared to play, but he clearly lost burst last season. Still, he was productive in 2019 with 1,804 scrimmage yards and 17 TDs.
- **2020:** I would guess that Moss starts significantly behind Singletary, but by the end of the season, they will be splitting carries pretty evenly.
- **Dynasty:** This is tough. I think Moss will be very productive as long as he's getting touches in Buffalo. I believe he has more upside than Devin Singletary as well. However, I view him a lot like I viewed Marlon Mack coming into the NFL. Mack really held his own in Indianapolis, but the Colts still chose to use a high draft pick on his eventual replacement. I view Moss as an RB4 in dynasty as a great bye-week and injury replacement.

Darrynton Evans, TEN (Appalachian State -- Round 3, Pick 93): Evans is the perfect complementary back to Derrick Henry. Evans is fast (4.41 40 time) who'll be a home-run hitter when the defense has been run down by Henry. If he gets to the 2nd level, he'll make guys miss, and he's a reliable outlet in the passing game. He'll probably be a factor in the return game as well.
- **2020:** It's going to be tough to actually pull Henry off the field. Evans is most likely just a handcuff for this season.
- **Dynasty:** This all depends on what the Titans work out with Henry. Henry will be playing on the franchise tag this year, and if he does walk after 2020, Evans would be the immediate replacement. Evans was a 3-

down back the last 2 seasons at App State, and he could serve as a lead back in the NFL, but he is much better suited for a changeup role.

Joshua Kelley, LAC (UCLA -- Round 4, Pick 112): Kelley has a lot of truthers out there, but I'm not one of them. Kelley does run downhill and will absolutely deliver his best effort. He was also productive in a hit-or-miss UCLA offense over the last 2 years, churning out 2,567 scrimmage yards and 25 TDs. His game is 'NFL average'; he's definitely good enough to play in the NFL, but I don't think he's going to stand out.

- **2020:** Limited upside for Kelley this year. Austin Ekeler will be the leader in the backfield for the Chargers, obviously, but Kelley will compete with Justin Jackson for secondary touches.
- **Dynasty:** I'm not excited about his long-term value. Ekeler isn't an unrestricted free agent until 2024, but Jackson is an RFA next year, and Kelley could become the 3rd-down back soon. I just don't think there's much upside for him outside of a situational back or handcuff.

La'Mical Perine, NYJ (Florida -- Round 4, Pick 120): Perine is an angry, punishing runner. I found him a little bit tough to evaluate, but I think his best trait is his attitude, followed up by his balance and receiving. Perine was always part of a committee at Florida, but last season was the first time he had over 150 touches (172, with 40 catches), and he had 11 TDs. Perine is an awesome complementary back.

- **2020:** His immediate value took a major hit when the Jets signed Frank Gore. Perine will probably be mainly a special teamer and 3rd-string RB this year.
- **Dynasty:** I actually like him long-term with the Jets. Gore doesn't have a lot left in the tank, and Adam Gase clearly wasn't happy with the Bell signing. Bell has an out in his deal after 2020.

Anthony McFarland, PIT (Maryland -- Round 4, Pick 124): I really like McFarland, and I'm really glad my Steelers took him in the 4th. McFarland didn't have a ton of opportunities at Maryland -- only 269 touches over the last 2 years -- but he averaged almost 7 yards per touch in that time. McFarland's a little bit of a project: He doesn't have much experience running routes or catching the ball. McFarland has a ton of speed, though (4.44 40 time), and he will make people miss in the open field. McFarland's ceiling is very high if he puts it all together.

- **2020:** McFarland is going to get a little work this year. He's behind James Conner and Benny Snell and will have to compete with Jaylen Samuels for snaps.
- **Dynasty:** Conner is a UFA after this season, and McFarland is way more enticing than Snell. He's my RB6 in a rookie draft this season and a mid-level RB3 for the long term.

DeeJay Dallas, SEA (Miami -- Round 4, Pick 144): Dallas was a high-school QB who was recruited as a WR to Miami and switched to RB his sophomore season. So it's fairly clear that Dallas is going to be a bit of a project. I really enjoyed watching his film; he flashes some real upside, and I really appreciate his effort. Dallas was part of a committee and never had more than 129 touches in any one season, but he did score 19 TDs on 293 touches. Dallas' best traits are his hands and effort, and the downside for him is experience. Athletically, he's probably NFL-average.

- **2020:** It was looking pretty good immediately after the draft. Chris Carson should be good to go by training camp coming off his hip injury, Rashaad Penny is most likely going to start on the PUP this year, and Travis Homer is mainly a special teams ace. Marshawn Lynch has been rumored to be in talks, however, and that may hurt Dallas' chance for touches this year. He does have experience running the Wildcat, so we'll see if they give him goal-line packages.
- **Dynasty:** I might take a swing at later in Rookie/Dynasty drafts. Carson is a UFA after this season. If Lynch signs, he will only be on a 1-year deal. Penny has missed 8 games over the last 2 seasons and is most likely to miss at least 6 to start the year on the PUP. I don't think Dallas will be an upper-echelon back, but he can carve out a decent role.

Jason Huntley, DET (New Mexico State -- Round 5, Pick 172): This pick surprised me. I feel like this had to be because Huntley returned 5 kicks for TDs and had 134 catches in college. I didn't even watch Huntley much at all going into the draft, and he wasn't invited to the combine, so he wasn't really on my radar. He's a legit pass-catching threat out of the backfield, but his athleticism is average.

- **2020:** The Lions have a ton on this roster at RB: Kerryon Johnson, second-round pick D'Andre Swift, Bo Scarbrough, Ty Johnson and Wes Hills. Huntley has the special-teams chops and receiving skills to make the roster, but I wouldn't be surprised if he's cut.
- **Dynasty:** He might be able to develop into a 3rd-down back, but that's about his ceiling. He might stay on the roster as a return specialist.

Eno Benjamin, ARI (Arizona State -- Round 7, Pick 222): I cannot believe Benjamin fell this far in the draft. His production at ASU was outstanding. In his first year as a starter, he had 1,905 scrimmage yards with 18 TDs and 5.7 yards per touch. Last season, with a true freshman starting at QB and defenses knowing Eno is the main piece of the offense, he had 1430 yards and 12 TDs. There are 2 legit knocks on him: (1) He is impatient when a block doesn't form right, failing to do enough to get outside, and (2) He doesn't have top-end burst/speed. Benjamin has great vision and balance, and he's served as a workhorse, with 77 catches over the last 2 years. The Cardinals got a steal.

- **2020:** 7th-rounders are of course easier to cast off if they don't perform in camp and the preseason, but I think Benjamin is a lock for the roster. That being said, he'll probably be 3rd-string and have to contribute somehow on special teams.
- **Dynasty:** I can't imagine a 7th-rounder inspires much confidence, but Benjamin is underrated and can work his way into a decent NFL role.

Raymond Calais, TB (Louisiana -- Round 7, Pick 245): Calais is a speed-only back, really (4.42 40 time). He did a great job in a 3-headed committee with Elijah Mitchell and Trey Ragas. Calais will most likely serve as a special teamer. Though he didn't do much of it in college, Calais has some potential as far as catching the ball. If I had to make a pro comp at this stage of his development, he'd be Tatum Bell.

- **2020:** Not much, even on the Bucs. Ke'Shawn Vaughn, Ronald Jones and Dare Ogunbowale are all more complete options.
- **Dynasty:** The Bucs most likely drafted Calais because he's an ace on kick coverage and has experience returning kicks. Anything else he does is a bonus.

Malcolm Perry, MIA (Navy -- Round 7, Pick 246): I love this pick. Perry was the starting QB for Navy the past 2 seasons, and most had him pegged to move to WR, but the Dolphins drafted him as a RB, which I think is a smart move. Perry ran for 2,017 yards in Navy's triple-option last year, and he has real wiggle and a nose for the endzone (21 TDs in 2019). Obviously, Perry is going to take time to develop with the position change, but he was a team captain at Navy, has returned kicks and will play on kick coverage.

- **2020:** Probably not much; he is moving positions, and the Dolphins have Matt Breida, Jordan Howard, Kalen Ballage and Patrick Laird still on the roster.
- **Dynasty:** "Former QB in a new position" almost never works. It's not something I would bet on.

WIDE RECEIVERS

Henry Ruggs, LV (Alabama -- Round 1, Pick 12): Speed on speed on speed: Ruggs ran a 4.27 40 time and was disappointed with that at the combine. The Raiders are desperate for a No. 1 wideout, and they have pegged Ruggs as that guy. Ruggs never had a 50-catch or 1,000-yard season at Alabama, but the Raiders have a good track record with Alabama committee players; RB Josh Jacobs registered 262 total touches for the Raiders last year and only 299 in 3 years at 'Bama. Ruggs isn't going to body up any corners (5'11", 188 lbs), but he doesn't have to in most cases. He's going to get free in his release off the line and torch the CB, in a lot of cases. Ruggs can take it to the house anytime he touches the ball.

- **2020:** He might have the skill to be the Raiders' best WR from the moment he steps on the field. Vegas will for sure find a way to get him the ball on short routes, bubble screens and reverses. The QB isn't that desirable no matter who comes down with the job between Derek Carr and Marcus Mariota, but Ruggs could make the QB actually want to throw it down the field.

- **Dynasty:** High ceiling but a low floor. Ruggs is my rookie draft WR4. I believe in Ruggs, but the Raiders organization has been rough as of late, and I don't think Carr or Mariota is the long-term option at QB. Ruggs playing with a QB that can't throw downfield is like being impotent and being married to a supermodel. Fantasy WR1 upside, but WR3 right now.

Jerry Jeudy, DEN (Alabama -- Round 1, Pick 15): He's my favorite WR from this class, with his spectacular route-running being the most polished I can remember for anyone right out of college. Jeudy also has decent size (6'1") and ran a 4.45 40 at the combine. He might not have top-10 speed like Henry Ruggs or crazy body control like CeeDee Lamb, but he's top-10% in just about everything. Literally the only knock I've seen on him is that he's average at contested catches (I'd say a little better than average), and he has some concentration drops. Jeudy was incredibly productive, putting up back-to-back seasons with 1,100+ receiving yards and double-digit TDs, despite having Ruggs, Devonta Smith and Jaylen Waddle in Alabama's receiving corps, along with loads of 5-star RBs. Of course, as with any other WR, Jeudy's upside is going to be up to the Denver's QB play, but he should make Drew Lock look good.

- **2020:** Hard to tell. Jeudy will definitely be the primary receiver, but the learning curve is pretty big for rookie WRs. Lock is a big question mark, as well; I wasn't fond of him coming out of college, but he seems to have learned a lot in just his rookie season (higher completion % than any of his 4 years at Missouri AND a way lower INT rate).
- **Dynasty:** Jeudy is the No. 1 dynasty player from this class. WRs are always tied to their QBs, but Jeudy will elevate Lock and become the possession guy as early as this year. While I wouldn't draft him as a WR1, I would be trying hard to make him my 2nd WR. The upside is tremendous!

CeeDee Lamb, DAL (Oklahoma -- Round 1, Pick 17): You'll hear scouts and evaluators rave about 2 things with Lamb: his catch radius and body control give him an impressive highlight reel. He's also big, fast and hungry – and not just for receptions; he'll mix it up in run blocking, and he'll do anything he can to get every blade of grass he can after catching the ball. Lamb isn't slow, but the main knock on him is that he doesn't have upper-tier speed. Still, he has enough burst in his initial push at the line to motor past a lot of DBs, and he can snap off a route quickly and leave the defender in the dust. This was a great pick for the Cowboys, even if it wasn't a need.

- **2020:** He's better than Michael Gallup right now. I don't know if that means we'll see him break out as the No. 2 option right away, but I would guess we'll see it by the end of the season. I would draft him as a fantasy WR4 and hope to see some of that upside sooner rather than later.
- **Dynasty:** Obviously, I think he's going to pass Gallup fairly quickly -- and I like Gallup, so that's no small accomplishment. I also think he'll eventually pass Amari Cooper. I wouldn't put all my eggs in the Lamb basket in a startup dynasty, but I would take him right behind Jeudy as a WR2 with room to grow.

Jalen Reagor, PHI (TCU -- Round 1, Pick 21): I am so excited to see what Reagor does with an NFL-caliber QB! Over his 3 seasons at TCU, the Horned Frogs had 6 QBs throw more than 50 passes. Outside of the awful QB play, the first thing I noticed when watching Reagor is not really the speed. (It's great, at 4.47 40, but he plays faster.) Nor was it the highlight-reel vertical he can pull off on high pointed catches. It's his instincts with the ball in his hands. TCU tried to get him the ball any way they could: He had 35 rushing attempts over the past 3 years, scoring on 2. Reagor also returned punts his sophomore and junior seasons, and he improved his average from 12.1 yards per return in 2018 to 20.8 last year with 2 TDs. Reagor is best as a vertical threat, and I don't think that he'll become a possession option, but he carries an absolute boatload of upside.

- **2020 Value:** As I've pointed out for a lot of other prospects, 2020 rookies are going to be behind without rookie camp and being able to meet with coaches and teammates before (most likely) training camp. However, because the Eagles brought in so many WRs to fix this issue they had last year, it affects Reagor even more. The Eagles drafted Reagor, Quez Watkins and John Hightower; traded for Marquise Goodwin; and still have Alshon Jeffery, DeSean Jackson and 2019 rookie JJ Arcega-Whiteside still on the roster. Reagor has the ability to beat everyone here, but I wouldn't bank on it for his rookie campaign. Probably a WR5 or 6 with a high 2020 ceiling.

- **Dynasty Value:** I like him way better here. Reagor is a high-ceiling, low-floor WR, and I don't think he's going to ever be a 100-catch guy, but he can have a DeSean Jackson-like career if he puts it all together: a nice WR3 or 4 to have when a good matchup is available.

Justin Jefferson, MIN (LSU -- Round 1, Pick 22): I was a little surprised to see Jefferson fall this far, but the landing spot is great. The Vikings are looking to replace Stefon Diggs since they traded him to Buffalo, and they used one of the 4 picks they got back in that swap to do it. Jefferson was expected to run in the 4.5s at the combine and started seeing real 1st-round lock buzz when he ran a 4.43 at the combine. He actually compares to CeeDee Lamb fairly well. Jefferson had better QB play with Burrow, of course, but they are about the same height -- and Jefferson is a bit faster. Jefferson also probably runs crisper routes than Lamb, and while Jefferson's best attribute is probably his hands, he's nowhere near Lamb's contested-catch ability. Jefferson was like other LSU WRs until 2019; when Burrow improved, so did everyone in the offense. Jefferson was tied with James Proche for most catches in college football with 111 and he had 18 TDs.
- **2020:** I don't know if he'll put up 100 catches at the NFL level, but he should quickly become the No. 2 behind Adam Thielen. I like new arrival Tajae Sharpe, but Jefferson is flat-out better.
- **Dynasty:** The offense is different. Cousins went from 38 passes a game in 2018 to 30 last season; Mike Zimmer wanted to run more 2-TE sets to improve the run game. Thielen will be 31 going into this season, and the Vikings have an out on his contract after this season. We could see Jefferson as Minnesota's No. 1 receiver at least as soon as next season.

Brandon Aiyuk, SF (Arizona State -- Round 1, Pick 25): Aiyuk had a fantastic senior year, showing off his great route-running technique and straight-line speed as he had averaged 18.3 yards per reception – all while playing with a true freshman at QB. NFL Network's Daniel Jeremiah referred to him as a route-running technician. The knocks on Aiyuk are getting off press coverage at the line and getting bodied up by bigger CBs. However, his routes, high-point ability, and creativity the ball in his hands make him a 1st-round talent. Aiyuk is exactly what the 49ers need at WR: a deep threat to pull safeties away from the box for that awesome run game and so George Kittle and Deebo Samuel can work over the middle. I don't know whether that it's a great fantasy fit, but Aiyuk has a ton of upside.
- **2020:** Not too high. Though his ability to pop off a big play makes him a tantalizing best-ball piece or bye filler, he'll still be just the 4th option behind the run game, Kittle, and Samuel.
- **Dynasty:** As much as I love Samuel, Aiyuk could pass him on the depth chart. Of course, with the Niners' cap issues, they may struggle to hang onto Kittle; in that case, Samuel and Aiyuk will have to pick up the slack. I have him firmly as a WR4 in a dynasty startup.

Tee Higgins, CIN (Clemson -- Round 2, Pick 33): Higgins is one of my favorite WRs in this class. He isn't going to burn anyone, but he's faster than expected, and at 6'3", 227 lbs., he boxes out and makes the contested catch as easily as Shaq grabs a rebound. It's his best tool, but the rest aren't bad. Higgins is a strong route runner, especially on anything deep (18.1 yards per catch in college). For his size, he has great body control to make every catch. He's one of the best at tracking balls in the air and getting under them on deep routes. Higgins probably won't need a ton of help tracking too many balls coming from QB Joe Burrow, who just had the highest single-season completion percentage in CFB history.
- **2020:** Higgins will have to beat out John Ross to be the 4th target at best with A.J. Green, Tyler Boyd and Joe Mixon on roster, so he's a last-round flier/waiver-wire addition.
- **Dynasty:** Green and Ross are UFAs after this season, and the Bengals might have to franchise Mixon, who is threatening to hold out for this season if he doesn't get a new contract. Higgins lines up as the big-play guy to Boyd's possession work starting next year. I see a lot of 60-1000-10 seasons in his future.

Michael Pittman, IND (USC -- Round 2, Pick 34): I like the Colts getting someone to help T.Y. Hilton; that role has been musical chairs for a few seasons. They missed getting Tee Higgins by 1 pick; if Higgins is an A+ match, Pittman is a B+. He's big-bodied at 6'4" with super-long arms. Like Higgins, he'll make contested catches. Pittman's lack of separation speed isn't a major problem; though he'll often see routes cut off when fighting for a catch, this could actually help him thrive in PPR formats. He needed 101 catches to get to 1,275 yards last year; it would have taken

Higgins 65 catches to hit that. While Pittman is better suited to get 100+ catches at the NFL level, I fear he won't fight off top cornerbacks.

- **2020:** Pretty good immediate landing spot. If he can beat out Zach Pascal, he should see significant snaps. With Philip Rivers taking Indy's snaps, Pittman could become a go-to guy.
- **Dynasty:** This is much cloudier. We have no idea how long Rivers plans on playing; he's already agreed to become a high-school coach as soon as he walks away from football. Not knowing the Colts' future QB will make this tough, though Pittman has ample PPR upside.

Laviska Shenault, JAX (Colorado -- Round 2, Pick 42): He's a one of my favorites from this class, and I'm excited to see him with an NFL-caliber QB -- but with Jacksonville, he might have to wait until 2021 for that. Shenault is a GM's nightmare: He has enormous upside, but he's injury-prone. Shenault had offseason core surgery, but he said he's 100%. Shenault is a Swiss-Army knife player, having run the ball out of the Wildcat at the goal line; he had 7 rushing TDs in the last 2 seasons. I wouldn't call Shenault great at any one thing, but he's above average at pretty much everything -- except staying healthy. It was tough to watch Steven Montez throwing to him; even Gardner Minshew is a huge step up.

- **2020:** On the depth chart behind D.J. Chark, he'll have veteran competition for snaps with Chris Conley, Keelan Cole and Dede Westbrook. I think Shenault is better than all of them, and he'll probably get some goal line Wildcat snaps next to Leonard Fournette.
- **Dynasty:** His injury history has to be the biggest knock on him before we even consider his surroundings. I think Shenault has much better skills than Michael Pittman, but I'll have Pittman ahead in my rankings because he can stay on the field. That being said, Shenault has proven he can stand out with bad QB play.

K.J. Hamler, DEN (Penn State -- Round 2, Pick 46): Positives first here: I liked Hamler way more than I expected to when I watched his film. From what I heard and read, I thought I was going to see a no-skills burner type, but I saw a great route runner who was surprisingly good in contested situations for his size (5'8", 178 lbs.) and dangerous with the ball in space. As far as short, slight WRs go, I'd say he's way more on the DeSean Jackson side than the John Ross side. Unfortunately, the landing spot is not ideal -- not because of Drew Lock, but because of the weapons already in place. Courtland Sutton was a Pro Bowler last year, Noah Fant and 2020 rookie Jerry Jeudy are 1st-round picks, they spent $16 million on Melvin Gordon, and Phillip Lindsay is still around.

- **2020:** Hamler will be a waiver-wire add if anything this year. Assuming all the players I listed above are ahead of him on the depth chart, he would still have to beat out DaeSean Hamilton and Tim Patrick for snaps in the offense. Hamler will be the kick and punt returner this year, and that's all I would expect.
- **Dynasty:** I love his skill set, but Jeudy, Sutton and Fant should be the top 3 receiving options. Hamler's talent is there, so I would spend a later pick if I could stash him for a little bit. Talent often, if not always, wins out.

Chase Claypool, PIT (Notre Dame -- Round 2, Pick 49): Claypool is the biggest boom-or-bust player from this class. He's enormous (6'4", 238 lbs), and because of his massive frame, some scouts wanted to compare him to Travis Kelce and said he should be moved to TE. The Steelers are going to use him as a WR, mainly on the outside, and they have always been fans of "99th percentile SPARQ score" types. His nickname is Mapletron; he has the same physical frame as Calvin Johnson, and he's from Canada. I thought the comparison to Allen Lazard was more apt than Megatron, but I think he has more upside than Lazard. Claypool had an impressive 40 time (4.42) and vertical (40.5") at the combine, but I wouldn't say his film matches those times. The biggest thing that flashes is his motor. The dude is relentless. He's a kick coverage ace and will run-block a DB into the next dimension. His best receiving trait, unsurprisingly, is his contested-catch ability; he'll box out just about anyone, and his hands are strong outside of a few concentration drops. Claypool needs to polish his routes, and he doesn't have much wiggle, but he can run through a lot of defenders.

- **2020:** The Steelers were terrible in the red zone last year; I'm guessing Claypool will see most of his snaps there. He'll cover kicks and punts. Probably a fantasy stash with big-play potential.
- **Dynasty:** I don't see where the gray area would be. He's most likely to be a big-time playmaker quickly or turn into Corey Davis 2.0. If he makes plays, he'll stay on the field to enjoy a returning Ben Roethlisberger.

He has all the physical traits we want in a big WR, and because he gives the effort everyone likes to see, I would give him a 60-40 chance to be an NFL starter.

Van Jefferson, LAR (Florida -- Round 2, Pick 57): Jefferson started to separate himself during the Senior Bowl, when he was constantly smoking cornerbacks in practice, but then he suffered a Jones fracture that required surgery and he missed the combine. I thought he would drop to the 3rd day, but the Rams pulled the trigger in the 2nd Round! His overall production at Florida, which topped out at 49-657-6 his senior year, kept him off the radar a little bit, but he wasn't playing for top-tier QB talent. Jefferson has an edge in Football IQ; his dad, Shawn Jefferson, played 13 seasons in the NFL and is now the Jets' WR Coach. His route running is outstanding, and while he might not be the biggest or fastest WR in this class, knowing where to be on every play is going to keep him on the field.

- **2020:** Asking the rookie to surpass Josh Reynolds on the depth chart is a pretty big ask. Jefferson can play in just about any system, but for the Rams, he'll have to wait a year to be productive.
- **Dynasty:** Cooper Kupp and Josh Reynolds are UFAs after 2020, and the Rams are already in cap hell. Both likely will walk. This could leave Jefferson as the No. 2 WR behind Woods next year.

Denzel Mims, NYJ (Baylor -- Round 2, Pick 59): Another big-bodied, possession WR in this class, Mims was getting a lot of 1st-round love leading up to the draft, so I was a bit surprised to see him slip to the end of the 2nd round. Mims is another contested-catch monster (6'3", 210) who has a nose for the end zone with 28 TDs over the last 3 seasons. With all that size, Mims still ran a 4.38 40-yard dash at the combine, jumped a 39.5" vertical, and registered the fastest 3Cone drill time among WRs. His ability to run-block is going to get him on the field, and making big plays is going to keep him there.

- **2020:** I like him as a late-round flier in redrafts. His competition includes Jamison Crowder, Breshad Perriman and Vyncint Smith. I wouldn't say he's better than anyone today, but by the end of the preseason, he can move past at least Smith, and if he makes some plays, he can overtake Crowder and/or Perriman by the end of the season.
- **Dynasty:** He has the most talent of any WR on this roster by a wide stretch. The Jets defense isn't exactly top-tier right now, so Mims should be able to pick up some garbage-time yards while the Jets are playing catchup. I'm pretty excited about Mims landing in New York with Sam Darnold throwing him the ball and no tough competition for long-term success.

Lynn Bowden, LV (Kentucky -- Round 3, Pick 80): Bowden has all kinds of superlatives: My favorites being thrown around include "unique," "unicorn," and "football player." If you haven't watched Bowden, he was All-SEC in 2018 over some big names like Henry Ruggs, Justin Jefferson and Van Jefferson, who were all drafted ahead of him. When Kentucky starter Terry Wilson was injured for the season in the 5th game of 2019, Bowden stepped in at QB and ended up with 1,468 rushing yards, 13 rushing TDs, and the Paul Hornung Award (most versatile player in college football). So the Raiders went ahead and drafted him as an RB. Weird move from the Raiders, but RB could make sense. I thought he was going to be a slot WR in the NFL. Whatever Las Vegas designates as his position, they should get the ball in Bowden's hands; he averaged 7.9 yards a carry in 2019 when everyone knew what was coming.

- **2020:** Played WR in '18, QB in '19, and now in his rookie season he'll be moving to RB at the pro level. Can't expect much this year.
- **Dynasty:** I hate it when players move positions to start their pro career, but Bowden has the chops to make it at pretty much any position he wants to play. I would hesitate to draft him unless I have a big bench or devy system where I can stash him.

Bryan Edwards, LV (South Carolina -- Round 3, Pick 81): I was really surprised by this one on draft day; I thought the Raiders had drafted Bowden to play WR, and they already had taken Ruggs in the 1st. Even more confusing: Bowden and Edwards are likely to play out of the slot, but now we know Edwards will be competing for snaps, and I really like his game. Edwards isn't fast or shifty, but he has a big frame (just under 6'3," 212), and he really can take advantage of a small CB or slow LB. Edwards actually fits better with Derek Carr than Ruggs; he ran a lot of short routes partly because he isn't top-shelf at separation, but he also had some rough QB play. Edwards might not have the raw athleticism that other rookies do, but he's a smart and high-effort player who will outwork the competition.

- **2020:** Well, Edwards' problem is that Vegas already has a scrappy slot WR in Hunter Renfrow. Not only is Edwards going to have to beat Renfrow for snaps, but the veterans the Raiders have in Zay Jones and Nelson Agholor are not going to just hand the job over to the rookie.
- **Dynasty:** Edwards has a much higher ceiling than those three WRs, but I'm afraid Bowden may eventually move back to WR, and I like him way more than Edwards. I don't know whether Edwards would hold off the next WR draft pick or a decent free-agent signing next offseason.

Devin Duvernay, BAL (Texas -- Round 3, Pick 92): Duvernay surprisingly went off for 106 catches for my Longhorns. Duvernay had 70 catches in his previous 3 years, but taking over the slot role made him the No. 1 target. As impressive as 100+ catches are, Duvernay does not have much experience against capable press defenders, and a lot of those snags were against soft coverage. That's why the landing spot is nice. If Duvernay slips behind some defenders biting on a play action, he'll have a big gain. The 4.39 40 at the combine is real: Duvernay won the 100 meters at Texas' high school state competition.

- **2020:** The Ravens seemed excited that Duvernay fell to them; John Harbaugh was pumping his fist like they had just won a game when the pick came through. That doesn't mean everything, and the Ravens are still a heavy run-first team. That isn't changing anytime soon. Marquise Brown remains the most talented WR on the roster, but No. 2 is up for grabs, and Duvernay should be given every opportunity to win a starting job.
- **Dynasty:** WRs are always tough dart throws, especially on run-centered teams. Even the No. 1 WR option in Baltimore will be behind TE Mark Andrews, at least 1 RB, and Lamar Jackson himself for targets/touches. Daniel Jeremiah said that the Ravens are building a 'track team' in Baltimore, and Duvernay could become a fantasy WR3, but that will probably be his ceiling unless Lamar Jackson starts throwing the ball a bit more.

Gabriel Davis, BUF (Central Florida -- Round 4, Pick 128): I wasn't expecting much before watching Davis' film, but I came away impressed. He plays bigger than his listed 6'2" size and is constantly getting the best of cornerback press with separation. He could stand to add more diverse routes to his vertical-centered game, and he's not often going to beat DBs with speed, but he most impressed me with his hand fighting when he's in tight spots or doesn't have much separation. I get real Robby Anderson vibes from Davis, but he wants to be the next OBJ pretty bad; he even has hair similar to Odell Beckham's.

- **2020:** I think he's better than a lot of Bills options, but he's going to have to earn playing time, and he's pretty limited to just deep-fly patterns, so I don't see that happening much this season.
- **Dynasty:** Stefon Diggs, Cole Beasley and John Brown are all on roster through next season, but Beasley and Brown are already on the wrong side of 30. If Davis improves his routes and impresses coaches, it could go a long way to expanding his playing time in 2021.

Antonio Gandy-Golden, WAS (Liberty -- Round 4, Pick 142): ANOTHER big-bodied, contested-catch magnet, possession type. This where the deep WR class gave some great bargains. AGG stacks up at 6'4", 223 lbs, and was highly productive at Liberty with 150-2433-20 over 2 years there. He probably slipped to the 4th round due to his pedestrian 40 time (4.6) and the fact that he played against mostly small-school competition. He has size and turns 50/50 balls into 80/20 balls, and his downfield routes are solid -- but they're not so hot in the short and intermediate ranges. Unless he can change that, he's going to rely heavily on big plays. Luckily, he'll be getting early experience landing with the Redskins.

- **2020:** Deep-league flier, standard league watchlist. Gandy-Golden has an opportunity. Terry McLaurin is the only sure thing; the group of Trey Quinn, Kevin Harmon, Steven Sims and Cody Latimer are all beatable. The biggest competition might be fellow rookie Antonio Gibson.
- **Dynasty:** Prove it this year, and that will go a long, long way for his success moving forward. You can say that for pretty much any rookie, but the Redskins are going to have high picks for '21 and most likely '22 as well. If they feel compelled to take a WR in the first round, that guy will be across from McLaurin, not AGG or Gibson.

Joe Reed, LAC (Virginia -- Round 5, Pick 151): I love this fit. Bryce Perkins was a scrambling type of QB who would buy time by scrambling, so Reed should know what to do when his QB is moving -- and he's going to get that from Tyrod Taylor and, whenever a switch happens, Justin Herbert. Now the harsh reality: This pick was probably more about Reed's kick-return skills than his receiving. Reed returned 5 kicks for TDs and has versatility as he had 34 rush attempts and 17 tackles covering kicks and punts.

- **2020:** K.J. Hill, the Chargers' 7th-round pick, has a better shot at WR snaps than Reed this year.
- **Dynasty:** Not much here. He'll have to earn his way on the roster as a special-teamer and stick around before we can think of him having a big role in the offense.

Tyler Johnson, TB (Minnesota -- Round 5, Pick 161): I really like this landing spot. Of course, Chris Godwin and Mike Evans are the top two receiving options for the foreseeable future, but Johnson getting 1-on-1s as the third WR sounds nice. Johnson was extremely productive at Minnesota and made a habit of making some highlight-reel catches, but the most impressive thing is his route running. He's going to have a tough time separating like he did in college, but he's big enough to body up most corners, and he can go up and get it when high-pointing.

- **2020:** Not much; Evans, Godwin, Rob Gronkowski and O.J. Howard will all be ahead of him for targets, and even passing vets like Justin Watson and Scotty Miller could prove difficult.
- **Dynasty:** I think he's a great option down the road, but he doesn't have special-teams experience, so he's going to have to make an impact soon to stay on the roster.

Collin Johnson, JAX (Texas -- Round 5, Pick 165): If Johnson would have declared last year, he would have been at worst a 2nd-rounder. Unfortunately, Johnson not only fell short of being WR on his team, but he also missed 6 games due to knee and hamstring injuries. Furthermore, he missed games and played at less than 100% when a lot of the other WRs that went ahead of him were stringing together great seasons. I like this pick. Johnson has upside as yet ANOTHER big-bodied WR with separation issues, but at 6'5 5/8", 222 lbs, he'll be a tough matchup for DBs and an instant red-zone asset.

- **2020:** If Johnson flashes potential, as I said with Laviska Shenault, all the WRs on the roster outside of D.J. Chark are beatable for snaps. I wouldn't bet on it, but it's possible.
- **Dynasty:** Knowing that Johnson would have been a lot higher last year (and the fact that I'm a Longhorns fan) makes me more bullish on Johnson than I probably should be. Johnson has size and a high football IQ. I get Preston Williams vibes from him, so keep him on your watch lists.

Quintez Cephus, DET (Wisconsin -- Round 5, Pick 166): Ohio State's Jeffrey Okudah, the top corner picked in the draft, described Cephus as the best WR he faced in his college career. High praise from a great opponent, but the 40 time at the combine (4.73) and some off-field issues pushed Cephus down the draft board. Cephus obviously isn't going to blow past DBs, but he runs good routes, effectively shoves off press coverage, and has great hands. Cephus was productive at Wisconsin: 901 yards there might as well be 1,500 yards anywhere else, considering how often the Badgers run the ball. Speed is obviously his biggest question -- it might kill his chance at an NFL career -- but if his game speed is enough for the NFL, the rest of the tools are there.

- **2020:** Not a lot, unless the Lions have some injuries. Kenny Golladay, Marvin Jones, Danny Amendola, T.J. Hockenson and D'Andre Swift are all well ahead of him in offensive weaponry.
- **Dynasty:** Golladay, Jones, Amendola and Geronimo Allison all have their contracts expiring after this year. Maybe Detroit keeps 2 of them, but even in that scenario, Cephus has room to step into a consistent role. Nice stash option in deeper leagues.

John Hightower, PHI (Boise State -- Round 5, Pick 168): As I mentioned earlier in the Jalen Reagor breakdown, the Eagles are throwing a lot of options at the wall and seeing what sticks at wideout. Hightower has real playing speed, is dangerous in the open field, and has great instincts after the catch to get everything he possibly can. Hightower's hands are his biggest issue: He has concentration drops, double catches and some attempts that will go straight through his hands. Those issues can be fixed with time and practice, and in the meantime, he can be productive in the return game; he averaged over 24 yards per return and took one to the house last year.

- **2020:** Not much, unless there are injuries, or all the players that should be ahead of him fail.

- **Dynasty:** He boasts speed and YAC potential that can't be taught, but he is a bit of a project.

Isaiah Coulter, HOU (Rhode Island -- Round 5, Pick 171): The Texans did something right! After a big offseason of perpetually screwing it up, they made a great pick here in the 5th round, but it was at a position that wasn't really on their list of needs. Coulter is a bit raw, but he got the nickname Big Play Zay because he can high-point the ball well, and he has made some great over-the-shoulder catches in his collegiate career. He was pushed down to the late 5th round because he played at the FCS level against lower-level competition and he has some issues getting separation. While he has good speed, he doesn't have wiggle to make guys miss. Coulter can use this season as a redshirt year to polish his game.
- **2020:** The Texans have too many WRs on the roster right now for Coulter to have a viable role this season. They attempted to trade Keke Coutee during the draft, but it didn't work, so now they have him, Will Fuller, Brandin Cooks, Kenny Stills, and Randall Cobb.
- **Dynasty:** Stills and Fuller are UFAs next year, and Cooks has an out in his contract, so Coulter could have a decent role in this offense as soon as 2021 if he can round out his skills.

Darnell Mooney, CHI (Tulane -- Round 5, Pick 173): At first glance, Mooney probably seems like a speed-only WR; he never had more than 49 catches and averaged 16.7 yards per reception at Tulane. Mooney is way crisper as a route runner than given credit for, and he started games all 4 years in college. Matt Nagy undoubtedly has a plan for the rookie, but Mooney is going to have to put on mass to avoid getting pushed around by physical corners.
- **2020:** Minimal. He's going to have to impress early to make the roster as he doesn't offer help in kick coverage or returns. Allen Robinson, Anthony Miller, Ted Ginn, Riley Ridley and Cordarrelle Patterson are all ahead of him in terms of targets and that's just at WR.
- **Dynasty:** We know that Nagy clearly values speed, considering he's stockpiling it. A lot of contracts are up after this year, including those for Robinson, Patterson and Ginn. I like Mooney, but I'm not going to be investing in him in too many leagues.

K.J. Osborn, MIN (Miami -- Round 5, Pick 176): Osborn transferred from Buffalo to Miami, and he wasn't bad, even with terrible QB play. Osborn can track the ball well and had a great 40 (4.48), but he was drafted to return punts and cover kicks. He's fairly one-dimensional. Osborn ran a limited route tree, mostly on free releases from the slot, so he doesn't have much experience against press coverage.
- **2020:** Not much, unless injuries strike. Adam Thielen, Justin Jefferson and Tajae Sharpe will be the top 3, and Osborn will be behind Chad Beebe, Bisi Johnson and probably Dillon Mitchell.
- **Dynasty:** Can't teach speed, so that's a nice tool, but he's a project. I'm not investing a lot here.

Donovan Peoples-Jones, CLE (Michigan -- Round 6, Pick 186): I was wildly surprised to see DPJ fall this far, even with one of the deepest WR classes ever. DPJ was a 5-star recruit that ended up some bad QB play at Michigan, but he's a complete WR. He runs through contact at the line, has great game speed, flashes sticky hands, and churns with a high motor. The only thing he doesn't really have is a lot of moves to make a defender miss, but he's big enough (6'2", 212 lbs) to muscle through many of them.
- **2020:** Even though the top 3 spots are taken by Jarvis Landry, Odell Beckham, and Rashard Higgins, DPJ could make an impact this year. Landry is coming off hip surgery, and Peoples-Jones has more than enough to beat out the other rosters in camp.
- **Dynasty:** I'm not going to break the bank for him, but I would take him over most of the 5th-round picks and anyone below him.

Quez Watkins, PHI (Southern Miss -- Round 6, Pick 200): More stockpiling by the Eagles here as they try to solve their WR issues. Watkins is a project, but he can offer help on special teams and has blazing speed (4.35 40 time). Watkins flashes being damn good at everything but hasn't perfected anything.
- **2020:** He likely won't see many offensive snaps. He'll spend most of his time on special teams.
- **Dynasty:** Nice deep-league lottery ticket, but I would only roster him with dev stash space.

James Proche, BAL (Southern Methodist -- Round 6, Pick 201): Proche led the nation in targets and catches, but he was mainly a beneficiary of the spread offense and matching up against lesser competition. Proche runs great routes, has steady hands, and is pretty good at contested catches, but he lacks NFL-level speed. He knew he probably wasn't going to test well at the combine, so he didn't run. The fit, as far as a WR goes in Baltimore, isn't very good.

- **2020:** Almost nothing for this year, barring a multitude of Ravens injuries.
- **Dynasty:** He's going to be a project, but he has a lot of upside. Even with that potential, the Ravens' run-oriented offense isn't going to bode well for any WR not named Marquise Brown.

Isaiah Hodgins, BUF (Oregon State -- Round 6, Pick 207): Hodgins has great size (6'3 5/8", 210 lbs), and he can make a catch in traffic. After that, however, he doesn't have a lot of meat left on the bone. Hodgins is not fast and doesn't have enough experience against press coverage to make an impact soon. He will be a bit of a project if he even makes the roster.

- **2020:** Not much. The Bills traded for Stefon Diggs and have John Brown, Cole Beasley, Robert Foster and fellow rookie Gabriel Davis to round out the WR corps. Hodgins doesn't have special-teams experience, either, so he's going to have to impress to stay on roster.
- **Dynasty:** A lot will depend on what he can put together this year, but I will not be investing.

Dezmon Patmon, IND (Washington State -- Round 6, Pick 212): Meh. Patmon was productive at Washington State, and he can provide a big target at 6'4", 225 lbs, but he doesn't do much beyond having size. Patmon had a great 40 time at the combine (4.48), but his game speed isn't that fast, he has problems fighting off press coverage, and he doesn't provide much in the way of special teams.

- **2020:** I would be surprised if he makes the roster.
- **Dynasty:** He's big and fast, so there's a lot to work with, but for him to be successful, he must work on the details in a hurry.

Freddie Swain, SEA (Florida -- Round 6, Pick 214): The Seahawks have been known to take relatively unknown WRs and make them decent producers, the most recent examples being David Moore and Malik Turner. That being said, Swain is almost purely a special-teamer. Swain has nice burst but wasn't productive at Florida. He's a project on offense but was a returner and covered on kicks and punts.

- **2020:** None really. He's on the roster because he'll have an instant impact on special teams.
- **Dynasty**: Not much here. He'll take a while to earn offensive snaps.

Jauan Jennings, SF (Tennessee -- Round 7, Pick 217): Shanahan loves to take projects, and Jennings fits that label. He's a big-bodied WR who may move to TE. Jennings ran a 4.72 40, and he displayed about the same game speed. Jennings made downfield plays and showed flashes against tough competition, but his inability to wrestle off press coverage and create separation will slow him down in the pros.

- **2020:** None. The 49ers have more than enough targets already.
- **Dynasty:** He joins and ranks behind fellow project Jalen Hurd. Don't expect an opportunity soon.

K.J. Hill, LAC (Ohio State -- Round 7, Pick 220): I'm reiterating that I like this match. The Bolts also took Joe Reed earlier, but I believe he will mainly be a special teamer. Hill, to me, is the opposite of former teammate Parris Campbell as a slot WR. Campbell is all speed, and Hill is finesse without Campbell's burst. Hill might not be able to box out well or blow past defenders with lightning speed, but he has great hands, knows where to sit in zone coverage, and runs great routes.

- **2020:** Chargers wideouts behind Keenan Allen and Mike Williams have an opportunity. TE Hunter Henry and RB Austin Ekeler will be ahead of the WR3 for targets, but someone has to win the job between Reed, Hill, Darius Jennings, and anyone else who makes the roster.
- **Dynasty:** Way higher than anyone else drafted in the 7th round, and the only 6th-rounder I like more than him is Donovan Peoples-Jones.

Tyrie Cleveland, DEN (Florida -- Round 7, Pick 252): Cleveland is a project at WR, but he has all kinds of physical tools, he's big at 6'2 3/8", 209 lbs, and he ran a 4.46 40 at the combine. The Broncos obviously have a ton on offense already, so Cleveland will be a special-teamer for the near future but will be working to develop into a viable receiving option.

- **2020:** Nothing for this year, he'll get some special-teams reps, but that's about it.
- **Dynasty:** He'll most likely have to make it on another team, but I think he has higher upside than your typical 7th-round flier WR.

TIGHT ENDS

Cole Kmet, CHI (Notre Dame -- Round 2, Pick 43): A lot of people (including me) lamented this TE draft class, but the Bears took a chance on a potential top-tier name in the 2nd round. The Bears of course had more pressing needs; they already have Jimmy Graham and Adam Shaheen on roster. Kmet may not be ready to start from Day 1, but he has tremendous potential. Kmet is going to have to get better blocking, but he can be useful in the receiving game right away. Kmet only had 17 catches going into his junior year but enjoyed a nice breakout with 43-515-6 even with some subpar QB play. Kmet runs solid routes, whether he is lined up in the slot or inline. He boasts great hands and will beat almost any defender in a contested-catch spot with his giant frame (6'6", 262).

- **2020:** Probably more of a redshirt year for Kmet, and he can learn from a vet like Graham. Even a polished TE like Noah Fant only ended up with 40 catches as a rookie.
- **Dynasty:** He has the talent to become a TE1, and I think he will be able to do it. He probably would have been better off staying at Notre Dame for another season, but learning at the NFL level and getting paid while doing it is definitely more appealing. I think Kmet will be pushed into a big-time role in 2021; Shaheen and Demetrius Harris are UFAs after this season. Graham is slated to make $6.9 million next year, and he likely will be cut.

Devin Asiasi, NE (UCLA -- Round 3, Pick 91): Asiasi is another project with all kinds of potential. A lot like Kmet, Asiasi had his first big effort last year. Going into 2019 with only 8 receptions, he ended with 44-641-4 for a UCLA offense that was inconsistent, to put it nicely. He does already have a decent skills base, but he will need a lot more polish, particularly in blocking and using his big frame to help him on contested catch spots. His best assets right now are (1) game speed, and (2) his tenacity to get every inch the defense will let him take when he has the ball in his hands.

- **2020:** He couldn't have landed in a better spot for immediate production. The Patriots are TE-desperate, so most of Asiasi's experience will be coming on the field rather than taking a redshirt year. He's still probably not worth drafting, but he should stay on your watchlist.
- **Dynasty:** TEs are more miss than hit, but when you combine his physical tools with the fact that he's going to get a lot of experience in Year 1, he could be worth a flier in some deeper leagues.

Josiah Deguara, GB (Cincinnati -- Round 3, Pick 94): Deguara is a great fit here. He's run routes out of the slot, inline and as an H-back. I know that Packers fans will hate this pick because it wasn't a WR, and I'll admit I thought it was a little weird; I really like what they have in Jace Sternberger, whom they drafted in the 3rd round last year. Deguara can already line up inside and in the slot, and he has pretty good hands, but I don't know whether he has a lot of upside. Not that Deguara needs to have a ton of upside, but there are some other TEs that were still on the board that have more upside. If the Packers were really concerned with immediate production, why wouldn't they have taken a WR?!

- **2020:** In 2-TE sets, Deguara might get some early run, and he has a lot of versatility, so he might be one of the more productive rookie TEs in this class. Still, he's best left for redraft watch lists.
- **Dynasty:** I don't see him ever becoming an upper-echelon TE, but I can see him being a useful piece for a while. He's the definition of "low ceiling with a high floor."

Dalton Keene, NE (Virginia Tech -- Round 3, Pick 101): This pick goes to show the Pats' desperation at the position. It's not a bad dart, but most teams don't spend many picks in the same round on the same position. Keene is a lot like Deguara as far as moving around goes, but he probably has more upside as a receiver than Deguara. The downside to Keene is that he struggled sustaining blocks in college, and that's definitely not going to get easier in the NFL. His progress there will determine his playing time.
- **2020:** Even with the Pats needing a receiving threat at TE, it's just really hard to predict playing time for rookies at this position. Keene being able to lineup all over the place could help him get on the field a little more than expected this year.
- **Dynasty:** I'm not going to be investing a lot in him. The Pats are looking down the barrel of a QB hunt, and Keene is the Pats' 2nd TE drafted in this class, so I would be looking elsewhere.

Adam Trautman, NO (Dayton -- Round 3, Pick 105): The Saints may not be in need of a TE, but with the most complete roster in the NFL, they aren't looking for a ton anyway. The Saints must have really liked Trautman; they traded 4 picks to move up in the 3rd to take him. Trautman succeeded at Dayton, but he fell because of he was merely beating up on small-school competition. Although Troutman displayed basically every tool you would want to see, the success against lower-level opponents makes scouts and GMs nervous. He wasn't impressive at the combine, but he was just about in line with the averages of most other TEs for times and measurements. Trautman was a high-school QB and played a lot of basketball, which means he's highly athletic but also inexperienced.
- **2020:** The Saints have Jared Cook and Josh Hill at TE, so Trautman will play sparingly this season.
- **Dynasty:** Right in line with Chicago's Cole Kmet. Trautman just needs a little more polish, which will come with experience, and I think he can be a big-time playmaker in this offense.

Harrison Bryant, CLE (Florida Atlantic -- Round 4, Pick 115): I was surprised to see some of the names that went before Bryant. I think he has a ton of upside! Being way behind the pack in blocking is most likely the reason he dropped: He was OK at FAU, but he would get overwhelmed sometimes. In fantasy terms, though, Bryant has great hands. While he did take advantage of scheme mismatches, he still runs solid routes. The worst part is his landing spot. The Browns didn't think he would be on the board and scooped him up, even after signing Austin Hooper, and they still have David Njoku on roster.
- **2020:** Not a lot here, unfortunately. Hooper and Njoku are already in town, and Odell Beckham, Jarvis Landry, Kareem Hunt and Nick Chubb will all be way ahead of Bryant for targets/touches.
- **Dynasty:** Dicey. I like him as a receiving option, but this roster has great TEs already. Njoku isn't a free agent until after 2021, and they just signed Hooper. Good players find a way, though, so I'm OK with investing in him in a deeper league, preferably with dev spots, as a stash.

Albert Okwuegbunam, DEN (Missouri -- Round 4, Pick 118): Albert O (because no wants to try that last name) is a hard prospect to pin down. I like that he landed in Denver. He certainly has the physical skills: Okwuegbunam was incredible at the combine, posting a 4.49 40 (the next closest at TE was 4.66). He needs a lot of work to earn consistent on-field reps, though. He doesn't body up LBs or DBs well at all for his size (6'5 ½" 258), and with all that speed, he didn't always have good separation, which is baffling.
- **2020:** He's a project, but even if he did get snaps, the Broncos have too many mouths to feed in the passing game. He wouldn't be too productive for fantasy purposes, anyway.
- **Dynasty:** He has the tools, but over 3 seasons with Missouri, he never had more than 43 catches or 500 receiving yards. He will be reunited with Drew Lock, however, which should at least help with familiarity. He's a "draft-and-stash" with a high ceiling and a low floor.

Colby Parkinson, SEA (Stanford -- Round 4, Pick 133): Stanford has historically had some great TEs, and Parkinson will fit right in for the Seahawks. Parkinson suffered through some rough QB play after K.J. Costello went down last season; he had more catches last season than he had in his first 2 seasons, but that was expected with the departure of JJ Arcega-Whiteside. Even with all those catches, he still only mustered one TD. Parkinson can box out receivers and block a little bit, but he really needs to smooth out the rough edges everywhere else before he sees significant work.

- **2020:** None. Greg Olsen, Will Dissly, Luke Willson and Jacob Hollister are already on the roster.
- **Dynasty:** Parkinson will need to sit and learn for a year or 2, and he will be afforded that with the depth at TE the Seahawks already have.

Brycen Hopkins, LAR (Purdue -- Round 4, Pick 136): Hopkins was the top TE on some boards coming into the draft. Hopkins improved every year he was in college, and I'm sure Sean McVay has a plan for him. Hopkins is another rookie who needs to gain technique at blocking but has great receiving skills.

- **2020:** Limited. Tyler Higbee finally broke out last year, and I expect him to build on that momentum. Plus, Gerald Everett is right behind him.
- **Dynasty:** Much better long-term bet than this year, given the Rams' cap problems. Everett is gone after this season, and I would expect Hopkins to step right in his TE2 spot.

Charlie Woerner, SF (Georgia -- Round 6, Pick 190): I doubt Woerner will have any fantasy impact; he only had 34 catches over 4 seasons at Georgia and got into the end zone once in those 4 years. Woerner was most likely brought into to be a blocker in 2-TE sets for the running game the 49ers like to utilize.

- **2020:** He's a blocking TE.
- **Dynasty:** See above.

Tyler Davis, JAX (Georgia Tech -- Round 6, Pick 206): Davis transferred from UConn to Georgia Tech after his junior year. Davis was originally recruited to UConn as a QB but moved to WR after his redshirt freshman year. He then switched to TE his junior year and stayed there as a senior. Davis no doubt interviewed well; he was elected team captain in his only season at Georgia Tech. He obviously needs work after moving around so much, but he is a high-effort player.

- **2020:** He'll be way behind on the depth chart. The Jags already have 3 viable TEs in Tyler Eifert, Josh Oliver and James O'Shaughnessy on roster already, but he'll get some special-teams reps.
- **Dynasty:** Guys that move positions a lot don't tend to last. Not rooting against him, but he has a tall mountain to climb.

Stephen Sullivan, SEA (LSU -- Round 7, Pick 251): I don't get it. I actually like Sullivan a lot. He reminds me of Cameron Brate: more of a slot WR than a true TE. But the Seahawks don't need him. If he gets cut, I could see him being scooped up by a team that needs a slot option. Still, he is a classic tweener: not big enough to block inline, but not fast enough to play WR.

- **2020:** He'll be on the practice squad at best
- **Dynasty:** Not much here. I'm guessing he gets kicked around the league for a little bit.

UNDRAFTED FREE AGENTS TO KNOW

Salvon Ahmed, RB, SF (Washington): I'm not sure why Ahmed wasn't drafted, but the 49ers got a nice 3-down back who can catch the ball out of the backfield. He's a longshot to make the roster, like most UDFAs, but any RB in SF has upside. How do you think Raheem Mostert climbed his way to the top?

Lawrence Cager, WR, NYJ (Georgia): Cager most likely fell off board because he couldn't stay on the field in his college days. He is a big WR (6' 4¾", 220 lbs) with great body control and good hands.

Thaddeus Moss, TE, WAS (LSU): I was genuinely surprised Moss didn't get drafted. He's a great run-blocker and an awesome short-route receiver. It came out after the draft that Moss had a Jones fracture that needed surgery, and those can linger. That and his lack of speed held him back.

Hunter Bryant, TE, DET (Washington): He was one of the best receiving TEs in this class, but a bad combine showing and the inability to run-block made him go undrafted. If he gets on the field, he'll mostly be used as a receiver, but the Lions already have T.J. Hockenson.

LOOKING AHEAD TO 2021

QUARTERBACKS

Trevor Lawrence, Clemson (Junior in 2020): Lawrence would have been the first pick after his freshman year, when he took Clemson to a national title. I can't remember a hype this big for a QB since Peyton Manning. Very mobile passer who looks to throw the ball downfield. It's hard to see a flaw in his game.

Justin Fields, Ohio State (JR): Looks like the No. 2 QB off the board right now. In his first starting year, he had a 41:3 TD:INT and took Ohio State to the playoffs. Stock is pretty high as it stands, so this season will be about cementing his spot near the top of the board. He's a taller Kyler Murray.

Trey Lance, North Dakota State (Redshirt Sophomore): 28 TDs and 0 INTs last year! NDSU is becoming a bit of a QB factory with Carson Wentz and Easton Stick before Lance, who looks like the next one. He's big listed at 6'3" with a rifle for an arm, and he's obviously accurate -- and he's a runner with over 1,000 on the ground last year and 14 TDs.

More to Know: Sam Ehlinger, Texas (SR); Jame Newman, Georgia (rSR); Brock Purdy, Iowa State (JR); D'Eriq King, Miami (SR); K.J. Costello, Mississippi State (SR)

RUNNING BACKS

Travis Etienne, Clemson (Senior): I don't know what his best tool is, but he has just about everything. He'll hit a 2nd gear and then a 3rd in the open field. Rarely ever goes down with 1st contact, will run over tacklers, and has the wiggle to put a move on them. The knock on him going into 2019 was that he only had 17 catches, but he had 37 last year with 4 TD catches.

Chubba Hubbard, Oklahoma State (SR): Vision and explosion jump out. He had 2,094 rushing yards last year, which was more than the leading passer at OK State. It was a little surprising that he didn't leave for the draft already, but he's in the conversation to be the 1st RB off the board next year.

Najee Harris, Alabama (SR): He reminds me of his former teammate Josh Jacobs with hints of Le'Veon Bell. He has great vision and can catch the ball downfield.

More to Know: Max Borghi, Washington State (JR); Kennedy Brooks, Oklahoma (rJR); CJ Verdell, Oregon (SR); Jermar Jefferson, Oregon State (JR); Demetric Felton, UCLA (rJR); Zamir White, Georgia (rSO); Kenneth Gainwell, Memphis (rSO)

WIDE RECEIVERS

Ja'Marr Chase, LSU (JR): Might have been the 1st WR off the board if he were able to declare this year. It will be interesting to see if he can get anywhere near the 84-1780-20 line he had with Joe Burrow throwing him the ball. He's explosive with the ball in his hands; eats up man coverage with ease; makes contested catches; and knows how to find holes in zones. His best asset might be his hands.

Justyn Ross, Clemson (JR): Ross isn't a burner, but he does have size at 6'3" and runs super-clean routes. Ross won't just beat DBs with his size; he's also really great at hand-fighting downfield to get himself in favorable position. He's been getting DeAndre Hopkins comps. I think that's a bit hyperbolic, but he does have the same style to his game.

Devonta Smith, Alabama (SR): Has good instincts to get open, and when he catches, he has a 2nd gear that leaves defenders in the dust. He's a bit skinny, but plenty of wiry WRs make it work.

Rondale Moore, Purdue (JR): Just get the ball in his hands and watch him make the play. He's undersized at 5'8", but he's an absolute pinball. I don't know if I've seen balance like his; he almost never goes down on first contact. Got RB snaps, and returns kicks and punts. He'll be used as an all-around weapon in the NFL.

Jaylen Waddle, Alabama (JR): He's got speed, but he also sets up downfield blocks well; he has a lot of experience taking short routes to get the ball in his hands. Waddle also has crazy ups; he'll go way over the top to haul in a 50/50 ball. He also has 3 return TDs in 2 seasons.

More to Know: Amon-Ra St. Brown, USC (JR); Rashod Bateman, Minnesota (SR); Sage Suratt, Wake Forest (rJR); Tylan Wallace, Oklahoma State (SR); Tamorrion Terry, Florida State (rJR); Tutu Atwell, Louisville (JR); Terrace Mitchell, LSU (JR); Anthony Schwartz, Auburn (JR)

TIGHT ENDS

Brevin Jordan, Miami (JR): The 2020 class didn't have top-tier TE talent, but the 2021 class is going to have a ton if they all declare, starting with Jordan. Jordan doesn't have the production to back up the talent, but that's more because of the musical chairs QB situation they had going. This year should be better with King. He was a 5-star recruit who can really become a great weapon. The Evan Engram comparison is pretty damn good.

Pat Freiermuth, Penn State (JR): Baby Gronk? That comparison is a bit tired, of course, but I think this one might end up fitting. Naturally, wherever Freiermuth lands, he won't get the best QB of all time throwing him the ball, but he is a big bully of a receiving TE. He is constantly torching coverage when he leaks out on a delayed short route and boxing out and high-pointing downfield. Freiermuth was productive last year (43-507-7). With WR K.J. Hamler gone, he should get a bigger share of the targets.

Kyle Pitts, Florida (JR): The Gators say he's a TE, and so does his frame, but most of his film says he's a WR. He's 6'6", 239 lbs, but he plays more slot and even split out wide a decent amount than on the line. Kind of a Devin Funchess type, and most of us were excited about Funchess coming out of Michigan, so I'm comparing to that and not the current-day pro mess we have. Pitts gets wide-open looks for being such a huge target and knows where to end his route so the QB has the best shot at getting him the ball.

More to Know: Charlie Kolar, Iowa State (rJR); Jake Ferguson, Wisconsin (rJR); Matt Bushman, BYU (SR)

Chapter 11

NFL WAGERING

Mike Randle

The NFL and sports betting make a perfect marriage. The combination of a weekly schedule and the unpredictability of a physical competition creates the precise balance of variables that entice millions of sports fans to search for ideal wagering opportunities.

NFL GAMBLING OVERVIEW

Here are five tips to keep in mind as you prepare your wagers for the 2020 NFL season.

1. Be objective.

To make sound betting decisions with positive EV (Expected Value), remain completely objective as a bettor. We all have predetermined allegiances to a favorite team or player, but each game has its own independent entity and should be examined as such. Before the season begins, become self-aware of your ingrained biases and analyze your ability to stay neutral. If you have a strong allegiance to a certain team, it may be best to avoid betting them completely.

2. Lean on homefield advantage.

While we still do not know whether fans will be able to actually attend sporting events in September, NFL squads have a historical advantage when playing at home as a favorite against the spread. Using data from BetLabs, here are the teams with the highest R.O.I. (Return On Investment) in those situations since 2003:

- New England (75-51-6), 59.5%, 16.4% ROI
- Green Bay (64-47-5), 57.7%, 12% ROI
- Minnesota (55-42-3), 56.7%, 10% ROI

Being aware of a historically successful team against the spread can be a profitable investment especially late in the season, when games have greater importance.

3. Late-season divisional games? Bet the Under.

Familiarity breeds contempt.

NFL teams are always focused on achieving dominance within their own division. When a club plays a divisional opponent late in the season, the game is often close.

Over the past two seasons, December underdogs in the AFC North, AFC West, NFC South, and AFC East have covered the spread at a 60.9% rate (42-27-6), with a 16.3% ROI. Regardless of season performance, divisional games toward the end of the regular season are usually tighter than expected, which provides savvy bettors with prime opportunities.

4. Monitor injury reports.

Injuries play a crucial role in handicapping an NFL game. For example, an injury to a key offensive lineman for a road underdog can play a critical role in the efficiency of that team's offense. Always take note of star players who leave a game because of injury and evaluate whether the opening line for the following week reflects that player possibly missing the subsequent game. This is particularly true for teams with a short turnaround to a Thursday Night game.

5. Target situational underdog spots.

There are times during the season when underdogs tend to give their best effort. One of those times is as a winless home team during Week 3. Over the past three seasons, teams that are 0-2 listed as a home underdog in Week 3 are 6-2 (75%) against the spread with an ROI of 42.1%. Only six teams since 1980 have made the playoffs after starting 0-3, making for live home underdogs after two consecutive losses to start the season.

Best Bets for 2020

Check your favorite web sites and casinos for a myriad of available wagers. While listings may rapidly change due to offseason and preseason news, including injuries, you can generally find patterns across multiple outlets that may, for example, be over- or undervaluing a team or player.

Look for the trends that you can manipulate, especially if you find something reflecting my favorite wagers of the 2020 season:

Over/Under for Team Win Totals

Los Angeles Chargers Under 7.5 Wins: For the first time since the start of the 2006 season, the Chargers will not have Philip Rivers as their starting quarterback. The reins have been passed to veteran Tyrod Taylor, with first-round rookie Justin Herbert serving as the primary backup. Coming off a disappointing 5-11 season that vastly underperformed their expected win total (9.5), the Chargers have plenty working against them for a .500 season.

Los Angeles will adjust to life without former starting running back Melvin Gordon, who produced 47 touchdowns over the past four years. Veteran wideout Keenan Allen relied more on his precise route-running and connection with Rivers, rather than his sub-standard athleticism (4.7 40-Yard Dash speed). The 31-year old Taylor and a diminutive lead running back in 5-foot-9, 199-pound Austin Ekeler represent a severe downgrade in offensive weaponry.

The Chargers also contend with one of the toughest groups of divisional foes. The Broncos and Raiders upgraded their offensive talent through the NFL Draft to join the Super Bowl-champion Kansas City Chiefs in one of the toughest divisions in football.

With a minimal homefield advantage and uncertainty on offense, the Chargers will be hard-pressed to improve by three wins. The schedule-makers have done Los Angeles no favors, as well, with non-divisional games against the AFC East and NFC South. A 7-9 record feels like the ceiling.

Tampa Bay Buccaneers Under 10 Wins: The Buccaneers made the biggest free-agent offseason splash with the signing of future Hall of Famers Tom Brady and Rob Gronkowski. Their seasonal win total and Super Bowl odds immediately skyrocketed. This is a prime opportunity to employ a classic betting strategy: fading the public.

While Brady will have some of the best offensive weapons of his career in wideouts Chris Godwin and Mike Evans, he will also turn 43 years old to start the 2020 season. As an immobile quarterback, Brady will rely on a Tampa Bay offensive line that only ranked 22nd in pass protection allowing a 7.6% Adjusted Sack Rate (FootballOutsiders). His fantasy points per game in 2019 (17.5) were also the lowest of his career since 2006.

Gronkowski has not played NFL football since the 2018 season after retiring as a result of constant injuries. His 1.82 fantasy points per target that season ranked just 18th among all NFL tight ends. The likelihood of an injury-free season for the 31-year old veteran seems low.

The Buccaneers reside in the NFC South and must therefore face the explosive offenses of the Saints and Falcons twice during the season. Tampa Bay has difficult non-divisional games against the Chiefs, Packers and Vikings. The last time the Buccaneers exceeded 10 wins was 2005. With Tampa Bay's difficult schedule, tough divisional opponents, and unproven offensive line, the public steam on a massive improvement looks unrealistic.

Buffalo Bills Over 9: I fully support a Bills team that has reached nine wins or more in two of the past three seasons. Buffalo's defense returns as one of the NFL's best, having ranked sixth in defensive efficiency that included a vitally important No. 2 rank against the pass. The Bills were second in points allowed per game (14.8) and totaled 44 sacks. Buffalo bolstered its pass rush by drafting defensive end A.J. Epenesa from Iowa with its second-round draft pick. The Bills also plugged the hole left from defensive tackle Jordan Phillips (Arizona) by acquiring Quinton Jefferson and Vernon Butler in the offseason.

Their offense should improve with the acquisition of top-level wideout Stefon Diggs from Minnesota. Running back Devin Singletary showed promise as a rookie, and he'll be joined by first-year thumper Zach Moss, who replaces veteran Frank Gore. I project big things for QB Josh Allen, one of the position's top dual threats, in his third season. He ranked first among quarterbacks with 9 rushing TDs and eighth in Deep Ball Attempts (72), per PlayerProfiler.

The Bills are coming off a 10-win season and consistently have one of the biggest late-season homefield advantages in Buffalo. With New England possibly taking a step back in the post-Brady era, I'm bullish on the Bills as one of the AFC's best teams.

San Francisco 49ers Over 10.5: I don't like betting overs on double-digit win totals, but I'll make an exception for the Super Bowl runners-up. The 49ers' physicality on both sides of the ball provides a consistently competitive gameplan for both home and away contests. San Francisco improved its offensive efficiency from 27th to seventh last season, while ranking second with 144.1 rushing yards per game.

The 49ers offense should be even better. San Francisco traded running back Matt Breida to Miami but should welcome back the talented Jerick McKinnon from knee surgery to join the strong Raheem Mostert-Tevin Coleman tandem. To replace veteran WR Emmanuel Sanders, they traded up to select explosive rookie Brandon Aiyuk with the 25th overall pick in the draft.

San Francisco strengthened the NFL's second-most efficient defense by selecting defensive tackle Javon Kinlaw from South Carolina, a pick acquired through the trade of DeForest Buckner to Indianapolis. With the fifth-most sacks (48) and fourth-most fumble recoveries (15), San Francisco has the perfect balance needed to return to the Super Bowl.

Player Prop Bets

Dak Prescott Over 4,375.5 Passing Yards: The Cowboys have assembled one of the most talented offenses in the NFL. With the addition of Oklahoma standout pass-catcher CeeDee Lamb, Prescott now has three elite wide receivers (Lamb, Amari Cooper, Michael Gallup), an All-Pro dual-threat running back (Ezekiel Elliott), and a high-efficiency tight end (Blake Jarwin), all behind one of the best offensive lines in football.

The Cowboys were 8-0 in games when they scored more than 30 points, and with Jason Garrett's conservative play-calling replaced by new head coach Mike McCarthy to pair with OC Kellen Moore, Prescott is a good bet to again approach the 5,000-yard passing plateau.

Davante Adams Over 1,200.5 Receiving Yards: Green Bay's decision to not draft a wide receiver greatly helps the target projection for Adams. The 27-year old wide receiver lost four games to a toe sprain last season. However, he still tallied 997 receiving yards, which projected for 1329.3 yards in a full 16-game season. This followed his 1,386-yard performance of 2018.

It's easy to see Adams finishing as the league's receiving leader. He still benefits from playing alongside Aaron Rodgers, one of the most accurate QBs in NFL history. Assuming health, this total projects just 75 yards per game for one of the NFL's most \accomplished QB-WR tandems.

Baker Mayfield Over 23.5 Passing Touchdowns: I'm buying Mayfield in the classic post-hype sleeper spot with a new coaching staff and improved offensive line. New head coach Kevin Stefanski graded out as the best play-caller in game-neutral situations last season, per PFF. By adding free-agent offensive tackle Jack Conklin and drafting tackle Jedrick Wills with the 10th overall pick, the Browns should greatly improve on last season's 30th-best protection rate (PlayerProfiler). With a full season for pass-catching running back Kareem Hunt to pair with Nick Hubb; wideouts Odell Beckham Jr. and Jarvis Landry; and depth at tight end with the addition of Austin Hooper, Mayfield only needs to slightly exceed last year's dismal performance (22 passing touchdowns) to hit this over total.

Chapter 12

OVERRATED & UNDERRATED 2020

MOST OVERRATED

QUARTERBACKS

Aaron Rodgers, GB: Household name aside, Rodgers isn't what he once was. Gone are the days of his 300-yard, 3-TD classic games. The Packers have failed to develop a secondary option behind Davante Adams in the passing game, and their commitment to a heavier rushing attack seems strong. Oh, and the Packers moved up to take another QB in the draft. Not that Jordan Love is an immediate threat -- he's not. Still, there are simply better fantasy QB1 options in 2020 than Rodgers. *--Joe Pisapia*

Aaron Rodgers, GB: Rodgers is being drafted as a QB1 despite finishing outside the top 12 in fantasy points per game last season. He had 7 games of 216 passing yards or fewer and only 3 games of more than 2 touchdowns. No weapons were added to the offense, and the Packers appear to favor the run game. *--Adam Ronis*

Drew Brees, NO: Brees is the first non-running quarterback off the board. I don't pay a premium for quarterbacks who don't add anything in the run game, and I am not going to do it with Brees this year. Quarterbacks who run are a cheat code. If you don't get one early, look to guys later who have that upside. *--Eliot Crist*

Aaron Rodgers, GB: Rodgers posted a career-low 17.4 FPPG (QB14) last season (his lowest mark dating back to 2007 when he became a starter). Rodgers had just 5 games in 2019 in which he totaled 15+ fantasy points, yet he's being drafted as a top-10 option according to ADP data. Green Bay did next to nothing in the offseason to add pass-catching weapons to the offense (sorry, Devin Funchess doesn't really count), so it's hard to see Rodgers returning top-10-QB value this year. *--Matt Franciscovich*

Matt Ryan, ATL: I know this is his "other" year and we're supposed to buy (2nd in '16, 15th in '17, 2nd in '18, 11th last year in Total Points at QB), but Ryan is getting long in the tooth, and the Falcons downgraded at TE with Austin Hooper out and Hayden Hurst in. If Todd Gurley is back up to standard, he'll eat into red-zone touches, too; the Falcons were 25th (51.7%) at coming away with a TD after entering the red zone last year. *--Scott Bogman*

Deshaun Watson, HOU: Watson will still likely be drafted in the top 5 at the position in 2020. This will be the main reason I'll be out on him. That, and he's missing one of the best wideouts in the game. I'm not sure what Bill O'Brien is doing in Houston, but they have a problem □. Watson does provide value as a mobile QB, but if David Johnson can remain healthy, they may lean on the run game from their RBs a bit more in 2020. Did I mention the awful coaching and absence of DeAndre Hopkins yet? *--Nate Hamilton*

Aaron Rodgers, GB: Rodgers will be drafted as a top-12 quarterback in fantasy, and considering last year's performance, that's too rich. Rodgers was the QB14 in fantasy points per game last year. With the Packers looking to run the ball more and failing to upgrade the weapons around Rodgers (no, Devin Funchess doesn't count), the arrow is pointing down. *--Derek Brown*

Aaron Rodgers, GB: QB9 last season, but outside the top 12 in fantasy points per game. Rodgers failed to hit the 300-yard passing mark in 12 of his 16 games, and he checked in at 216 or under in 7. He also only had 3 games with more than 2 passing touchdowns. As stated by others, the Packers did him zero favors this offseason. Where's the upside? The position is too deep to take A-Rod in the top 12. *--Chris Meaney*

Teddy Bridgewater, CAR: After some time as Drew Brees' understudy, Bridgewater finally landed himself another starting gig. Moving to Carolina gives him access to an arsenal of weapons in Christian McCaffrey, D.J. Moore, Curtis Samuel and now Robby Anderson. The issue is his low ceiling. Bridgewater was QB22 in the 5-game stretch that he started in 2019, even with elite pass-catching options like Michael Thomas and Alvin Kamara at the helm. He'll be drafted in superflex leagues, but buyer beware. --*Kate Magdziuk*

Deshaun Watson, HOU: While Watson is a talent in his own right, it shouldn't be understated how big a loss it is to no longer having DeAndre Hopkins. Brandin Cooks will help mitigate the loss, but he and Hopkins aren't even in the same stratosphere. Couple that with the fact that you just can't rely on Will Fuller to stay healthy, and there's plenty of concern if you're someone expecting Watson to once again finish as fantasy's QB4 or better. --*Chris McConnell*

Josh Allen, BUF: Sure, Allen finished as the QB6 last year. That's all fine and dandy. It's like Frank Gore finishing as the RB12 back in 2016 while rushing for 1,026 yards and four touchdowns. Ask anyone who owned Gore in 2016 or Allen in 2019 if they were worth where they finished. The answer would be no. Allen posted top-12 numbers just 43.8% of the time, the same as Jared Goff. --*Mike Tagliere (FantasyPros)*

Drew Brees, NO: No one will deny that Brees is still among the top real-life quarterbacks, but fantasy is about volume. Over his last 3 seasons, Brees has thrown just 33.4 passes per game, which comes out to only 534 over a full season. Even if he puts up his career YDS/ATT and TD% in his age-41 season, we'd still only be looking at around 330 fantasy points, which would have been QB6 last year. Brees doesn't run, either, so QB6 is his upside. --*Bobby Sylvester (FantasyPros)*

RUNNING BACKS

Nick Chubb, CLE: Chubb had a fantastic total rushing season in 2019. However, when Kareem Hunt showed up in Week 10, Chubb's targets went south, and that trend will likely hold in PPR. Chubb should still be good for yards and TDs, but having Hunt from the jump of the 2020 season is going to eat into his touches. That's not a good thing. --*Pisapia*

Mark Ingram, BAL: Much of Ingram's production last season came from 10 rushing touchdowns and 5 receiving scores. He had 202 carries and 26 receptions. He turns 31 in December, and the Ravens drafted running back J.K. Dobbins in the 2nd round. Everything was prefect for Ingram last season, and it's unlikely to repeat. --*Ronis*

Nick Chubb, CLE: Kareem Hunt is a thorn in Chubb's thigh, and there is no getting around it. Without Hunt last year, Chubb averaged 4 targets a game, but that was cut in half with Hunt's return. He went from RB6 the 1st half of the year to RB15 the 2nd half without receiving work. Without passing-game upside, Chubb is overpriced. --*Crist*

Joe Mixon, CIN: Look, I love the talent here. I just think it's absolutely nuts to target a running back in the first round of your fantasy draft who plays on a team that averaged 16.4 points per game last season, dead-last in the NFL. Plus, rumors have been swirling all offseason that Mixon could hold out, as the 23-year-old seeks an extension. If that happens, you'd be taking an RB in a potentially terrible offense that could miss several weeks of playing time. No thanks. --*Franciscovich*

Clyde Edwards-Helaire, KC: I know, the rookie guy should not be bashing the rookies, and this absolutely has nothing to do with CEH's talent level; it's still high. 15 Fantasy Pros experts have ranked him as a RB1 already. Sure, he *can* finish there, but knowing what we know about Andy Reid's backfield games, I can't predict Edwards-Helaire to be an RB1 and probably even an RB2 in his rookie year. We did this same bit with Darwin Thompson, Mecole Hardman and LeSean McCoy all because they are playing with Patrick Mahomes in the best offense in the NFL. He's probably going to be a top-tier RB in KC soon, but I won't be investing at his current price this year. –*Bogman*

Miles Sanders, PHI: I'm not denying the talent of the player, but Doug Pederson has shown us time and time again that he just can't help himself when it comes to destroying the fantasy value of his running backs. He's in love with the committee approach. There's been a lot of Sanders being "easily a top-10 back" talk going around, and I just can't put my stamp on that given the history of his head coach. --*Hamilton*

Leonard Fournette, JAC: Fournette survived last season with volume and his pass-game role. With the Jaguars attempting to trade him all offseason, and Chris Thompson in the building now, neither of those factors are sure things. With the uncertainty surrounding Fournette, there's no way I can rationalize drafting him as a top-15 running back. *--Brown*

Nick Chubb, CLE: This pains me, because I absolutely love Chubb. I think he's terrific, and I believe he can handle 3-down work. It was on full display at the beginning of the season. Unfortunately, we can't ignore Kareem Hunt, who is also terrific. In the final 8 games of the season, Chubb's numbers and opportunities -- including those in the red zone -- dipped with Hunt on the field. *--Meaney*

Aaron Jones, GB: The #FreeAaronJones movement almost looked to be gaining speed in 2019. He finished as the RB2 in PPR leagues after finishing with 1,558 scrimmage yards and 19 total touchdowns. However, his workload and production splits with and without fellow running back Jamaal Williams were significant. In 2020, Green Bay will bring to the mix rookie A.J. Dillon, who has a significantly larger frame and is bound to see some goal-line action. A 3-way committee is all but a death sentence for your fantasy rosters. *–Magdziuk*

Aaron Jones, GB: This one should be quite obvious. The regression should be large. Jones could still find his way to be an RB1 in 2020, but he's going to be tied for the league lead in rushing TDs again (16) on his way to doing it. His fantasy season was propped up by all those TDs, and with rookie A.J. Dillon now in the fold as the epitome of a goal-line back, those TD numbers aren't likely to be anywhere close this season. He's a perfect keeper sell-high candidate if you can pull it off. *--McConnell*

Derrick Henry, TEN: He's a good running back; I won't deny that. However, we cannot simply ignore the first few years of his career to a much smaller 6-game sample size to close out the 2019 season. Did you know that heading into Week 10 last year, Henry hadn't topped 100 yards rushing on the season? When investing a late-1st or early-2nd-round pick on a running back, you need him to offer a higher floor than Henry does. His lack of involvement in the passing game simply presents too much downside. *–Tagliere*

Clyde Edwards-Helaire, KC: Eliot Crist is going to send me hate mail for this, but I won't have any shares of CEH if he continues to go in the early 2nd round. I won't deny that his upside is tremendous, but wasn't the same true of LeSean McCoy, the last rookie RB that Andy Reid drafted early? McCoy was extremely efficient, yet Reid gave him just 195 touches his rookie year. You can hope CEH will get 280, but Damien Williams nearly won the Super Bowl MVP, so this probably won't be anything other than a split backfield for the 1st half of the season. *--Sylvester*

WIDE RECEIVERS

Rookie Wide Receivers in Redraft '20 Leagues: Look, the COVID-19 pandemic took away OTAs and a lot of important time for young WRs to gain rapport with their QBs. I love the talent of this year's rookie class, but I'm more bullish about the chances of these prospects in dynasty/keeper leagues, as opposed to redrafts in 2020. Some probably could break through, but it's likelier to happen as the season progresses. That makes them better early trade targets than early draft targets. *--Pisapia*

Mike Evans, TB: Evans has relied on volume and big plays. Both should decline with Tom Brady at quarterback. Jameis Winston took shots down the field, and Brady won't do that as often and could rely on shorter passes to Chris Godwin and Rob Gronkowski. The Buccaneers' defense has improved, and Brady won't turn it over as much. Evans won't finish as a top-10 WR, and that's where he's being drafted. Evans had 568 of his 1,157 yards in 3 games last season. *–Ronis*

Michael Thomas, NO: Coming off a year when he set the receptions record, Thomas is a beast; there is no doubt. However, he is being drafted over guys like Ezekiel Elliott and Dalvin Cook, and receiver is a far deeper position. Thomas saw 66.7% of the receiver targets in New Orleans -- nearly 15% higher than the next closest player in Allen

Robinson. With Emmanuel Sanders in town, the targets will spread out just enough that Thomas is closer to Pick 6 than Pick 3 off the board. *--Crist*

Mike Evans, TB: If you for one second think that Evans will see anywhere near his career average of 9.3 targets per game (118 targets last year in 13 games), you're going to be let down. While Evans remains one of the top WRs in the NFL ability-wise, Tom Brady is not going to throw 30 picks like Jameis Winston did last year. That means less passing volume. A lot less. Add Brady's ball security to the fact that Rob Gronkowski is likely to soak up red-zone targets, and you can see why Evans is not worth his hefty draft price this season. *--Franciscovich*

D.J. Moore, CAR: This one hurts. I have been a bell-ringer for Moore since he came out of Maryland in 2018, but he is being ranked as a WR1, and I can't get on board. The Panthers have a new head coach in Matt Rhule, a new QB in Teddy Bridgewater, and new WRs in Robby Anderson and Seth Roberts. Moore finished 17th in PPR PPG last year, and I think because CMC probably won't get as many snaps under Rhule and the QB situation is better than last year, people want to move him up. I won't bury him, but he won't be a WR1 on my board. *–Bogman*

DeAndre Hopkins, ARI: I can't believe I'm saying this. Hopkins was the only viable target in Houston for so many years. He finds himself on his second NFL team, which has more weapons than his previous club. As exciting as it can be for a player to change scenery, it doesn't always immediately translate. That's my fear with one of my favorite WRs in the game for 2020. I expect some growing pains in his first year with the Cardinals. Hopkins hasn't dealt with those variables yet, and I'd rather go even safer with my 1st-round pick. *–Hamilton*

A.J. Brown, TEN: After Ryan Tannehill took over as the Titans' starter (week 7), Tennessee still ranked 31st in pass rate during neutral game script ahead of only the Ravens. Tannehill averaged only 27 pass attempts per game over that stretch. Brown was a stud last year, but considering prospective volume in Tennessee's passing offense, anyone drafting him as a top 12-15 wide receiver is doing so at or above his ceiling. *--Brown*

A.J. Brown, TEN: I typically like to take care of the RB position pretty early in drafts, so when I see Brown sitting there in the 3rd as a potential WR1 or even WR2, it's an easy pass for me. Brown had a phenomenal rookie season, and he has all the tools to be a great wideout in this league, but I'm concerned about the volume. Brown's 5.2 targets per game last season ranked 64th among wideouts. He had 6 games with 2 or fewer catches (8 if you include postseason) and 4 or fewer targets in half of his contests (10, including postseason). He showed his big-play in 4 of his final 6 games, but I'm looking for a bit more consistency. Plus, there were games against top corners, when Tannehill didn't even bother looking Brown's way. I don't think the Titans will surprise too many teams with their play-action this year. *--Meaney*

DeAndre Hopkins, ARI: Though Hopkins continues to hold the title of "best hands in the league," circumstances caution me not to think this will translate to fantasy in 2020. He'll have to make ample adjustments as he heads to Arizona: a new scheme, coaching staff, quarterback, playbook and verbiage. It's bound to be all the more difficult to make those adjustments with the limited activities in the NFL offseason amidst the COVID-19 outbreak. The talent will still be there, but I don't expect Hopkins to continue averaging 160 targets per season as he's seen in Houston -- at least not in 2020. *--Magdziuk*

DeVante Parker, MIA: Parker is a fine candidate for back-end WR2/high-WR3 numbers in 2020, but if anyone is expecting anything close to what he did after Week 9, they're in for a rude awakening. Preston Williams will be back healthy; was out-producing Parker across the board before tearing his ACL in Week 9; and was essentially already establishing himself as their alpha receiver. Parker may be looked at by many as The Guy going into 2020, but for me, Williams is the WR to own on this team. A single hot streak after being outplayed by a teammate isn't going to suddenly make me believe the lightbulb has turned on for Parker. *--McConnell*

Amari Cooper, DAL: You won't find a bigger Cooper fan than me from a pure talent standpoint, but in fantasy, he's overvalued. Cooper has never posted WR1-type numbers in more than 31.3% of his games in a season, and in fact, has never posted WR2-type numbers in more than 50% of his games in a season. Still, he's being drafted as a top-

10 option. The lack of elite targets has been the problem and will continue to be the issue now that CeeDee Lamb has been added to the mix. —*Tagliere*

D.K. Metcalf, SEA: We write and talk often about TD rates for quarterbacks, but the same applies to wide receivers. Boom players in the past like Will Fuller have had unsustainable TD rates, so analysts faded them the following season. Metcalf is the same fools' gold, and unless he sees a major target-share uptick in this run-heavy offense, he has slim chances of out-producing Keenan Allen, A.J. Green or Stefon Diggs, who are all being selected later in drafts. --*Sylvester*

TIGHT ENDS

Zach Ertz, PHI: Ertz is a fine TE and a great PPR asset. However, Dallas Goedert is still around, and the Eagles are hoping Jalen Reagor and a healthy Alshon Jeffrey (if that's even a thing) can help this offense be more aggressive downfield. It's not that I'm anti-Ertz; I just don't like him at his ADP. I think his 2019 stats are more repeatable than his 2018 numbers (which are still driving that ADP too high). --*Pisapia*

Austin Hooper, CLE: Players changing teams often struggle in that first season, and the lack of offseason activities will make it tougher in 2020. Hooper benefitted from a pass-heavy offense in Atlanta and averaged 7.4 targets per game last season. He won't see that volume in Cleveland. --*Ronis*

Evan Engram, NYG: The issue with Engram isn't the talent. It's health. In the last 2 years, he has shown up on the injury report with 6 different issues and has missed 12 games in the last 2 seasons. His season ended needing a Lisfranc surgery, and he has had issues with his MCL, hamstring, knee and ankle in the last 2 years. Engram is a beast when on the field but doesn't see it enough to pay a premium for him. Leave him to your DFS lineups. --*Crist*

Zach Ertz, PHI: After George Kittle and Travis Kelce are off the board, Ertz is the next-best TE available. He's got a Round 4 asking price, and that's simply too rich for what Ertz will provide in return. You want to spend that pick on a RB or WR, and let someone else waste it on Ertz. He saw a significant decline in targets year over year from 2018 to 2019, and he's simply not as consistent of a fantasy option as he once was, especially with Dallas Goedert on the rise and the Eagles bringing in more threats at wide receiver, including rookie Jalen Reagor. --*Franciscovich*

Evan Engram, NYG: Engram is a stud, no doubt about that; he has finished 4th in '17, 7th in '18, and again 7th '19 in TE PPR PPG. FantasyPros has him ranked at what looks appropriate as the 6th TE, but he has just missed too many games to be counted on at that level. TEs miss games almost every year; it's a brutal position. 4 of the 5 guys above Engram missed at least 1 game last year, but Engram missed 8 in 2019 and 5 in 2018. I'll take Engram, but his price has to drop. --*Bogman*

Austin Hooper, CLE: Yes, Hooper had success in the Falcons offense but has since moved to Cleveland. He caught 75 of Matt Ryan's 97 targets in 2019. His new QB, Baker Mayfield, targeted the TE position just 69 times and completed just 41 of those passes. Baker's top TE was Ricky Seals-Jones, who had just 14 receptions on the year! I wouldn't pay up for Hooper in 2020. --*Hamilton*

Darren Waller, LV: Waller is facing an uphill climb to repeat the 117 targets he saw last year. When Hunter Renfrow was active, Waller's target share dropped from 24% to 20.9%. Expect a further dip this year with Renfrow back and the team drafting Henry Ruggs, Lynn Bowden and Bryan Edwards. --*Brown*

Evan Engram, NYG: Engram has the talent, and we've seen him produce TE1 numbers when healthy, but he's missed 13 games in the last 2 years for multiple reasons. I think you'll see the Giants turn to a heavier run offense, and we don't even know if Engram will be ready Week 1 as he recovers from a dreaded Lisfranc injury. --*Meaney*

Austin Hooper, CLE: Hooper was incredibly productive in Atlanta, finishing as the TE6 in each of the past 2 seasons. Now he joins the Browns, where he joins the tight-end room with former first-rounder David Njoku. Though Njoku seems to have fallen out of favor with Cleveland, he is bound to see a share of snaps and create more competition for targets. Baker Mayfield should have no excuses heading into his 3rd season with the weapons in that offense, but I worry that Hooper won't see the target volume to make him worth his draft cost in 2020. --*Magdziuk*

Tyler Higbee, LAR: Look at the games in which Higs went on his fantasy tear: During the entirety of said tear, Gerald Everett wasn't on the field. Expecting Higbee to continue where he left off, especially after the Rams said that they want to get Everett more involved, is a bad business decision. The fact is, when Everett is on the field, we can't point to anything Higbee has done that is significant. They also drafted the talented TE Bryce Hopkins in the 4th round, along with WR Van Jefferson in the 2nd round and still having Josh Reynolds around to fill the void left by Brandin Cooks. With all these factors considered, we have the epitome of a sell-high candidate and a situation from which to stay far, far away. --*McConnell*

Austin Hooper, CLE: Going back to 2009, just 11 tight ends have finished top-10 without seeing a minimum of 80 targets, which might be difficult for Hooper to come by with his new team. Not only does Cleveland have Odell Beckham, Jarvis Landry, Nick Chubb, and Kareem Hunt, but Hooper is now part of a crowded tight end room with David Njoku and Harrison Bryant (whom they drafted in the 4th round). Kevin Stefanski's offense in Minnesota did run a lot of 2-TE sets, but their top 3 tight ends combined for just 105 targets, and none had more than 48 targets. –*Tagliere*

Evan Engram, NYG: Unless you think Daniel Jones is going to break out into a Year 2 superstar, there are just too many mouths to feed for Engram to return draft value. Sterling Shepard, Golden Tate, Darius Slayton and Saquon Barkley may all come before Engram on the pecking order. As if that weren't enough, Engram hasn't been the epitome of efficiency in his career, putting up just 1.04 fantasy points per target -- which is 32% less than O.J. Howard, for instance. --*Sylvester*

MOST UNDERRATED

QUARTERBACKS

Carson Wentz, PHI: Wentz finished as fantasy's QB10 last year, and that's with a wide receiver corps that grossly underperformed. Still, Wentz's 4K yards, 27:7 TD:INT and 5 300-yard games marked a strong 2019 line and a realistic 2020 expectation. Fun fact: Wentz had at least 1 passing TD in all 17 regular-season games last year. Patrick Mahomes, Deshaun Watson, Lamar Jackson, Dak Prescott etc. … none of them can say that. –*Pisapia*

Daniel Jones, NYG: Jones didn't play one game when all of Saquon Barkley, Evan Engram, Golden Tate, Darius Slayton and Sterling Shepard were healthy or not suspended last season. The Giants improved the offensive line, and Jones had 24 passing TDs and 2 rushing TDs in 13 games. He will have to cut down on the turnovers after 12 interceptions and 11 lost fumbles last season, but he elevates his floor since he can run. He had 279 rushing yards on 45 carries last season. *--Ronis*

Gardner Minshew II, JAC: I want quarterbacks who offer upside with their legs, and Minshew does just that. Minshew finished 6th in carries, 5th in carries per game, 5th in rushing yards, and 11th in rushing attempts in the red zone, but never got in the end zone. The Jags will be bad, meaning he will be in a lot of pass-heavy situations, and he isn't scared to use his wheels. *--Crist*

Tyrod Taylor, LAC: Get the 2018 Browns version of Taylor out of your mind. Think way back to 2015-2017 when Taylor was starting full seasons with the Bills, rushing for 500+ yards per season with 4-6 rushing touchdowns, combined with his passing production. That's who's underrated here. He's surrounded by the best weapons he's ever had in his career on a revamped Chargers offense and, yet again, has a fresh chance at being his team's starter all year. You want this Los Angeles version of Taylor in your mind, especially if you like to wait on QBs in your draft. *--Franciscovich*

Joe Burrow, CIN: The rookie guy is back on track to hype up a rookie again! Burrow is coming off the most accurate season for a QB in college football history, throwing 60 TDs over his 15 games last year. Burrow also walks into a pretty damn solid receiving corps with A.J. Green, Tyler Boyd, John Ross, rookie Tee Higgins and RB Joe Mixon. The Bengals defense is still going to be working out the kinks so the offense might be forced to play catch-up a lot. Burrow is a QB2 with a high ceiling. *--Bogman*

Baker Mayfield, CLE: Admittedly, I am not Mayfield's biggest fan, but I know value when I see it. Too much was expected out of that offense in 2019. Things just don't click right away when you stockpile on talent. It's time for this offense to gel. It will be Mayfield's 3rd season, but 2nd second year with guys like Odell Beckham Jr. and Kareem Hunt. He'll add one of the few "elite" options at tight end in Austin Hooper. This offense is looking scary (for real this time) especially with a full season of Hunt as a pass-catching RB. *--Hamilton*

Matthew Stafford, DET: Stafford is quietly coming off one of the best seasons of his career. Last year, Darrell Bevell's offense fit Stafford's strength to a tee, dialing up play-action and deep passing. With Stafford's downfield weapons intact, he possesses top-5 upside at the position that will fall yet again to the later rounds. *--Brown*

Baker Mayfield, CLE: I think we all nailed Mayfield as an easy pass and one of the most overrated QB's last season, when he was getting drafted as a top-5 QB. What a difference a year makes; he's going outside the top 12 in 2020. Everyone was in on the Browns. Now, it seems most are out, despite a solid coaching hire in Kevin Stefanski, a full upcoming season with Kareem Hunt, and a strong addition in TE Austin Hooper. Mayfield failed to throw more than one TD pass (7 total) in his first 8 games, during which he averaged 12 fantasy points per game. However, in his final 8 contests, he tossed 15 and averaged 17 fantasy points per game, flashing a bit of that upside. It's not a coincidence his numbers started to get better when Hunt was activated. *--Meaney*

Matthew Stafford, DET: Stafford is coming off a career season, and unfortunately one that ended his streak of 136 consecutive starts. He was placed on injured reserve in December after sustaining back fractures, but not before balling out. Stafford ranked 4th among QBs in fantasy points per game in 2019 while producing a career-high 8.6 yards per pass attempt and a touchdown rate of 6.5%. His surrounding cast only continues to improve, which gives him a genuine shot of being your most undervalued quarterback in 2020 drafts. --*Magdziuk*

Daniel Jones, NYG: With a revamped offensive line, one of the best stables of weapons in the NFL and Eli Manning no longer being in the locker room breathing down his neck, Jones knows this is his team now and he's the leader. He's got a higher floor than most due to his great ability when he takes off to run and he flashed over and over again in 2019. If his weapons stay healthy, Jones is going to be on the QB1 radar in 2020, and at his likely ADP, I want all the shares I can get. --*McConnell*

Joe Burrow, CIN: I won't often draft a rookie quarterback, but if you're looking for someone who you can platoon, Burrow is going to be a fantasy factor in 2020. He's walking into a situation where he'll be throwing to A.J. Green, Tyler Boyd, John Ross, Tee Higgins, Auden Tate, and Joe Mixon. He's also going to be getting last year's 1st-round pick Jonah Williams to protect his blind side. Yes, Burrow has a great arm, but he can also use his legs, which is something you want when looking for a potentially underrated late-round quarterback. –*Tagliere*

Tyrod Taylor, LAC: No, this isn't only for Superflex leagues; I'm drafting Taylor to be my QB1. He was a QB1, after all, with no weapons in Buffalo, outscoring all but 5 other quarterbacks per game. Now, he has Keenan Allen, Austin Ekeler, Mike Williams and Hunter Henry at his disposal, plus all the free fantasy points he'll compile from rushing. Most importantly, though, every single one of his first 9 matchups are streamer-worthy. --*Sylvester*

RUNNING BACKS

Kenyan Drake, ARI: I spent the last few years screaming into the abyss about how good Drake was and could be. Finally, last year, the devil got his due. From Week 9 onward, he was fantasy's RB4. This Cardinals offense is going to give opposing defenses fits, and Drake is going to earn the respect of the fantasy community. --*Pisapia*

Tevin Coleman, SF: Coleman had 22 carries for 105 yards with 2 touchdowns in the Divisional round against the Vikings and hurt his shoulder in the NFC Championship game. While Raheem Mostert was more efficient, Coleman will still get touches and is the cheaper of the pair. With Matt Breida gone, Coleman could be more involved in the passing game, pending the status of Jerick McKinnon. The 49ers were 3rd in rush percentage, run often in the red zone, and added left tackle Trent Williams. This is a run game to invest in with the value backs. --*Ronis*

Clyde Edwards-Helaire, KC: I know he isn't cheap, but he is the latest back in the draft who has a real shot to be a top-3fantasy asset. Andy Reid hadn't taken a back in the 1st round in his previous 22 years and compared him to Brian Westbrook, who had 87 targets in 4 straight years under Reid. 1st-round backs get on the field, and this is football's best offense. When Damien Williams has played 60% or more of the snaps for the Chiefs, he's averaged 25.3 PPR points per game. That's what Edwards-Helaire is walking into. --*Crist*

Austin Ekeler, LAC: Ekeler is the epitome of a stud fantasy running back. Last year, he gathered 993 receiving yards, as he soaked up 108 targets for 92 catches and 8 receiving TDs. Ekeler also rushed 132 times for 557 yards and 3 scores. He finished as the RB4 overall in PPR scoring and averaged 19.3 FPPG -- more than Saquon Barkley and Alvin Kamara. The dude is literally a league-winner, and he's going as the RB18 according to some early ADP data. Don't let him fall down draft boards. --*Franciscovich*

Derrius Guice, WAS: I know some people are going to roll their eyes and move on from this one, and I can't really blame them. Guice has only played 5 games over his 1st 2 NFL seasons with multiple knee injuries. Guice didn't miss a game in college, though, and while Rivera has said that he predicts all RBs to have a role this season … if Guice outperforms old man Adrian Peterson and Bryce Love, he could see a significant amount of touches (see

Christian McCaffrey). Guice didn't qualify to be ranked in PFF grades, but he would have been 15th overall and 7th in pass blocking among RBs. Take a chance on him as your RB3/4. --*Bogman*

Kareem Hunt, CLE: Fewer than 2.3 fantasy points (.5 PPR) separated Nick Chubb and Hunt in 5 of the 8 games Hunt played in 2019. The total fantasy points in those 8 games for each player? Chubb 98.3., Hunt 82.9. Although Hunt is in a backfield with another stud RB, he still provides a ton of value in fantasy. Especially in PPR. Now, there are talks of Hunt being used in the slot for 2020 ... [insert fire emoji]! --*Hamilton*

David Montgomery, CHI: Montgomery finished last year with the 12th-most touches among RBs. If volume is king, Montgomery will be one of the most overlooked sources of it after he burned fantasy investors last year. Montgomery will challenge for 300 touches in 2020 with zero competition for early-down work. --*Brown*

Phillip Lindsay, DEN: A lot of the underrated RBs (James Conner, Raheem Mostert & Clyde Edwards-Helaire) have been touched on by this great crew, so I'll go off the board here with Lindsay, who is getting drafted in the 8th round. I think that's fantastic value for a back who has hit the 1,000-yard mark in each of his first two seasons. Melvin Gordon will take some touches away, likely in the passing game and on the goal line, but Gordon has been underwhelming of late. He has 1 full season on his resume and 1 year in which he topped 3.9 YPC (4.0 for his career). Lindsay has a 4.9 Y/A average over his first 2 seasons and was extremely productive again last season; I think it's easy to overlook him with the addition of Gordon. Heck, we and the entire football world have been overlooking Lindsay. James White and Tarik Cohen are getting drafted ahead of Lindsay -- seriously? He'll make for a great depth piece, and we already know he has RB2 upside should something happen to Gordon. There aren't too many backs going outside the position's top 35 with that kind of upside. --*Meaney*

Raheem Mostert, SF: Mostert tied with Tevin Coleman for 137 attempts in 2019, yet somehow managed to gain 228 more yards. He was the picture of efficiency within Kyle Shanahan's zone scheme, leading the 49ers RBs in avoided tackles, yards after contact, rushing touchdowns, and tackles avoided. Former teammate Matt Breida was traded to the Dolphins during the draft, leaving 142 touches to the rest for the taking. Though there's bound to be some rotation in the backfield, Mostert carries favor with the coaching staff and proved himself to be their most efficient asset. He is an RB2 with weekly RB1 upside. –*Magdziuk*

James Conner, PIT: I'm not buying a single word of the coach-speak that Benny Snell will be heavily involved or Anthony McFarland could take the starting job. Let's get down to brass tacks here: What's not to like about a 25-year-old workhorse RB who has performed at the highest level and is also getting Ben Roethlisberger back under center in what will be an excellent offense? Oh, you're worried about injuries? Guess what? He's a running back. RBs get hurt. It's the riskiest position in all of football. Worry about injuries with ALL RBs. Conner was fantasy's RB6 in 2018 while not even having 1,000 rushing yards, but that was mainly because he was too busy adding receiving stats to your fantasy box score. If I can get an elite RB1 season out of a guy at his price point? I'll buy low on Conner and sleep like a toddler. --*McConnell*

Kenyan Drake, ARI: It's crazy to see Drake not getting the respect he deserved when he performed the way he did under Kliff Kingsbury last year. Since coming over in Week 9, he was the No. 4 running back through the remainder of the fantasy season, and the Cardinals liked him enough to move on from David Johnson and not draft a running back until the 7th round. I might draft him over someone like Derrick Henry, especially in a PPR format. --*Tagliere*

Raheem Mostert, SF: After being handed the starting job in Kyle Shanahan's magical offense, Mostert went for 792 yards and 15 TDs in just 8 games. Folks, that pace would have made him a full 65 points above the next best RB not named Christian McCaffrey. Mostert is going as an RB3, friends. You know what to do. –*Sylvester*

WIDE RECEIVERS

A.J. Green, CIN: I love when people have short-term memory loss. Green sat out a whole season, and he was rewarded with Joe Burrow. Green isn't "elite" at this stage of his career, but he's capable of plenty of WR1 games in 2020. There will be a cloud of negativity attached to his ADP, and the farther he falls, the safer he becomes to acquire. --*Pisapia*

Marvin Jones, DET: Jones had 42 catches for 535 yards and 6 touchdowns in 8 games with Matthew Stafford last season. Jones has scored 9 touchdowns in 2 of the last 3 seasons and was on pace for 9 last year before getting hurt. Jones has been a top-30 WR in points per game for the last 3 years. --*Ronis*

Terry McLaurin, WAS: McLaurin caught 32.7% of Washington's total passing yards in games he played. He was extremely efficient as a rookie and has next to no competition for targets. The Redskins offense is pedestrian at best, but "F1 McLaurin" is going to be fed and will be up in at the top of the leaderboard in target and market share among receivers. --*Crist*

DeVante Parker, MIA: The arrival of rookie QB Tua Tagovailoa in Miami should lift the production of the entire offense. But for some reason, Parker, his projected No. 1 wideout, is being drafted in Round 7, which is absolutely criminal. Bet you didn't know that in his last 8 games of 2019, Parker ranked 2nd among all NFL receivers in PPR fantasy points behind only Michael Thomas. --*Franciscovich*

Courtland Sutton, DEN: AGAIN! I went with Sutton last year, and I'm going to go back to the well this season. Sutton finished 19th in total PPR points last year. That was with 3 different QBs, and they traded Emmanuel Sanders after 7 weeks, leaving Sutton to get doubled up. This year, Denver will have Drew Lock going into his 2nd season, 1st-round rookie Jerry Jeudy, 3rd-round rookie K.J. Hamler, TE Noah Fant going into his 2nd season, and free-agent arrival Melvin Gordon. I don't know that Sutton gets all the way to a WR1, but I bet he nudges right up against that tier. --*Bogman*

D.K. Metcalf, SEA: Last year, Metcalf finished the season with just 157 receiving yards fewer than his teammate -- and WR1 in the offense -- Tyler Lockett. He had 7 TDs, to Lockett's 8. Metcalf was able to accomplish this production with 24 fewer receptions than Lockett. Not to mention last year was Metcalf's rookie season! Metcalf has plenty of room to improve as an NFL wideout, and I believe he'll take a big step in the right direction. -- *Hamilton*

Robert Woods, LAR: Woods is a quiet volume monster with the 7th-most targets among wide receivers over the last two years (269). Woods will again be overlooked despite 3 consecutive seasons of top-20 per-game WR production in fantasy points (PPR). Over the last 3 years among wide receivers that played 8 or more games, Woods was the WR18, WR16, and WR13 in that metric. --*Brown*

Marvin Jones, DET: There's a ton of value at WR this season, but I'm locking in Jones. Quarterback Matthew Stafford has a decent price tag, as well, and Jones is his 2nd-favorite target -- though it's close, as Jones averaged 7.1 targets last season (31st among WR), and Kenny Golladay averaged 7.2. Marv has a team-high 23 touchdowns in his last 3 years with Detroit. --*Meaney*

Diontae Johnson, PIT: Johnson's rookie season was plagued with poor quarterback play, yet he still managed to shine. He led 2019 rookies with 59 receptions and outperformed studs like Marquise Brown, D.K. Metcalf, Darius Slayton and Terry McLaurin in yards after catch per reception. Quarterbacks Mason Rudolph and Devlin Hodges ranked 25th and 30th, respectively, in terms of average depth of target, but he was able to produce with smooth routes and elusiveness. With a healthy Ben Roethlisberger, Johnson has a real shot at finishing as a fantasy WR2 in 2020. --*Magdziuk*

A.J. Green, CIN: Oh look, another player scaring fantasy drafters because of past injuries. Green is back and is as healthy as ever. He has the best QB prospect since Andrew Luck throwing him the football, and by the looks of what he's done with Andy Dalton in the past … yeah, Green is going to be just fine. He's coming at a dirt-cheap price for someone of his caliber. If you pass on nabbing a potential fantasy WR1 at his price, you're just not playing smart fantasy football. The reward greatly outweighs the risk. --*McConnell*

A.J. Green, CIN: When I saw Green was going outside the top 25 receivers, I thought I'd missed something about an offseason injury. Since coming into the NFL, Green has posted WR2 or better numbers in 59.1% of his games, a number that has only been topped by 4 others. Those players are Michael Thomas, Julio Jones, Antonio Brown and Odell Beckham Jr. If Green plays all 16 games, he'll finish as a top-12 wide receiver. There's risk, sure, but the reward is well worth it. –*Tagliere*

A.J. Green, Bengals: I was astonished when I saw just how low most others were ranking Green. Sure, he has more injury risk than the next guy, but we are talking about someone who has been a WR1 in fantasy points per game all 8 years of his career. Now he has the best QB in his career in rookie Joe Burrow, and everyone suddenly expects him to drop down to a WR3? C'mon! --*Sylvester*

TIGHT ENDS

Noah Fant, DEN: Young QBs tend to check down and favor TEs early in their career. Fant caught 12 of the 14 targets he saw in the final few weeks of 2019 after Drew Lock took over. Fant is flying completely under the radar and will be a decent late target should you miss out on the top TEs. --*Pisapia*

Hayden Hurst, ATL: Hurst will take over for Austin Hooper, and it's a great spot. The Falcons led the NFL in pass attempts last season, and Hurst will get a lot of favorable matchups with Julio Jones and Calvin Ridley getting so much attention. Falcons offensive coordinator Dirk Koetter tends to use his tight ends heavily. -*Ronis*

Blake Jarwin, DAL: Tight end becomes a wasteland in a hurry. If you miss out on the top 5 guys, you likely want to wait till the end of drafts and grab a few dart throws. The athletic Jarwin spent 39% of his snaps in the slot last year and averaged 8.9 yards per target. With Witten gone, he steps into a full-time role and has TE1 upside at a TE2 cost. --*Crist*

Eric Ebron, PIT: Ebron popped for 13 TDs back in 2018. Last year, however, his season was marred by a nagging ankle injury, and he only appeared in 11 games, starting just 3. He's due for a bounceback with his new team, and honestly, I would not be shocked if Ebron sees somewhere around 100 targets with the Steelers, as the team has yet to replace the target volume left behind when Antonio Brown departed two seasons ago. --*Franciscovich*

T.J. Hockenson, DET: 2019 was a tough year all the way around for Hockenson. Over the first 4 weeks, he as on a pace to finish as the No. 8 TE, but Matthew Stafford broke down, and then shoulder and knee injuries slowed Hock down; he played through them and finished as the No. 31 overall and 27th in per-game average. TEs usually take a little bit to get rolling going from college to the NFL, but Hockenson has a TON of upside, and he and Stafford are coming into the season healthy and ready to rock. Hockenson provides TE1 upside you can snag at the end of the draft. --*Bogman*

Jack Doyle, IND: Doyle has two things in his favor for the 2020 season. First, he no longer has Eric Ebron to steal the show and vulture TDs. Second, he will not be catching passes from Jacoby Brissett. Philip Rivers steps in under center. Historically, Rivers loves to target his pass-catching backs and, more importantly, tight ends. This 2020 Colts offense is expected to score more than it did in 2019, and that bodes well for the No. 1 tight end on the roster. --*Hamilton*

Mike Gesicki, MIA: Gesicki is a slot receiver masquerading as a tight end. Last year, Gesicki lined up in the slot on nearly 70% of his snaps. With the Dolphins adding zero pass-catchers early in the draft, Gesicki is locked into a sizable target share with a coordinator (Chan Gailey) who has fed the slot in previous stops (hello, Eric Decker and Quincy Enunwa). --*Brown*

Hayden Hurst, ATL: Hurst is getting drafted as a Top 12 TE in NFC leagues, but he won't get selected as one in your average home league. Matt Ryan's 616 passing attempts in 2019 were the third-most in the league, and his 41 attempts per game led all QB's. He finished third in attempts in 2018 as a well, and Atltanta still has some major holes on defense. Plus, Austin Hooper and his 185 targets over the last two years are gone. Hurst may not hit the 70 plus catch mark like Hooper did in each of his last two seasons, but he'll double the 30 he received last season in Baltimore as the third TE. He'll also get some soft coverage with most of the attention going to Julio Jones and Calvin Ridley. --*Meaney*

Tyler Higbee, LAR: My friend Chris McConnell just gave you the case against Higbee, but I'll agree to disagree. Though he wasn't as prolific with another TE there to siphon targets, Higbee smashed once teammate Gerald Everett went down with a knee injury in Week 12. After being cleared from the injury report, Everett accumulated 4 offensive snaps in the next 2 games; it was The Higbee Show. Higbee finished as the TE1 in Weeks 13-17, over which he saw his greatest shares of offensive snaps, and he'll only have more opportunities with the departures of Brandin Cooks and Todd Gurley. --*Magdziuk*

Hayden Hurst, ATL: While Hurst hasn't yet proven himself, he's stepping into a phenomenal situation in Atlanta where the TE is heavily utilized. We saw what Austin Hooper did in 2019, breaking out and being fantasy's TE1 for a portion of the season; Hurst could easily do the same. After all, he's a bigger, faster version of Hooper and is no longer stuck in Baltimore's 3-man rotation at TE with Mark Andrews and Nick Boyle. The position is all his, and he'll have an abundance of targets. --*McConnell*

Hayden Hurst, ATL: Opportunity means everything to a tight end, and Hurst will walk into plenty of it. The Falcons have used their tight end quite heavily over the last couple years, and they really didn't replace Mohamed Sanu. Instead of trying to re-sign Austin Hooper, they decided it'd be better to trade a 2nd-round pick for Hurst, showing just how much they valued him. Don't think he's not talented just because he played behind Mark Andrews. He should see 80+ targets in 2020 en route to a top-12 TE finish. --*Tagliere*

Austin Hooper, CLE: I get it. Hooper is splitting targets with Odell Beckham Jr., Jarvis Landry and Kareem Hunt now, but he wasn't he just splitting targets with Julio Jones, Calvin Ridley, Mohamed Sanu and Devonta Freeman? Before his injury, Hooper was the No. 1 fantasy tight end through 9 weeks! Cleveland paid him as though they, too, will make him a priority in the offense. --*Sylvester*

Chapter 13
TEAM PREVIEWS

AFC EAST
Matt Franciscovich

BUFFALO BILLS

Key Losses: RB Frank Gore

Key Additions: WR Stefon Diggs

Gore's exit may not seem significant, but the old man logged 166 carries a season ago. That's significant volume that will be up for grabs this year. Buffalo also traded for a true No. 1 wideout in Diggs, giving QB Josh Allen a top-tier receiver to work with. Diggs will automatically be the team's WR1.

Drafted Players of Fantasy Note: RB Zack Moss, WR Gabriel Davis, QB Jake Fromm, WR Isaiah Hodgins

Buffalo clearly invested in offense depth during the draft, picking up 2 receivers, a running back and a quarterback. The one player who will likely have immediate fantasy impact is the 3rd-rounder Moss out of Utah. With Gore gone, Devin Singletary slots in as the team's RB1, but his diminutive size raises some concerns about workload and durability. Moss brings power and tackle-breaking abilities to the table, where Singletary is more of an elusive speed back. Those aforementioned 166 carries (and maybe more) vacated by Gore could easily fall into Moss' lap, making him an interesting late-round dart throw at RB.

Offensive Outlook: Allen is a matchup-based QB in fantasy, while his ability to extend plays and use his legs to gain additional yards on the ground provide a solid floor to fantasy rosters on a weekly basis. The aforementioned Diggs joins a Buffalo receiving corps with incumbent speedy deep threat John Brown and slot man Cole Beasley. The main fantasy concern with this receiving corps is the mediocre aerial production. Allen ranked 21st last season in pass attempts with 461, and a 58.8% completion rate, ranking him last among 32 QBs who threw 240+ attempts. Buffalo averaged a mediocre 200-ish pass yards per game in the regular season. Still, Diggs should see the majority of the team's targets, and he can produce solid WR2 numbers. Brown, who posted a 72-1060-6 line on 115 targets (WR19) a season ago as the team's No. 1, will likely see a dip in production. This isn't an offense that's going to produce 2 1,000-yard receivers.

Defensive Outlook: Heading into Week 17 last year, the Bills boasted the 2nd-ranked scoring defense (16.4 PPG allowed) and 3rd-ranked total defense (300.1 YPG allowed). The Bills defense remains a top-10 fantasy D/ST given its success the past few seasons -- coupled with the fact that they play some of the league's worst offenses in the NFL twice per season in the Jets and Dolphins. And with New England's outlook questionable as the team moves on from QB Tom Brady, they can add two more divisional games against a potentially lackluster opponent.

2020 Outlook: Buffalo has been trending upward for 2 straight years, and the team added much-needed offensive depth this offseason to balance out a strong defense. The Bills could easily take the AFC East, but once they get out of their division is where issues could arise in the playoffs. Buffalo will face some true tests in the regular season with matchups against both of last years' Super Bowl teams in the Chiefs and 49ers, among others. But the Bills should, at worst, repeat their 10-win campaign and could finally get an elusive playoff win.

MIAMI DOLPHINS

Key Losses: RB Mark Walton, RB Zach Zenner

Key Additions: RB Jordan Howard, RB Matt Breida

After Miami sent RB Kenyan Drake to the Cardinals midseason, the team pieced together a terrible excuse for a backfield between no-names like Mark Walton, Patrick Laird, Kalen Ballage and Myles Gaskin. Who? Yeah. Veteran QB Ryan Fitzpatrick ended up leading the Dolphins with 243 rushing yards. That's absolutely embarrassing. So the team added proven veterans Howard and Breida. The tandem will likely split the workload in 2020, with Howard specializing as an early-down and short-yardage guy, while Breida's versatility will work in passing situations.

Drafted Players of Fantasy Note: QB Tua Tagovailoa

With the 5th overall pick, Miami (finally?) got its QB of the future in Tagovailoa. The Alabama product has some health concerns (coming off hip surgery), so whether he'll start under center in Week 1 is yet to be determined. When healthy, the reliable and mobile QB offers accuracy from the pocket and on the run, with sound decision-making and athleticism. Tua should be a boon for the entire Miami offense from a season ago, and with veteran WR and RB support, he could thrive as a fantasy option.

Offensive Outlook: In addition to the upgrades at RB and QB, the Dolphins have brought back the key contributors in their receiving corps. DeVante Parker, Allen Hurns, Albert Wilson and Preston Williams -- along with TE Mike Gesicki -- offer options for the team's rookie signal-caller. Parker led the team last year with a 72-1,202-9 line, posting his first career 1,000-yard season (about time). In his last 8 games played, Parker ranked 2nd among all NFL WRs in PPR fantasy points behind only Michael Thomas. He has a strong case to be a top-15 WR in fantasy drafts given his production last year and the hype surrounding Tua's arrival, but initial draft rooms remain skeptical. Outside of Parker, none of the aforementioned receiving options posted more than 500 receiving yards in 2019, for various reasons. Gesicki ranked 2nd on the team in targets with 89 that he converted into a solid 570 yards and 5 touchdowns, all of which were scored in the final 6 weeks of the season. He should ride that momentum into 2020 and become a low-end TE1.

Defensive Outlook: Whatever the Dolphins rolled out last year wasn't an NFL defense. The unit ranked last or near last in total defense, scoring defense, passing defense, rushing defense, sacks, yards per play and turnover differential. It actually became a joke.

The unit will look drastically different in 2020; Miami went nuts re-signing and adding players to its defense in free agency (Byron Jones, Kyle Van Noy, Shaq Lawson, and Xavien Howard) and the draft (1st-round pick Noah Igbinoghene).

2020 Outlook: After last season, it's difficult to predict how this new-look Miami team will work out. But honestly, there's nowhere to go but up. Let's just agree to call whatever happened in Miami last year rock-bottom, on both sides of the ball. A 1st-round rookie QB in Tua should inject some much-needed energy into this team and its fanbase, and with the Patriots potentially dethroned, things could get interesting in the AFC East this season.

NEW ENGLAND PATRIOTS

Key Losses: QB Tom Brady

Key Additions: QB Brian Hoyer

Arguably the biggest news of the NFL offseason was the departure of Tom Brady, who signed with Tampa Bay in free agency. Following Brady's departure, New England displayed little to no urgency to acquire an actual starting-caliber QB in the offseason. In turn, the entire Patriots offense could be more stagnant than we've seen in literally 2 decades this season without some kind of boost under center.

Drafted Players of Fantasy Note: TE Devin Asiasi

New England traded up to get Asiasi. The UCLA product is likely to immediately slot into the No. 1 passing-down TE role but has work to do as a blocker, according to NFL Draft pundits. Still, without much competition at the position in New England, Asiasi is worth a look as a late-round option or streamer and could become a productive fantasy TE, no matter who winds up as the Patriots quarterback.

Offensive Outlook: Without a solid starting QB (it's between 24-year-old Jarrett Stidham and veteran journeyman Brian Hoyer, unless the team lands a free agent like Cam Newton), the Patriots offense could sink fantasy rosters, especially when it comes to the receiving corps (Julian Edelman, Mohamed Sanu, N'Keal Harry).

The running back room remains headed by early-down plodder Sony Michel and passing-down specialist James White. Rex Burkhead (seemingly always injured) is also lurking for touches, though second-year bruiser Damien Harris could get an extended look if the Pats decide to slow down their offensive pace. As is always the case with Patriots RBs in fantasy, it's a fool's game to predict which back will produce in a given week. However, if you're throwing darts in the middle-to-late rounds, they can make for solid bench stashes that you can plug-and-play in favorable matchups, though there looks to be far fewer of those on the schedule this season.

Defensive Outlook: The Patriots finished the 2019 campaign at or near the top in the league in total defense, scoring defense, passing defense, yards per play allowed and turnover differential. They also had one of the easiest schedules one could dream up for the first 8 weeks. However, 5 of New England's matchups through Week 11 of the 2020 season include 2019 playoff teams like Seattle, Kansas City, San Francisco, Baltimore and Houston.

With 3 key members of New England's front 7 leaving this offseason, the team was forced to focus on bulking up on defense. They grabbed a couple of rookie linebackers in the draft, and their top pick was used on DB Kyle Dugger. Veterans like Stephon Gilmore and Devin McCourty will also return as starting CBs. Safe to say, this defense just got a lot younger. Any way you look at it, however, New England's D will be taking a step back in 2020.

2020 Outlook: Without a solid starting QB and with potential holes in a retooled defense, the Patriots have a shaky 2020 outlook. Honestly, White might be the best fantasy player to pluck from the New England offense. It will be tough to rely on Michel, who got a lot of his production from goal-line situations the past couple of seasons. It's tough to say how Edelman will produce without Brady slinging to him, so even at his Round 8 ADP, he presents risk. Watch for Harris as you round out your bench.

NEW YORK JETS

Key Losses: WR Robby Anderson

Key Additions: RB Frank Gore, WR Breshad Perriman, WR Josh Doctson

With the loss of speedy Anderson in free agency, the Jets revamped their receiving corps, adding former 1st-round picks Perriman and Doctson to the mix. Perriman popped late last year, finishing with 3 straight 100+-yard games and 5 TDs in his 4 four outings (when Buccaneers teammates Mike Evans and Chris Godwin were out with injuries). Perriman should slot in as the Jets' No. 1 receiver, while Doctson's role remains up in the air. Veteran ironman Gore was added to the backfield for depth behind Le'Veon Bell, but it's tough to see him providing a ton of fantasy value outside a change-of-pace role. The now 37-year-old averaged just 3.6 yards per carry on 166 attempts last season in Buffalo.

Drafted Players of Fantasy Note: WR Denzel Mims, RB La'Mical Perine

Mims was drafted in the 2nd round and brings size (6'3", 207 lbs.), speed (4.38 40-yard dash), and impressive athleticism to a Jets offense needing a lift. He was also wildly productive at Baylor, racking up nearly 3,000 yards and 28 touchdowns over the last 3 seasons. Mims could easily plug in as the Jets' No. 2 receiver, and with 96 targets vacated by Anderson, there should be enough volume to go around. Perine was taken in Round 4. The Florida product was effective as both a runner and a receiver with the Gators, compiling 938 scrimmage yards on 172 touches in his final collegiate season. He'll have to fend off Gore and Trenton Cannon for snaps behind Bell, but his versatility could earn him more playing time sooner rather than later.

Offensive Outlook: New York's offense was a joke last year, ranking last or near last in the NFL in total offense, scoring, rushing, passing, third downs, sacks, big plays and yards per play. Big yikes.

Entering his 3rd season in the NFL, quarterback Sam Darnold clearly has room to improve. Last year, he posted just a single game with more than 2 touchdown passes and registered a 19:13 TD:INT. You might remember him "seeing ghosts" during a now infamous Week 7 game against the Patriots when he threw 4 picks. It was bad. Unfortunately, the rest of the Jets' skill-position production is in Darnold's hands. Bell will be the first Jets player off fantasy draft boards, but we saw how the Jets' lack of overall offensive production sunk Bell's fantasy value last year: 245 carries, 789 yards, and 3 TDs with a career-low 3.2 yards per carry, plus 461 receiving yards on 78 catches and 1 receiving touchdown. And with the additions of Gore and Perine, this could curse the fantasy world with a committee situation.

On the bright side, New York majorly retooled its offensive line in the offseason and added depth at WR in both free agency and the draft. We've yet to mention incumbent slot WR Jamison Crowder, who posted career highs across the board with New York last year (78-833-6) on a team-leading 122 targets. Between Crowder, Perriman, and Mims, Darnold at least has an improved set of weapons around him.

Defensive Outlook: The Jets' rushing defense finished last year as the 2nd-ranked run D in the NFL. Shocking, I know. The team allowed just 3.3 yards per carry to opposing teams all season. But that was really the only bright spot. Still, the unit has potential. It's fronted by All-Pro DB Jamal Adams, as long as he's not traded. Defensive coordinator Gregg Williams is entering his 2nd year with the team and should have more flexibility to impose his coaching style with some of his guys, which should be an upgrade over last year. The Jets don't exactly have a favorable schedule on paper to start the year, though, facing the Bills, 49ers and Colts to start.

2020 Outlook: Improvements in the receiving corps, newfound RB depth, and a defense on the rise should lead to a more successful season. Lest we forget, Darnold missed a good chunk of the beginning of last year, as he was out with mono. If he can hit the ground running with a fresh set of weapons, we might see the Jets truly take off.

AFC NORTH

Nate Hamilton

BALTIMORE RAVENS

Key Losses: TE Hayden Hurst

Key Additions: None

The Ravens were quiet from a fantasy standpoint in offseason moves. Why wouldn't they be? They have an amazing team that made it to the playoffs under the leadership of Lamar Jackson. It was Jackson's 1st full season as the starting QB, and we've only begun to see the potential of this offense.

Hurst isn't really a key loss; however, the Ravens were able to use the pick involved in trading Hurst to draft J.K. Dobbins.

Drafted Players of Fantasy Note: RB J.K. Dobbins, WR Devin Duvernay

The Ravens decided to use their 2nd-round pick (acquired through the Hayden Hurst trade) to draft a running back. Mark Ingram will turn 31 this season, and although he was still productive for the Ravens in 2019, the team is getting younger. Dobbins should be more involved than Ingram owners would like to see in 2020, which deducts from the veteran's value a bit this year. Don't forget about Gus Edwards and Justice Hill.

Wide receivers don't typically produce enough to be super-fantasy-relevant in their rookie year, but Baltimore doesn't have much at the position outside of Marquise Brown that pushes the 3rd-rounder Duvernay down the depth chart. If you're looking for a late-round flier at WR, Duvernay could surprise many in this offense.

Offensive Outlook: The Ravens have a decent, young group of wideouts; a veteran leader at RB; one of the best backs from the 2020 draft, an elite tight end; and one of the most explosive, versatile QBs in the NFL. This team is scary for so many reasons. It's extremely difficult to plan against this offense thanks to Lamar Jackson. He can beat teams on the ground and through the air. As I said, this team is getting younger, which typically poses promise for the future, but that future could be as soon as 2020 with someone like Jackson leading your offense.

Defensive Outlook: The starters on this defense remained intact for the most part. The Ravens did make plenty of moves to their defensive line which further proves they are moving in the right direction. The only negative is that this defensive line could need some time before it gels, which doesn't bode well for the pace in which you want your offensive stars on the field. If this defense can click before the start of the season, the Ravens will find themselves in the hunt again this year.

2020 Outlook: The Ravens have the easiest "strength of schedule" in 2020 with their opponents combining for a .438 winning percentage last year. Of course, a lot can change from year to year, and it's difficult to determine how easy a team's schedule is based off data from the previous season. At the end of the day, I'm sure the Ravens will take any breaks they can get and be competitive regardless of the opposing team. Jackson and Co. are primed to provide us with another exciting season full of fantasy points.

CINCINNATI BENGALS

Key Losses: QB Andy Dalton

Key Additions: None

The writing was on the wall with the release of quarterback Andy Dalton. Once the Bengals drafted Joe Burrow, Dalton's time in Cincinnati ended shortly after.

Drafted Players of Fantasy Note: QB Joe Burrow, WR Tee Higgins

Burrow finds himself on the worst team in the NFL, which is often the case for the No. 1 overall pick. Expect growing pains in the first year, but he still has plenty of fantasy potential thanks to his surrounding weapons.

Higgins will likely be the 3rd or 4th look for Burrow in 2020 if the returning A.J. Green can stay healthy. I wouldn't expect much out of the 33rd overall pick for fantasy purposes this season -- unless of course, Green goes down; then he'll be a huge waiver-wire pick up.

Offensive Outlook: This offense has the least appeal in the AFC North. A rookie QB to begin the season with limited weapons and no one worth noting at the TE position. It will be interesting to see how much time these players will have together leading up to the season given the state our world is in. A rookie QB always adjustments and time, and I wouldn't expect anything else for the Bengals. There isn't much quality depth behind running back Joe Mixon -- assuming he doesn't hold out -- and if Green does go down, you're looking at Tyler Boyd and the 1st-year Higgins to carry the pass-catching load. I love most of these guys for dynasty, but in redraft, I'm fading most, if not all, Bengals.

Defensive Outlook: The Bengals were one of the worst defenses in 2019. They ranked last against the run and finished the year 24th overall. The Bengals addressed their needs in the draft and free agency. This defense will look starkly different than last year's unit, and defensive coordinator Lou Anarumo is hoping to change the culture in his second year as DC for the Bengals. If the Bengals defense can't keep games close, it's going to be another long season.

2020 Outlook: Picking Burrow could prove to be what this organization needed to compete in this division. The Bengals are likely to find themselves at the bottom of the AFC North in 2020, but that doesn't mean they are doomed forever. It's difficult and often unlikely to go worst-to-1st in an NFL division, but the Bengals have some life in them and are ready to move forward in the Burrow era. I'd expect Cincy to be trailing often, which will lead to fantasy production from this offense.

CLEVELAND BROWNS

Key Losses: None

Key Additions: TE Austin Hooper, QB Case Keenum

Baker Mayfield targeted the tight end position just 69 times in 2019, completing just 41 of those passes. His top TE in 2019 was Ricky Seals-Jones, who caught 14 passes on the season. The Browns would like to see an increase in production out of the position. They have signed Hooper to a 4-year, $42 million contract that includes a $10 million signing bonus and $23M guaranteed. It was the only offensive position (from a pass-catching perspective) that needed attention. Hooper provides Mayfield with a big-bodied target and could quickly become one of Mayfield's favorite targets in 2020.

It's a stretch to call Keenum a "key addition," but he does provide the Browns with a solid veteran backup quarterback. I don't expect the fantasy assets to see a major drop in production should Mayfield miss any time this year.

Drafted Players of Fantasy Note: OT Jedrick Wills Jr.

The Browns wasted no time to improve their O-line as they drafted the highly regarded Alabama lineman with the 10th overall pick. They desperately needed to protect their franchise QB and allow him more time to get the ball into the hands of his surrounding talent.

Offensive Outlook: The Browns are set to finally show everyone what we thought they were. Mayfield has a new toy at tight end, will have his second season with Odell Beckham Jr., an upgraded offensive line, and 1 of the NFL's best 1-2-punch backfields. It was proven that Nick Chubb and Kareem Hunt could be fantasy-relevant when they are both on the field, and we will get the chance to see it potentially for 16 games in 2020. If there is a year to buy the Browns as a true threat in the NFL, this is it. The Browns offense is the post-hype sleeper in 2020.

Defensive Outlook: Myles Garrett is a game-changer and the backbone of this defense. He applies so much pressure on the opposing quarterback, which leads to yardage loss, turnovers, and great field position for the Browns offense. The Browns also spent 3 of their top 4 draft picks on defensive players to beef up the talent around Garrett. They are finished being 1 of the laughing stocks in the league.

2020 Outlook: Mayfield will have to take a step forward in 2020 if we are to see the full potential of this offense. The organization has moved on from Freddie Kitchens. Kevin Stefanski, former Vikings offensive coordinator, has plenty of talent on this roster to make this squad a real contender in 2020. If the Browns can't succeed with this offense, the organization may need to blow up the team after the season.

PITTSBURGH STEELERS

Key Losses: None

Key Additions: TE Eric Ebron

Ben Roethlisberger will enjoy having another reliable vet to target in the red zone in 2020. Ebron is just one season removed from 750 receiving yards and 14 TDs. He was the No. 4 TE in .5 PPR formats with Andrew Luck at QB. Unfortunately, for Ebron, he had to catch passes from Jacoby Brissett in 2019. Big Ben is a major upgrade, which should lead to a bounce back year for the 27-year-old. Big Ben also looks like a great late-rounds value with his new receiving option.

Drafted Players of Fantasy Note: RB Anthony McFarland, WR Chase Claypool

The Steelers may not re-sign James Conner and/or JuJu Smith-Schuster after this season. Both are unrestricted free agents ahead of 2021. The Steelers only added fuel to that fire when they drafted McFarland and Claypool. I'd find it hard to see Roethlisberger not heavily target JuJu this upcoming season, but the Steelers certainly have plenty of talented pass-catchers on the roster should they decide to sample what it would be like without Smith-Schuster in the mix.

I believe Conner is more affected by this draft class than Smith-Schuster in 2020. The league is quickly trending in the "running backs don't matter" direction, and it appears the Steelers plan on dividing the backfield workload. Talent will often win out, but if there isn't a significant difference in production between Conner and the other RBs, we should expect to see more of a RBBC in Pittsburgh.

Offensive Outlook: There is a ton of fantasy goodness here for 2020. Diontae Johnson and James Washington are looking to feed off their momentum from 2019. Smith-Schuster is healthy, gained some muscle this offseason, and is playing for a new contract. Roethlisberger is back with some new weapons to utilize. The Steelers have a lot going on in this offense. They will not only provide fantasy rosters with plenty of value but should absolutely be in the "Super Bowl contender" conversation in 2020.

Defensive Outlook: With a full season of Minkah Fitzpatrick on the roster, the Steelers will likely be on the top of many defensive projections for 2020. It's almost unfair when you add T.J. Watt, Joe Haden, and Cameron Heyward to the list of talented defensive players on 1 team. If this defense can slow offenses, it may lend more importance to the Steelers' running backs.

2020 Outlook: Sadly, we must preface our sentences often with "if healthy," but this is the nature of today's game. So, if this core group of talented players (on both offensive and defensive sides) can stay healthy in 2020, there is no reason this team can't make a deep playoff run -- all after becoming one of the top fantasy-producing teams in the NFL.

AFC SOUTH

Chris Meaney

HOUSTON TEXANS

Key Losses: WR DeAndre Hopkins, RB Carlos Hyde, RB Lamar Miller, CB Johnathan Joseph

Key Additions: RB David Johnson, WR Brandin Cooks, WR Randall Cobb, DT Timmy Jernigan

You don't need me to tell you the loss of Hopkins is awful for QB Deshaun Watson. He'll get drafted as a top-5 QB, and he may be forced to use his legs more than the Texans would like. But there's a real chance he'll be alone out there at times, given the injury history of David Johnson, Cooks, Will Fuller and Keke Coutee. If healthy, Cooks could churn out his 5th 1,000-yard season in the last 6 years, but that's a big if. His cheap price tag is a result of his concussion history, just know you should proceed with caution. Cobb may end up being the most consistent wideout for Watson, but he'll be nothing more than a fantasy WR3.

As for D.J., health is a major issue. Johnson has a 3.6 YPC over his last 2 seasons on 352 attempts. I'd be surprised if he can rack up 1,000 yards on the ground like Hyde did last season, but you have to believe he'll be given a shot to do so. Hyde only finished as RB27 in a half-point PPR setting with as strong as he looked on the ground. Johnson's value lies in the passing game as he has at least 36 catches in four of his five seasons.

Drafted Fantasy Players of Note: WR Isaiah Coulter

Houston failed to get a first-round pick for Hopkins, and they traded their 2020 1st-rounder, and 2021 1st-rounder in the Laremy Tunsil trade, so they only had 5 picks in the draft. Coulter is the only skilled position player they came away with, and they rook him in the fifth. He could make good if an opportunity presented itself, given the uncertainty with Cooks and Fuller. Coulter could turn out to be one of Watson's favorite targets in the red zone.

Offensive Outlook: Now that Hopkins is out of the picture, a lot is riding on Watson's shoulders. He's finished as a top-5 QB in each of his past two seasons. He's also been linked to one of the best wideouts in the game. It's hard to imagine him surpassing the 26 TDs he's thrown in each of his last 2 seasons, but he may give owners an extra boost on the ground. Watson has 964 rushing yards and 12 rushing scores over his last 2 seasons. The Texans' offense has a boom-or-bust feel to it, and it makes me uneasy. One hit could sideline Cooks for good; Fuller has missed 22 games over his 4 years; and DJ is far removed from being considered an elite back.

Defensive Outlook: The Texans coughed up the 4th-most passing yards in 2019, and their PASS DVOA defense ranked 26th, according to Football Outsiders. They also surrendered the 8th-most rushing yards. Houston allowed the 4th-most fantasy points to QBs and the 6th-most to RBs. I'm not sure they'll improve on those rankings. J.J. Watt and Zach Cunningham are top-20 players in IDP formats, but Watt has only played 1 full season in his last 4 years.

2020 Outlook: Bill O'Brien has done a number on this team over the past few years, but they've made the playoffs in 4 of the last 5 seasons. The AFC South is completely up for grabs, and it shouldn't shock anyone if they win the division. Though the Texans' offense isn't appealing from a redraft standpoint, Houston has several options to consider for those who play in best-ball leagues or are looking for home-run lineups in DFS.

INDIANAPOLIS COLTS

Key Losses: TE Eric Ebron, WR Devin Funchess, WR Chester Rogers, WR Dontrelle Inman, QB Brian Hoyer, K Adam Vinatieri

Key Additions: QB Philip Rivers, TE Trey Burton, DT DeForest Buckner, CB Xavier Rhodes

Rivers' 4,615 passing yards (288 per game) in 2019 were the most he's thrown since 2015, but his 23 passing TDs were his fewest in a season since 2007. He also threw 20 interceptions, 1 shy of his career worst. Rivers and Frank Reich are very familiar with each other from their time together in San Diego, and I believe the former OC -- now head coach -- can get the most out of Rivers, to the point where the Colts compete for a division title. The 38-year-old will be well-protected behind a solid line, but he won't have the same weapons at his disposal in Indy as he had in Los Angeles. Don't expect much of an improvement on his QB18 fantasy finish from 2019, though, and you can feel better if he's your 3rd superflex QB.

Trey Burton reconnects with Reich, as well, and the 2 I'm sure will reminisce over the Philly Special, but there's really no appeal here from a fantasy standpoint. Eric Ebron and his 17 touchdowns over the last 2 seasons are gone, but Jack Doyle will quickly become one of Rivers' favorite targets.

Drafted Fantasy Players of Note: RB Jonathan Taylor, WR Michael Pittman Jr., WR Dezmon Patmon, QB Jacob Eason

Early reports suggest a "1-1 punch" at running back between Taylor and Marlon Mack. While I don't believe they are on the same page talent-wise, I do believe that's possible for the first couple months of the season. Don't let this chase you away from drafting Taylor, who is the far superior back. He doesn't have a lot of upside in the passing game, but he should control the bulk of the 1st-down carries and goal-line work. Taylor will be linked to a strong offensive line and offensive coach for years to come, making him appealing with the 2nd pick in rookie drafts. While Rivers has a history of checking down to the running back (see Austin Ekeler and Danny Woodhead), it's not a given that Nyheim Hines will play that role. He's the best pass-catcher of the three backs, but Mack hauled in 21 passes as a rookie.

Pittman can be that big-body wide receiver in the red zone, and he may end up in an even bigger role considering T.Y. Hilton missed 6 games last season and 2 the previous year. Eason is 3rd on the QB depth chart behind Jacoby Brissett.

Offensive Outlook: Only the Ravens, 49ers, Seahawks and Vikings ran the ball more than the Colts last season, and I can't see things changing much in 2020. If Rivers can take care of the football, the Colts will control the clock with their run game. They played at the 9th-slowest pace in neutral situations last season, according to FO.

Hilton's production (career-worst 50 YPG & 11.1 Y/R in 2019) and price tag continue to drop, but Rivers boosts his game. His fantasy WR2 days are likely finished, but if he's going to fall to the 7th round, consider it a worthy gamble. Parris Campbell is an underrated WR to consider.

Defensive Outlook: The Colts were friendly to fantasy QBs and WRs last season, but they were one of the better teams in the league when it came to stopping the run. They've finished outside the top 10 in sacks over the last two years, but they've been a top-15 fantasy defense in each of those seasons. They usually make for a decent streaming option, and that begins as early as Week 1 when they get the Jaguars. They also draw the Jets in Week 3. You may end up hanging on as they have Top 10 upside and they'll get overlook in drafts. Buckner is a huge addition on defense and Darius Leonard is the best IDP asset in the game.

2020 Outlook: The Colts offense looks much better heading into 2020 than it did in 2019. Turns out it's not easy replacing Andrew Luck. Indy has done a great job over the years of acquiring talented players on defense and has added capable pieces on offense through the draft this season. I'll call it a 1-2 punch, but I believe the run game will be strong. Taylor may be one of the better buy-low candidates after the first few weeks.

JACKSONVILLE JAGUARS

Key Losses: QB Nick Foles, DE Calais Campbell, CB A.J. Bouye

Key Additions: TE Tyler Eifert, RB Chris Thompson, LB Joe Schobert

There's not much to see here as the Jags continue to lose talented players on defense, though Schobert was a nice get, and he's a strong IDP target. Eifert hasn't been fantasy-relevant since 2015, but he did play in all 16 games last season. He's the TE1 on the depth chart, but Josh Oliver is a name you should get to know. Foles is gone. so Gardner Minshew has the keys for Week 1. He'll be looking to build on his QB19 fantasy finish as a rookie. (More below.)

The Thompson signing isn't a huge deal, but he'll rejoin former Washington head coach Jay Gruden, who was hired to be the new OC in Jacksonville. Thompson averaged 41 catches and 55 targets over his last 5 seasons with Gruden in Washington. It's important to note CT missed 20 games over those 5 years. Just something to keep in mind when projecting targets for Leonard Fournette; he may not repeat the 100 looks and 76 grabs he had last season.

Drafted Fantasy Players of Note: WR Laviska Shenault, WR Collin Johnson, QB Jake Luton, EDGE K'Lavon Chaisson, CB C.J. Henderson

Shenault has all the tools to succeed, and he could easily pass Chris Conley and Dede Westbrook in targets by the end of the season. There's still some inexperience in play QB, and neither Conley nor Westbrook were consistent enough to roster with confidence last season. Shenault has WR2 upside in dynasty formats, but he may be nothing more than a WR4/5 in Year 1. If you play in IDP leagues, Chaisson should be high on your dynasty radar. He could end up having a huge impact right away assuming Yannick Ngakoue gets his wish. Chaisson and Josh Allen form a young, explosive tandem at the edges for years to come. If he gets some snaps at linebacker, all the better for his redraft value. Henderson will get plenty of work in his 1st season and should be the first CB off the board in IDP rookie drafts.

Offensive Outlook: Minshew surprised many with his play when Foles went down, and he earned himself the right to be the opening-week starter in 2020. Don't ask me about 2021. The Jags played at the 3rd-slowest pace in neutral situations last season, and although they want to run the ball, their offensive line ranked 27th, according to Football Outsiders. It's a big reason why they only scored 3 rushing TDs. Jacksonville will be one of the worst teams in the league; the Jags will be battling from behind in a lot of their games this season. Don't be shocked if Minshew finishes in the top 12 in passing attempts and D.J. Chark repeats as a fantasy WR2.

Jacksonville doesn't plan on moving forward with Fournette after this year -- if at all. There's an opportunity for the Jags to give him as many touches as he can handle, but health and off-the-field issues remain areas of concern. I expect some positive regression when it comes to his touchdowns, but the Jags will remain one of the NFL's lowest-scoring teams. It's a risk that could pay off if you're looking for a volume back in the 4th round, though.

Defensive Outlook: Jacksonville ranked 31st in RUSH DVOA as they allowed the 5th-most rushing yards per game (139) in 2019. They coughed up the 2nd-most fantasy points to running backs, and you can expect teams to attack them on the ground again om 2020. Jalen Ramsey's departure was a big reason the Jags' overall defense finished 29th.

2020 Outlook: The Jaguars are obviously in rebuild mode, which didn't take long considering they are 3 years removed from having the league's best defense. If you remember, they were 1 half away from beating the New England Patriots and heading to the Super Bowl in 2017. A lot has changed since then, including a number of key players lost on defense. Take the under on the win total.

TENNESSEE TITANS

Key Losses: T Jack Conklin, RB Dion Lewis, QB Marcus Mariota

Key Additions: TE Delanie Walker, CB Logan Ryan, CB Johnathan Joseph, EDGE Vic Beasley

Conklin is clearly the biggest loss, but as you'll see below, the Titans addressed his departure through the draft. They also replaced depth pieces like Lewis and Mariota.

Drafted Fantasy Players of Note: T Isaiah Wilson, RB Darrynton Evans, CB Kristian Fulton, QB Cole McDonald

Evans fills the Lewis role, which consisted of 79 touches (25 catches) last season. Evans caught 21 balls, and 5 of his 23 touchdowns in 2019 at Appalachian State came through the air. Let's make one thing clear, though: This is Derrick Henry's backfield.

Fulton is a solid-looking corner out of LSU to help replace the loss of Ryan.

Offensive Outlook: There are so many question marks with teams. What will they do on offense? Will they run more? Will they pass more? Up-tempo? The Titans know exactly what they want to do on offense: Run the football with Henry. It's taken some people longer than they want to realize, but Henry is one of the safest players in fantasy. Believe it or not, people will overlook him in PPR leagues again, but he's seen an increase in catches in each of his past 3 seasons. He also doesn't need to catch more than 24 balls to flirt with RB1 overall. Consider selling high soon in dynasty leagues, but he has another 300 touches in him at a high level.

The run game clearly opened up the play-action pass for Ryan Tannehill and A.J. Brown. Tannehill is not getting the respect of a top-10 QB, which he was from the time he took over for the struggling Mariota. I'm not sure if it's because he only played 12 games last season, or people see the low passing attempts and expect regression from him and Brown, but Tannehill is not getting drafted as a QB1. There's really no doubt Tannehill will regress; his 9.6 YPA was the highest mark from a QB since Kurt Warner's 9.9 Y/A with the Rams back in 2000. That kind of production is not repeatable. He does have a sneaky rushing ability, though, which makes him a solid QB2 in superflex leagues. As for Brown, he'll have some inconsistent games, but he's the No. 1 option in the passing game, and he'll win you weeks with his big-play ability. Shoutout to Jonnu Smith, who has the ability to emerge as a TE1.

Defensive Outlook: The Titans allowed the 9th-most passing yards per game last season but ranked 9th-best against the run. They were a top-12 fantasy D, finishing 13th in sacks and 9th in interceptions. Tennessee's best IDP player is linebacker Jayon Brown.

2020 Outlook: The Titans placed the franchise tag on Henry and extended Tannehill to a 4-year, $118 million contract. Tennessee will get overlooked again in the fantasy community and the betting landscape. This squad came away with playoff wins in New England and Baltimore last season, only to squander a 10-point lead against the Kansas City Chiefs in the AFC Championship Game. However, out of all the playoff teams last season, they are probably the least likely to repeat their success.

AFC WEST
Matt Franciscovich

DENVER BRONCOS

Key Losses: QB Joe Flacco, RB Devontae Booker

Key Additions: RB Melvin Gordon

It's not like Flacco was a difference-maker in fantasy football, but his exit from Denver mainly due to a neck injury leaves 2nd-year QB Drew Lock under center to start the year. In his 5 starts last season, Lock posted a 7:3 TD:INT ratio with 1,020 pass yards on 156 attempts and averaged a mediocre 13.6 FPPG. He's working with some young WR talent around him (2 potential rookie starters, see below), so don't count on a massive uptick in fantasy production. Denver landed Gordon in free agency, and the veteran projects to lead the Broncos backfield as the bell cow. Gordon held out until Week 5 to start last season, but he still managed 9 total touchdowns with the Chargers. He presents added value as a pass-catcher, having soaked up 55 targets last year.

Drafted Players of Fantasy Note: WR Jerry Jeudy, WR K.J. Hamler

With their 1st- and 2nd-round selections, the Broncos tried to fill a dire need for WR talent. The Alabama product Jeudy (6' 1", 193 lbs.) was one of the top receiver prospects in the class: He's drawn comparisons to Calvin Ridley and Stefon Diggs and projects as an immediate starter opposite Courtland Sutton. Penn State product alum Hamler is a smaller, quicker, slot specialist capable of big plays and should also slide into a starting role, given the squad's lack of veteran pass-catching talent.

Offensive Outlook: Denver's offense ranked near the bottom of the NFL last year in points per game (17.6) and yards per game (298.6). The Broncos actually scored the fewest passing touchdowns in the league -- just 16 for the season -- and the team's RB tandem was a frustrating (for fantasy purposes) 50-50 split between Phillip Lindsay and Royce Freeman.

Lindsay (224/1011/7) finished last year as fantasy's RB19, but all of his productive games were TD-dependent and difficult to predict due to the lack of overall offensive production and the 50/50 split with Freeman. But Gordon should put an end to all the uncertainty in this backfield, as he's likely to see at least 70% of the team's backfield snaps on a weekly basis.

Tight end Noah Fant struggled with consistency as a rookie, as young TEs usually do in the NFL. But he's an athletic freak who provides another outlet for Lock, especially in the red zone.

One true bright spot in Denver's offense on whom fantasy owners should be able to rely is Sutton. He was a low-key WR2 in 12-team leagues last season, finishing as the WR22 overall with a 72-1,112-6 line. His numbers should only improve as he builds chemistry with Lock and some of the defensive attention is focused on the new weapons.

Defensive Outlook: The Broncos defense is loaded with talent and could be in for a bounce-back year as a unit. Obviously All-Pro linebacker Von Miller is a household name at this point. And former 1st-round draft selection Bradley Chubb should be back healthy after tearing his ACL early last season. Pro-Bowler Kareem Jackson anchors the Denver secondary and will reunite with former Texan teammate A.J. Bouye. With newfound health and added support, the unit will look to build upon its top-ranked red-zone defense from last year and its pass defense that ranked 6th in the NFL.

2020 Outlook: Lock could, for lack of a better word, unlock the Broncos offense this season. The young QB will look to take a step forward with more talent -- albeit inexperienced talent -- around him. The backfield was a constant headache, but Gordon solves that. Other than the Chiefs' domination in the AFC West, there's no real clear expectations for the division standings. So with some youth on offense and some new support on defense, the Broncos could surprise a lot of fans, as long as they don't get out to an 0-4 start like they did last year.

KANSAS CITY CHIEFS

Key Losses: None

Key Additions: RB DeAndre Washington, RB Elijah McGuire

When the curtain closed on the NFL free-agency period, it became clear that the Super Bowl-champion Chiefs are looking to repeat. They're bringing back 20 of their 22 starters from 2019, so they haven't had significant movement that factors into fantasy football, save for a couple of running-back depth adds. In mid-May, the Chiefs had 6 RBs on the roster, not all of whom are going to make the team. But we'll break down one of the most fantasy-relevant additions at the position now.

Drafted Players of Fantasy Note: RB Clyde Edwards-Helaire

With the final pick of the 1st round of the NFL Draft, the Chiefs selected the dynamic Edwards-Helaire. The LSU product posted a 225-carry, 1,414-yard, 16-TD line on the ground and added 55/453/1 receiving last season. Widely considered the highest-rated receiving back in the 2020 class, Edwards-Helaire has drawn copious amounts of praise from the Chiefs front office and coaching staff. Though the rookie will have to earn his reps behind veteran Damien Williams, it he may not need much time to take over a 3-down role. Early ADP data already showed CEH as the RB35, but that was probably before it started skyrocketing after he was picked by KC. Either way, he should have immediate impact as the No. 2 option (at worst) in the most explosive offense in the NFL and could wind up as a weekly RB1 by the end of the 2020 season.

Offensive Outlook: The Super Bowl LIV champions have a handful of skill-position players who'll be hot commodities in fantasy football drafts, for obvious reasons. QB Patrick Mahomes changed the game when he became the team's starter 2 seasons ago. He's the glue that holds the high-octane scheme together and has generated one of the highest-scoring offenses in the NFL the last two seasons. Mahomes was the QB7 in fantasy last year, and he even missed a few games with injury. Mahomes still posted 28 total TDs (a far cry from his 52-TD campaign in 2018) with just 5 picks and 4,031 yards.

The main beneficiaries of Mahomes' magic under center are TE Travis Kelce, arguably the TE1 in fantasy football drafts (if not George Kittle), and WR Tyreek Hill. This pass-catching tandem combined for 12 TDs in 2019. Hill missed 4 regular-season games with injury, and his fantasy production can be highly volatile on a week-to-week basis, but he can still be drafted as a low-end WR1 with week-winning upside every Sunday. Kelce should be off draft boards within the first 2 rounds given his consistency. He stands as the fantasy TE1 for 2 straight seasons and has seen 97 and 103 targets the last two campaigns. That's some bankable fantasy value that you can set and forget, which is priceless at the TE position.

Defensive Outlook: The Chiefs defense wasn't particularly strong in any area overall last season, and given the amount of points the team puts up on offense, the defense didn't need to be a top unit in the NFL. But if you were paying attention, you'd know that the Kansas City defense locked up down the stretch, allowing just 9.6 points per game to opposing teams from Weeks 11-16. But the run defense was a major weak spot, and offseason reports point to the Chiefs focusing on improving there.

2020 Outlook: There's no arguing the sky-high potential of the Chiefs offense. The combination of coach Andy Reid's genius, Mahomes' magical ability under center, Hill's game-breaking speed, Kelce's unwavering consistency, and the aforementioned upgrades to the backfield make this offense virtually unstoppable. If the team can improve its run defense, one of last season's biggest flaws, there's no stopping another Super Bowl run.

LAS VEGAS RAIDERS

Key Losses: RB DeAndre Washington

Key Additions: QB Marcus Mariota, WR Nelson Agholor, TE Jason Witten, RB Devontae Booker

None of the listed key additions above project to be starters, except for maybe Agholor. Mariota was added for depth behind Derek Carr. Booker is buried on the depth chart. And Witten is just plain old. Don't go rushing to grab any of these guys for your fantasy squad. They're all waiver-wire fodder for now.

Drafted Players of Fantasy Note: WR Henry Ruggs III, WR Lynn Bowden Jr., WR Bryan Edwards

The Raiders took 3 wideouts in the draft, showing a clear need at the position. Ruggs was the team's 1st pick, at 12th overall, and the 1st WR off the board in the draft. He brings elite speed, having clocked a 4.27 40-yard dash at the combine. He should be an immediate starter and will have definite fantasy value. Bowden and Edwards were both 3rd-round selections. Edwards has some injury concerns, but his collegiate production at South Carolina was elite. Bowden was announced as a running back when the Raiders selected him, and he played QB at Kentucky for much the 2019 season. His skill set has been compared to that of Taysom Hill: a Swiss Army knife who will keep defenses guessing. Not quite sure how all of that will translate to fantasy production, so let's see how Bowden's role pans out before we go crazy for him on waivers.

Offensive Outlook: The Raiders averaged just 19.6 points per game (24th) and 363.7 yards per game (11th) last season. Then-rookie Josh Jacobs finished the year with a 242-1,150-7 line on the ground as fantasy's RB18. Early ADP data shows Jacobs as a top-10 option heading into the 2020 campaign, and that's tough to dispute. He's a straight-up workhorse.

Among a misfit group of receiving options, TE Darren Waller stood out, posting a 90-1,145-3 line last season. That low TD number is of most concern for fantasy purposes; Waller's production in PPR leagues was weekly starter material, but he failed to find the end zone from Week 9 through the end of the regular season. The team has added depth at WR to last year's decent duo of Tyrell Williams and Hunter Renfrow, so Waller might have more competition for targets. Still, Waller is a talent that can't be ignored by Carr, so he'll get his. Waller projects as a top-5 fantasy TE.

Defensive Outlook: The Raiders defense was pretty bad last year, to put it bluntly. The unit ranked bottom-3rd or worse in most significant categories, including red-zone defense, yards per play allowed, third downs, scoring and passing. But some offseason moves create room for optimism. The signing of LB Cory Littleton is a major upgrade to the linebacker room. The team also acquired Prince Amukamara to add some experience to a young cornerback room. And defensive tackle Maliek Collins was added to the interior and is set to make a name for himself.

2020 Outlook: Look, it's tough to have high hopes for the Raiders this year. They still seem to have a lack of depth on the offensive side and a ton of youth and inexperience on defense. The team doesn't have an easy schedule to start the year, either, with matchups against the Saints, Bills and Chiefs early on. The couple of players you want to target in fantasy drafts are Jacobs, Waller and, as a late flier, Ruggs. Don't mess around here otherwise.

LOS ANGELES CHARGERS

Key Losses: QB Philip Rivers, RB Melvin Gordon

Key Additions: CB Chris Harris

The Chargers are going to look a lot different on offense in 2020. Rivers landed in Indianapolis, and Gordon found his way to Denver in free agency. That leaves Tyrod Taylor as the team's starting quarterback (at least to start the season) and Austin Ekeler, whom the team re-signed to a lucrative 4-year deal as the lead running back. Taylor won't be as productive of a passer as Rivers; his style is more of a game manager than a gunslinger. But he can rack up fantasy points with his feet, so that adds value.

Drafted Players of Fantasy Note: QB Justin Herbert, LB Kenneth Murray, RB Joshua Kelley, WR K.J. Hill, WR Joe Reed

The Chargers took Oregon's Herbert with the 6th overall pick. They'll look to groom him as their QB of the future, but all signs point to this being Taylor's job to lose. Kelley could make waves with his speed and quickness, but he will have to work on his power running to become a reliable fantasy asset. Meanwhile, Reed projects as an asset in the red zone, while Hill profiles as more of a slot specialist.

Offensive Outlook: Taylor has arguably the best set of weapons at his disposal in his career, with support from WR1 Keenan Allen, TE1 Hunter Henry and RB1 Ekeler. That skill-position trio is one of the best in the NFL, and when you add in the big body of wideout Mike Williams and the youth the team snagged in the draft, there's depth and a great mix of size and speed. Los Angeles will look to improve upon its 32nd-ranked turnover differential from last season, and Taylor is a good candidate to help that mission. He could be a sneaky late-round grab at QB.

Defensive Outlook: The Chargers had a strong pass defense last year and ranked 6th in total defense. And the team added Chris Harris to lurk in the secondary with the beastly Derwin James. Defensive ends Melvin Ingram and Joey Bosa are weekly game-changers, and the team added Murray in the 2nd round, out of Oklahoma to the mix. This D/ST could be a fantasy gem, and with divisional foes like the Raiders and Broncos still finding their way, the Chargers defense has a chance to make waves.

2020 Outlook: While the Chargers lost some key veterans on offense (Rivers, Gordon), it was time for a revamp. Allen, Ekeler and Henry remains a stellar foundation, and the draftees paint a promising picture of the future. On paper, the Chargers' regular-season schedule doesn't look extremely difficult, save for a couple of matchups against the Chiefs and Saints in the 1st half of the year. With a new quarterback, stadium and uniforms, the Chargers should improve on last year's 5-11 finish.

NFC EAST

Chris Meaney & Chris McConnell

DALLAS COWBOYS

Key Losses: WR Randall Cobb, TE Jason Witten, C Travis Frederick, CB Byron Jones, DE Robert Quinn, DT Maliek Collins, HC Jason Garrett

Key Additions: QB Andy Dalton, K Greg Zuerlein, DT Gerald McCoy, S Ha Ha Clinton-Dix, DT Dontari Poe, CB Maurice Canady

The loss of Pro Bowl center Frederick to retirement is a big deal. The Cowboys jumped in front of the Bengals in the draft, via a trade with the Eagles of all teams, to replace Frederick with Tyler Biadasz, but he has some big shoes to fill. Ezekiel Elliott is a strong runner, but the offensive line takes a hit. Dallas lost a lot of players on defense, but they addressed some holes through the draft, and McCoy shores up the middle of the field. It took them long enough, but Dallas finally moved on from Jason Garrett, and incoming head coach Mike McCarthy gives them a much-needed new look.

Drafted Players of Fantasy Note: WR CeeDee Lamb, CB Trevon Diggs, OL Tyler Biadasz

I don't think many had the Cowboys taking Lamb with the 17th overall pick. Not that they wouldn't jump on the opportunity if he were there, because we all know how much Jerry Jones loves his toys, but the fact he was free for the taking was one of the most surprising takeaways of the draft. Lamb is an absolute stud, but it's a crowded receiving corps in Dallas. We should see a dip in targets for Elliott and Michael Gallup, but it's a win for the Cowboys and Dak Prescott, who finished as fantasy's QB2 in 2019.

Offensive Outlook: The Cowboys are loaded on offense, and they'll be one of the highest-scoring teams in the NFL this season. It may be hard to pinpoint which wide receiver will get theirs on any given Sunday, especially when you include TE Blake Jarwin in the mix. Amari Cooper has the highest ceiling, but he hasn't been the most consistent wideout over the years. Elliott may lose a few more targets, but he may also get a few more touches in the red zone. Don't overlook Zeke and the safety he brings owners. Prescott has a significant price tag, and it's warranted if you play in superflex leagues.

Defensive Outlook: Dallas' defense ranked 21st in fantasy points last season, and their 7 interceptions were tied for dead-last. In 2018, they finished 23rd in fantasy points and 27th in INTs. LBs Jaylon Smith and Leighton Vander Esch are top-10 assets in IDP.

2020 Outlook: Prescott threw 42 more passing yards per game at home last season than on the road, and his TD:INT disparity between games in Dallas and away contests over the past 2 years is noticeable (34:10 at home, 18:9 elsewhere). It's Dak's only question right now. Can he win the big road game? He'll have a lot to prove if he wants to get paid, and you better believe Dalton would be a fantasy QB1 in this offense should something happen to Prescott. The Cowboys are slight favorites over the Eagles for the division, which seems right, but it'll be a fight between them to top the weak NFC East. *--Meaney*

NEW YORK GIANTS

Key Losses: WR Cody Latimer

Key Additions: CB James Bradberry, LB Blake Martinez, OC Jason Garrett

OK, so Latimer may not count as a "key" loss, but it's one of the things to like about the Giants: They really don't have "key" losses. New York didn't say goodbye to any significant pieces on either side of the ball, so they didn't have to focus on filling any major holes.

As for Latimer, he's never been anything more than an end-of-the-active-roster player, and even while starting 10 games in 2019, he amassed only a career-high 300 yards. He won't be hard to replace.

The defense needed a boost, and boy, did New York get it. Bradberry comes over from the Panthers after signing a 3-year, $45 million deal. He has a ton of experience covering some of the best WRs in the NFL, including Michael Thomas, Julio Jones and Mike Evans. New York's 2019 1st-round pick DeAndre Baker is better slated as a CB2, so they should form a formidable duo and make life difficult for the likes of Amari Cooper, CeeDee Lamb, Alshon Jeffrey, DeSean Jackson and Terry McLaurin -- assuming Baker's offseason legal troubles are resolved.

Martinez signed a 3-year, $30 million deal after leaving the Packers. New York desperately needed a reliable second-level force on the inside. Garrett takes over as offensive coordinator after being dismissed as Dallas head coach. We've seen Garrett shine in this role before.

Drafted Players of Fantasy Note: LT Andrew Thomas, S Xavier McKinney, OT Matt Peart

The Giants took zero offensive skill position players, instead opting to bolster areas where they needed help. A certified beast out of Georgia, Thomas was their 1st-round selection and will be tasked with protecting Daniel Jones' blind side. McKinney helps strengthen a secondary that has been burned for years. 3rd-rounder Peart out of UConn joins Thomas on the OL, the Giants' biggest area of need for the last few years.

On paper, this team has the looks to be one of the more fun fantasy offenses. A revamped O-line means Jones should be in an even better position to take another step forward. I believe he becomes a fantasy QB1 in his sophomore season, and he has the weapons to do it, starting with RB Saquon Barkley, who will likely be the only player fighting Christian McCaffrey to be the No. 1 overall fantasy pick.

2019 5th-round sensation Darius Slayton could end up as the team's WR1, and he'll be joined by Golden Tate and Sterling Shepard at WR to give Jones a rock-solid, reliable big 3 at WR. While Slayton is the best fantasy bet among the talented trio, Tate and Shepard should have plenty of fantasy relevance as well.

Evan Engram's caveat is staying healthy, but if and when he's on the field, he'll yet again be in the fantasy TE1 mix.

Offensive Outlook: The key to this offense doing anything is going to be the offensive line. It's been revamped by adding two early-rounders and bringing in Cowboys castoff Cameron Fleming, who reunites with Garrett. The offense has no other glaring weakness, so as long as Jones is protected and has time to make decisions, an offense that ranked 23rd overall in 2019 should skyrocket up the league's ranks and become at least a top-15 unit in 2020.

Defensive Outlook: If the offensive line was the biggest problem for this year the last few years, the defense as a whole is a close second place. But that should improve two-fold in 2020 as long as everything comes together. Bradberry, Martinez and McKinney are high-quality additions to a defense that desperately needed all the help it could get. If this unit can improve from its bottom-8 finish last season, this will be a solid football team.

2020 Outlook: The Giants look like a good team on paper. With a new HC in Joe Judge, a new OC in Garrett and plenty of new faces on defense, they do have a lot of areas that need to come together this year to make the playoffs. My bold prediction for the season is that they do just that and clinch one of the NFC wild-card spots in what will be an expanded playoff field moving forward. More importantly than anything, however, Jones' progress under center will set the course for the season. --*McConnell*

PHILADELPHIA EAGLES

Key Losses: RB Jordan Howard, RB Darren Sproles, WR Nelson Agholor, S Malcolm Jenkins, T Jason Peters

Key Additions: CB Darius Slay, CB Nickell Robey-Coleman, DT Javon Hargrave

The biggest takeaway from the Eagles' offseason, besides shaping up the secondary, is that they've done nothing (yet) to replace Howard or Sproles. Will Doug Pederson lean on Miles Sanders? He's not known to ride a single back, but Pederson arguably hasn't had an RB as talented as Sanders. Boston Scott has earned the 3rd-down role, and Corey Clement was re-signed, but Sanders may have an opportunity to build off his fantasy RB15 rookie showing.

Drafted Players of Fantasy Note: WR Jalen Reagor, WR Quez Watkins, WR John Hightower, QB Jalen Hurts, S K'Von Wallace

Reagor gives the Eagles much-needed speed and youth at wide receiver. A 50-catch debut year feels like his ceiling, should everyone stay healthy. If not, we may see Watkins and Hightower do more work. Maybe the biggest shock of the draft came in the 2nd round, when Philadelphia selected Jalen Hurts. It's a high price to spend on a backup quarterback, but if any team knows how important it is to have a solid fallback plan under center, it's the Eagles. Wentz played in all 16 contests last season, but he hasn't had the best track record when it comes to health. Wentz owners in dynasty formats may want to think about spending a pick on Hurts.

Offensive Outlook: The offense finished 12th in points per game and 11th in passing yards last season, despite dealing with plenty of injuries. The offensive line ranked No. 1, according to Pro Football Focus. Jason Kelce, Lane Johnson, Brandon Brooks and Isaac Seumalo all graded among the top 10 at their respective positions.

Health always seems to play a big part with the Eagles. Wentz was finally healthy in 2019, but Alshon Jeffery and DeSean Jackson missed a combined 19 games. It didn't seem to faze Wentz, who became the first QB in NFL history to throw for 4,000 yards without a wideout registering 500 receiving yards. He'll be fine regardless of what Jeffery and Jackson have left to offer, and the Eagles did a great job of surrounding Wentz with playmakers at the draft. TE Dallas Goedert will take another step forward, but Zach Ertz will remain Wentz's favorite target.

Defensive Outlook: As noted above, the Eagles revamped their secondary with the additions of Slay and Robey-Coleman. Philly allowed the third-fewest rushing yards last season and ranked fourth in RUSH DVOA. This trend will continue in 2020. For years, though, they've slotted among the worst teams for allowing fantasy points to wideouts. That may finally change with some of the additions. As bad as the defensive backs have been, Philly has always been a decent fantasy defense; the Eagles get after the quarterback and have playmakers. The Eagles are the perfect streaming defense to draft in the last round: They get Washington for Week 1.

2020 Outlook: The million-dollar question fantasy owners want answered, when it comes to the Eagles, is will Pederson finally allow one of his backs to flirt with 300 touches? That back would be Sanders. Only he and Christian McCaffrey finished 2019 with at least 800 rushing yards, 500 receiving yards, 50 catches and a 4.6 YPC. Sanders averaged 19 touches in the final 8 games of the season without Howard in the lineup, and they refused to re-sign Howard or address the RB position at the draft. The answer, though, is no. I think you'll see Sanders get the bulk of the touches, but he won't flirt with 300. The Eagles could very well bring in a veteran back to lighten the workload, which would be smart on their part. If this does happen, don't let it shy you away from selecting Sanders at the end of the 2nd or early 3rd as even 15 touches a game in that offense is valuable. *--Meaney*

WASHINGTON REDSKINS

Key losses: LT Trent Williams, QB Colt McCoy

Key additions: LB Thomas Davis, CB Kendall Fuller, CB Ronald Darby, QB Kyle Allen

The months-long standoff with Williams finally came to a close when the Redskins traded the star tackle to the 49ers, via which the 'Skins picked up a 2020 5th-rounder and 2021 3rd-rounder.

Washington will hope that 4th-rounder Saahdiq Charles out of LSU can become a strong replacement for Williams. Colt McCoy departed for the Giants' backup job, so with the uncertain future surrounding Alex Smith (leg), they filled the backup void, and perhaps even upgraded, by acquiring Allen from Carolina.

The three biggest additions for Washington came on defense, where help was desperately needed. New HC Ron Rivera added a staple from his former Panthers defenses by signing Davis. While he can still play (122 tackles with the Chargers in 2019), his addition is likely more so for locker-room leadership. Fuller is fresh off a Super Bowl season with the Chiefs, and Rivera believes he can turn Fuller, still 25, into the team's top CB. Regardless if he is or not, he's definitely an upgrade for this secondary that also welcomes Darby, who has struggled with injuries for a while now, but should be highly motivated while playing on a 1-year deal.

Allen will support Dwayne Haskins, though he could see some starting snaps this season if Haskins doesn't step up in Year 2.

Drafted Players of Fantasy Note: DE Chase Young, RB/WR Antonio Gibson, WR Antonio Gandy-Golden

For as good as Young is, he's going to be a popular pick in all IDP leagues. The blue-chip pass rusher should have an instant impact as a fine supplier of sacks.

Gibson gives the Redskins a great weapon they can move around the offense. He primarily played WR at Memphis, but many believe he'll settle in as a RB more than anything. The truth is, he'll be a Swiss Army knife. Unfortunately, that usually doesn't equal consistent fantasy output. Gandy-Golden was drafted in the 4th round and was on a lot of offseason "sleeper" lists. In a weak Redskins WR corps, he has a great chance to carve out a real role early on.

Terry McLaurin is the name on the offense everyone is most excited about. In a breakout rookie season that saw him explode for 919 yards and 7 TDs on 58 catches, he finished 2019 as fantasy's WR29. He'll look to build on that in 2020, but Haskins will have to take his own step forward to support that goal. Haskins had some OK moments, but they were fleeting. He hasn't yet shown that he can be a franchise QB, and with a new regime in town, Haskins probably won't have a long leash before he's pulled in favor of Rivera recruit Allen.

RB Derrius Guice is a great buy-low dynasty option this offseason, and he has a chance to finally breakout in Year 3, but will still be joined by Adrian Peterson (unless Washington cuts him) and even Gibson.

Offensive Outlook: Let's be clear: The offense is only going to be as good as the quarterback. Haskins will need to take a big step forward in Year 2 to have any shot at a starting job in Year 3. There's already talk of Rivera signing free-agent QB Cam Newton at some point. Whether that happens, the fantasy success of McLaurin will hinge upon whether whoever is at QB can play with more consistency than what was seen in 2019. He'll certainly have improve last season's 31st-ranked offensive unit.

Defensive Outlook: The offense wasn't alone in craving help. The defense ranked 27th in 2019. So adding Davis, Darby, Fuller, and Young will certainly work to fix those issues. Whether it'll be good enough to give the Eagles, Giants and Cowboys fits is a completely different discussion.

2020 Outlook: The Redskins won't come close to playoff contention. In fact, they'll likely be closer to the No. 1 overall pick in 2021 with a shot at Clemson QB Trevor Lawrence than they will of a wild-card berth. Both sides of the ball have to grow, though the defense is likely closer to that goal than the offense. It doesn't help matters that the COVID-19 pandemic has prevented the Redskins players and personnel from taking part in offseason workouts, and that's an even bigger point of contention with a new coaching staff in tow.

If anyone can navigate these types of waters, however, it's Rivera. From a fantasy standpoint, McLaurin and Guice will be tasked with helping put this O on the radar. --*McConnell*

NFC NORTH

Derek Brown

CHICAGO BEARS

Key Losses: WR Taylor Gabriel, TE Trey Burton, CB Prince Amukamara, OLB Leonard Floyd, G Kyle Long, S Ha Ha Clinton-Dix, DT Nick Williams

Key Additions: TE Jimmy Graham, QB Nick Foles, S Tashaun Gipson, WR Ted Ginn, LB Robert Quinn, CB Artie Burns

The Bears lost more integral pieces on the defensive side of the ball, with the exit of two-run stoppers in Floyd and Williams and critical parts of their secondary in Clinton-Dix and Amukamara. On the offensive side of the ball, the losses weren't as substantial. Burton was a bundle of injuries and under-performance during his time in Chicago. Gabriel was never a consistent contributor. His vanishing act was more well-rehearsed than his ability to pull a rabbit out of a hat.

In Graham and Ginn, the Bears brought in names who won't be confused with cubs. It's fair to wonder if either is a starting-caliber player at this stage. Sadly, the Jaguars learned the hard way last year that Foles is not the answer at quarterback. Foles' familiarity with Matt Nagy's system, I'm sure, played a part in the beer-goggles trade Chicago executed. The majority of the remaining moves were on defense with Quinn, Gipson and Burns.

Drafted Players of Fantasy Note: TE Cole Kmet, CB Jaylon Johnson, WR Darnell Mooney

The Bears have quickly become the land of a thousand tight ends with the drafting of Kmet on top of the signing of Graham and Demetrius Harris. The likelihood of any of these additions being difference-makers is low. Graham is washed at this stage of his career. Harris is a raw part-time player. Kmet faces the uphill struggle that all rookie tight ends do in adjusting to the league.

Offensive Outlook: Regardless of who is under center come Week 1, a Bears quarterback is not the signal-caller to lead your fantasy team to the promised land. That being said, Foles and his immobility could mean good things for David Montgomery in the passing game. Montgomery already has the early downs on lockdown after rolling up the 13th most carries in the NFL last year (242). The statue-esque Foles bumped Leonard Fournette's target share from 15.9% to 21.4%. The same can happen for Montgomery this season; his receiving acumen was underutilized last year. Tarik Cohen has carved a consistent role in this offense with back-to-back seasons of a 17%+ target share.

Allen Robinson remains underappreciated in fantasy circles. Robinson was the WR8 in point-per-reception scoring last year and one of only seven wide receivers (also Michael Thomas, Keenan Allen, DeAndre Hopkins, Julian Edelman, Julio Jones and Cooper Kupp) to finish with 90+ receptions; 1,100+ receiving yards; 5+ receiving touchdowns; and a 60%+ catch rate. Anthony Miller also offers some late-round appeal after flashing his upside last year. Miller was electric after Nagy reintegrated him into the passing game more often in Weeks 11-15, finishing as the WR8 in PPR over that 5-game stretch.

Defensive Outlook: Chuck Pagano was a reliable hire last year with Vic Fangio bolting to the Broncos' HC job. The Bears still were a top-10 defense versus the run and pass. Chicago did a passable job overcoming losses in its defense, replenishing through the draft and free agency. Quinn won't help against the run but can assist in pressuring the quarterback. Johnson or Burns will have to step up alongside Kyle Fuller as a starter for the Bears to remain a top-10 unit.

2020 Outlook: The Bears' season will hinge on two critical factors: quarterback and offensive-line play. Foles and Mitchell Trubisky have had their runs of impressive football. The skill players on this team need steady, not elite play to hit their ceilings. If Trubisky or Foles can achieve that in 2020, this could be an offense with sneaky value. Montgomery's 2019 was littered with inefficient volume behind a bottom-5 offensive line. While the Bears did nothing to improve their line in the offseason, if (big if) the Chicago line can be league-average in 2020, Montgomery could have upside on volume alone.

Robinson and Miller will rely on their QB to deliver accurate and timely passes -- which Foles and Trubisky have struggled to do consistently. Robinson is the unquestioned alpha, but Miller has upside as a low-end WR2 if everything breaks right. No tight end on this roster is worth my consideration.

DETROIT LIONS

Key Losses: CB Darius Slay, DT Damon Harrison, T Ricky Wagner, DT Mike Daniels, LB Devon Kennard, CB Rashaan Melvin

Key Additions: CB Darryl Roberts, QB Chase Daniel, S Duron Harmon, WR Geronimo Allison, LB Jamie Collins, DT Danny Shelton, DT Nicholas Williams

The Lions retooled a defense that collectively was arguably a bottom-5 unit. Detroit allowed the most passing yards (4,551) and second-most total yards (6,406). Together the defense isn't immensely improved even with the additions of Roberts, Shelton, Harmon, Collins, Williams, and highly touted draft pick Jeff Okudah. Roberts and Justin Coleman are coming off atrocious 2019 seasons.

The Lions offense is going to be called upon to keep pace with the opposition if Detroit has any prayer at success. Detroit added a collection of middle-of-the-road talent to fill out the depth chart. Allison at best will back up Danny Amendola as roster filler and a big slot option. Daniel offers a steady hand behind Matthew Stafford, but Daniel cannot be expected to even keep the boat afloat in times of crisis. The defensive additions are reliable, but none move the needle as a transformative piece.

Drafted Players of Fantasy Note: RB D'Andre Swift, CB Jeff Okudah, WR Quintez Cephus, RB Jason Huntley

Detroit investing 2nd-round equity in Swift signs the death certificate of Kerryon Johnson's workhorse hope. It's difficult to argue that the Lions improved in any area through the draft; the process can more adequately be described as a series of filling self-imposed holes instead of strengthening areas of weakness. Detroit jettisons Slay to draft Okudah, loses J.D. McKissic to draft Huntley, and will conceivably mitigate picking Swift by imposing a production-limiting committee.

Offensive Outlook: The offensive output for the Lions needs a bit of context. During the 1st half of last season, Detroit was an upper-echelon offense. Before Stafford was lost to injury, the Lions were averaging 25.5 points per game, which would have finished 7th in the NFL. After losing Stafford, the offense went into the trash can, only cresting above 20 points once over the last 8 games. Stafford was QB6 in fantasy points per game over the 8-game stretch he played.

With Stafford's cast of skill players intact and fortified, he is primed to continue the high-end production this upcoming season. Stafford is one of the best values in all of fantasy football.

Swift and Johnson will form a frustrating committee, with Swift being the presumed leader. These backs in tandem are better for the offense as a whole, but ultimately, they will hinder each other in fantasy production. Kenny Golladay pulled off his best DeAndre Hopkins impression last year, continuing top-20 WR production (WR11 with Stafford, WR16 without Stafford) despite hauling in passes from Jeff Driskel and David Blough.

Marvin Jones and his enticing stat line deserve a more fleshed-out context, however: His blow-up Week 7 stat line (10 receptions, 93 yards, 4 touchdowns) heavily puffed up his numbers. With Stafford under center (Weeks 1-9), Jones turned in 16.4 fantasy points per game (WR9 in fantasy points per game), including the Week 7 barrage. Looking at Jones' production pace over his 7 games not including his monstrous outlier performance, we find a receiver that was averaging 12.65 fantasy points per game (WR32). Jones is a fine option in the later rounds of a draft and holds WR2 upside, but drafting him with any ideas or presumptions his production can reach WR1 heights is incorrect.

With the return of Danny Amendola, T.J. Hockenson is left to scuffle for underneath targets. Last year with Amendola on the field, Hockenson's target share dipped from 13.2% to 9.2%.

Defensive Outlook: The Detroit defense needs Okudah to hit the ground running, Roberts to play the best football of his career, and Coleman to bounce back. The likelihood of all these stars aligning is slim. The Lions secondary is best viewed as a unit to pick on with secondary receivers as streaming options this season. The rush defense isn't any prettier; the Lions replaced aging vets in Harrison and Daniels for middling producers in Shelton and Williams.

2020 Outlook: The Lions were playing near .500 football with Stafford under center last year. After losing Stafford, the entire team went into the tank with 8 straight losses. Stafford in the Darrell Bevell offense heavily predicated on play-action and deep passing will be among the leagues' best again for as long as he stays healthy. Golladay has a top-5 fantasy wide receiver upside in a full season paired with Stafford. Golladay's deep prowess is also underscored by him leading the NFL in targets inside the 10-yard line last season (13). If everything breaks right for the Lions, they could be sniffing 9 or 10 wins this season despite their defense. That's how good this offense could be.

GREEN BAY PACKERS

Key Losses: TE Jimmy Graham, WR Geronimo Allison, T Bryan Bulaga, CB Tramon Williams, LB Blake Martinez

Key Additions: WR Devin Funchess, T Ricky Wagner, LB Christian Kirksey

The losses of Graham and Allison leaves Green Bay with 23% of their 2019 red-zone targets up for grabs. However, for a team that looks to be moving to a run-first, run-always approach, Bulaga is the most significant loss. He's a top-10, run-blocking tackle and will be replaced by Ricky Wagner, who, at the peak of his performance, is a league-average talent.

Considering the state of the Packers' receiving depth chart, this addition list is laughable at best. Injuries and ineffectiveness have plagued Funchess over the last few seasons. He was last seen as a productive fantasy asset in 2017 when he was WR21 (PPR scoring). Funchess was the new flavor of Kelvin Benjamin that season as an inefficient producer whose value was predicated on volume and touchdowns. Neither is a given with this landing spot.

Drafted Players of Fantasy Note: RB A.J. Dillon, QB Jordan Love, TE Josiah Deguara

Aaron Rodgers remains entrenched as the Green Bay QB. Love will likely collect dust this season unless Rodgers is injured.

The Packers sunk a second-round pick into Dillon with Aaron Jones entering a contract year. This backfield could be an absolute mess with Jones, Dillon and Jamaal Williams vying for touches. Last year Williams ate into Jones' workload on early downs with 26% of the team's rushing attempts. Dillon is an early-down grinder with the size to carve out a red-zone role that would likely hinder Jones more than give Dillon standalone value.

Offensive Outlook: Rodgers' once upper-echelon ceiling has evaporated quickly over the last 2 seasons. He has lived off touchdown percentage efficiency for his entire career, but he has finished with the lowest marks of his career in that department in back-to-back seasons (4.2%, 4.6%). The volume inside the 20 was present last year as Rodgers finished 5th in red-zone passing attempts (78) and 8th in passing attempts inside the 10-yard line (36). With his passing weapons outside of Davante Adams still lacking, this trend is doubtful to change. Rodgers will likely cobble together a few "ceiling games" to reach top-12 quarterback status.

Jones finished as the overall RB2 in point-per-reception scoring last year on touchdowns and a blistering finish. Jones closed the regular season with 136.6 total yards per game over his final 4 games with 5 touchdowns. Dillon's newfound presence is concerning for Jones, who last year had the goal-line role locked down, dwarfing Williams in this department with 13 carries (7th in the NFL) to Williams' 2. Dillon could upset that stranglehold: He's a mountain of a man at 247 lbs.

Adams has minimal competition for targets in this offense and has overall WR1 fantasy upside. After returning from injury last season, Adams ranked behind only Michael Thomas in target share (33% vs. 31%). Adams' 11.3 targets per game over that 8-game stretch would have led to 182 targets over a full season (Thomas had 185 targets). Funchess and Lazard possess intriguing late-round appeal, but Adams' elite target share and the Packers' average volume (16th in pass attempts in 2019) leave them as nothing more than dart throws at best. The shiniest dart in the bag, though, is TE Jace Sternberger. Sternberger possesses the size and pass-catching ability to garner red-zone work.

Defensive Outlook: Aside from Martinez's exit, the core of the Packers defense returns this season. Green Bay fielded a top-10 pass defense in 2019, with Za'Darius Smith and Preston Smith applying the pressure, and Kevin King and Jaire Alexander locking down the secondary. The Packers rush defense was exposed for its Swiss cheese self last year. Green Bay allowed the 10th-most rushing yards (1,921) and 12th-most rushing touchdowns (15). Not much is likely to change in that area this year: Mike Pettine defenses have a long history of ranking at or near the bottom of the league in rushing stats allowed.

2020 Outlook: The Packers were not nearly as dominant as their 13 wins might've implied in 2019. The Pack played 8 teams with losing records while also winning 4 games by 5 or fewer points. The Packers draft class feels more like tossing pennies in a wishing well for 2021 than fortifying a team for a playoff run in 2020. Outside of Adams becoming a human vacuum for targets this season, the Packers offense looks like a giant question mark. Can Rodgers will himself to another top-12-QB finish? Can Jones hold off Dillon and Williams, or are HC Matt LaFleur's hijinks in the cards? Will this team flame out in spectacular fashion hurtling toward a 6-win result?

MINNESOTA VIKINGS

Key Losses: WR Stefon Diggs, DT Linval Joseph, CB Xavier Rhodes, DE Everson Griffen, G Josh Kline, CB Trae Waynes, S Andrew Sendejo, CB Mackensie Alexander, WR Laquon Treadwell, S Jayron Kearse

Key Additions: WR Tajae Sharpe, DT Michael Pierce

Diggs takes his 41% air-yard share and 21% target share to Buffalo, leaving a void in the Vikings' air attack. With the departures of Diggs and Treadwell, 110 looks are up for grabs. The Vikings are replacing a large portion of their secondary with the losses of Rhodes, Alexander, and Waynes. Two rookies (more on them in a bit) will be tossed into the Week 1 fire.

While the Vikings were 30th in passing attempts last season, they were top-10 in passing rate when trailing by 9 points or more. If the Vikings' pass defense struggles out of the gate, Kirk Cousins and his pass-catchers could see an early-season volume bump.

The Vikings signing list is the equivalent of a C.J. Ham handoff: short and disappointing. Sharpe is just another warm body in the receiver room who will be lucky to break camp. After spending the 2019 season flush against the salary cap, the Vikings left their significant moves for the NFL Draft.

Drafted Players of Fantasy Note: WR Justin Jefferson, CB Cameron Dantzler, CB Jeff Gladney, WR K.J. Osborn

Jefferson enters a Vikings passing game that saw a dip of 162 attempts from 2018 to 2019. That being said, the Vikings are in line for positive regression of volume. Jefferson and his 1st-round draft capital will slide in next to Adam Thielen as a starter in 2-wide-receiver sets. Thielen has battled hamstring, ankle, back, and calf injuries over the last 2 seasons. It's not far-fetched that Jefferson could see an extended stretch as the alpha receiver should Thielen miss games again.

Offensive Outlook: Dalvin Cook will again be the straw that stirs the drink in Minnesota. Before getting dinged up with a shoulder injury in Week 13, Cook was second to only Christian McCaffrey in fantasy points per game (23.3, PPR). Cook will reprise his role as a matchup-proof elite RB fantasy start.

Cousins has returned mid- to high-end-QB2 value in the last 2 seasons (QB18, QB13). Cousins was able to do so last year with ultra-efficiency in the TD column. In 2019, Cousins finished with the highest touchdown percentage of his 5 years as a starter (5.9%), which was also the 6th-highest mark in the league (100 or more attempts). Cousins is best viewed as a midrange QB2 with early-season streaming potential or during weeks when the betting game total creeps up.

The Vikings' pass offense will be a concentrated group with Thielen and Jefferson leading the way, while Kyle Rudolph, Irv Smith, and Cook compete for targets behind them. Rudolph and Smith accounted for 41.1% of Minnesota's red-zone targets last season. Smith is a fantastic end-of-draft stash, especially for picking teams early in the preseason. If Rudolph were to miss time, Smith has top-5 fantasy TE upside.

Defensive Outlook: Replacing Joseph and Griffen will be no small task for a Vikings defensive line that struggled at times to stop the run. Minnesota gutted its secondary, letting go of 3 of their top 4 corners. Rhodes and Waynes were roasted repeatedly last season, so the downgrades there could be minimal. Alexander, however, was a top slot corner and easily the best of the bunch. Depending on how the Vikings address his loss, streaming slot WRs versus Minnesota could be a profitable fantasy strategy.

2020 Outlook: The Vikings boast one of the best rushing attacks in the NFL with Gary Kubiak at the controls. In his 22 years as a head coach or offensive coordinator, Kubiak's offense has finished in the top 10 in rushing yards 14 times. Volume is the big question mark with the Vikings' passing options. The Minnesota pass-catchers all represent great values if the volume surpasses expectations. This concentrated passing attack can yield high-end results as the season rolls along if the dice rolls unexpectedly. The Vikings likely will continue to at least sniff a playoff berth, if not run away with the division depending on Green Bay's performance.

NFC South
Chris McConnell

ATLANTA FALCONS

Key Losses: TE Austin Hooper, RB Devonta Freeman, EDGE Vic Beasley, CB Desmond Trufant

Key Additions: RB Todd Gurley, TE Hayden Hurst, EDGE Dante Fowler

Hooper enjoyed his best season by far of his short career, proving to be a playmaker. He also enjoyed some time as the TE1 in all of fantasy, but after missing a few weeks during the season, eventually he settled in to finish the year as TE6. This earned him a large contract with the Browns, who hope Hooper's breakout season wasn't just a mirage. The Falcons hope Hurst can fill the vacancy in fine fashion. Freeman was released and remains unsigned as of publication.

Beasley heads to the Titans to try and revive his own career as a former double-digit sack specialist.

Knee issues prompted Gurley's fall from grace with the Rams. A 1-year, $5.5M deal was enough to convince a now-healthy Gurley to come home to Georgia jump-start a run game that has been lacking since the 2016 Super Bowl run. The reward clearly outweighs the risk with the team-friendly contract.

Hurst never lived up to his 1st-round draft capital in Baltimore, but his early-career injuries forced Mark Andrews into the spotlight, and Hurst wasn't able to take that next leap forward as a backup option. Now healthy and traded to Atlanta with no competition for TE targets, Hurst will have every opportunity to prove he can be one of the best young TEs in the NFL. The workload will be there, and the bigger, faster replacement for Hooper makes for an intriguing late-round TE flier.

Atlanta has needed a consistent, strong pass-rusher for years but could never seem to find it. Fowler broke out with the Rams last season and finally lived up to his 1st-round reputation, playing alongside the best DT in the league in Aaron Donald. Now, as the Falcons' most important offseason find, he gets to play with the 3rd-best DT in the NFL in Grady Jarrett, which could mean Fowler is the answer to the Falcons' prayers after many years of searching for a QB wrecking ball.

Drafted Players of Fantasy Note: CB A.J. Terrell, DL Marlon Davidson, OL Matt Hennessey

Atlanta went heavy on defense in the draft, with 4 of its 6 draft picks coming from that side of the ball. Hennessey was drafted in the 3rd round to bring further stability to the offensive trenches and eventually take over at center for Alex Mack. The two drafted players most likely to make a fantasy impact (in IDP leagues) are 1st-rounder Terrell, who'll the underachieving Trufant, and 2nd-rounder Davidson, who made a habit of wrecking SEC offensive lines for Auburn.

Offensive Outlook: A top-5 offense in both total yards and YPG in 2019, Atlanta should come close to those rankings and possibly be better in 2020, possibly coming close to the O from its 2016 Super Bowl run. That quest will start in the trenches by protecting Ryan and opening running holes for Gurley. The passing game is an essential lock to be dynamite, but bringing it all together up front is what will make the Falcons deadly on offense again this year.

If the Falcons can do this and keep their franchise signal-caller's jersey clean, the offense should have no issue humming in 2020. Julio Jones will be Julio Jones, and Calvin Ridley looks to take that next step as a top-tier young receiver. Gurley has early indications of fantasy RB2 status with high-end-RB1 upside at a huge discount in fantasy drafts. Ryan will make it all come together as another season of a top-flight QB1 is in the plans.

Defensive Outlook: This has been the Achilles' heel for Atlanta since even before the Dan Quinn era. The Falcons have not been able to find consistent pass rush from multiple players in over a decade. But look closer and you will see a defense with all the makings of the potential to blast off with the addition of Dante Fowler off the edge. A healthy Keanu Neal will bring that tough, hard-hitting attitude back to the secondary, and Neal pairing with speedy Deion Jones could be a problem for opposing offenses. But if they can't pressure the QB yet again, the defense won't be able to stop anyone.

2020 Outlook: On the surface, there's not a lot to dislike about the Falcons. The biggest problem is that even if they're able to bring everything together and play well in the trenches, the NFC South is loaded with talent and should be among the most competitive divisions in the league. The key will be to protect Ryan and stay healthy. The Falcons were quietly one of the best 3 NFC teams in the league through the final 8 games last year, going 6-2 overall (4-0 on the road) and closing out the season with a 4-game winning streak. If they can carry that momentum from the second half into 2020, they will be competing for a wild-card berth with an expanded playoff field. If they can't, not only will they be sitting toward the top half of the draft order again, but they will also be in the market for a new head coach and general manager.

CAROLINA PANTHERS

Key Losses: QB Cam Newton, LB Luke Kuechly, DL Mario Addison, DL Vernon Butler, CB James Bradberry, TE Greg Olsen

Key Additions: HC Matt Rhule, QB Teddy Bridgewater, WR Robby Anderson

New regime, new rules: Newton was cut and remains without a team as of our publication. Perhaps the most shocking news of the offseason happened with Kuechly's retirement, and now the Panthers will have to find a way to replace the production of arguably the best linebacker in the NFL. Addison and his consistency (9 sacks last year) head to Buffalo. Butler joins Addison with the Bills after setting career highs in sacks, QB hits, and tackles for a loss in 2019. Carolina will have to replace its top CB after losing Bradberry to the Giants on a 3-year, $45M deal. Ian Thomas takes over at tight end for Olsen, who joins the Seahawks.

Rhule, the former Baylor HC, replaces Ron Rivera (now with the Redskins), bringing in a new offensive philosophy and new QB. Carolina handed Bridgewater $63 million over 3 years to be the new triggerman. The Panthers want to surround him with as many quality weapons as possible, so they also went shopping at WR to purchase the services of lid-lifter Robby Anderson on a 2-year, $20 million deal.

Drafted Players of Fantasy Note: DT Derrick Brown, DE Yetur Gross-Matos

All 7 picks were on the defensive side of the ball. There may be some surprising IDP value from each of these guys. Gross-Matos has an incredible motor off the edge, while Brown is a monster up the middle.

Offensive Outlook: The Panthers finished 19th in total offense in 2019, and in what should be a faster, faster-tempo offense, we should see them battle to top that in 2020. They certainly have the weapons to do it and with what should be a more consistent QB under center, the Panthers offense has all it needs to surprise everyone this season ... if they can keep Christian McCaffrey healthy and the electricity that keeps this offense alive.

Even in this spread offense, Bridgewater is still likely to only garner backend-QB2 value. He's a better real-life addition than fantasy gem, and he should deliver merely a safe, consistent, and unspectacular season. McCaffrey will be the most popular No. 1 pick in fantasy drafts, and for good reason. He'll have no problem remaining a top-5 RB1 in fantasy, especially in Rhule's RB-friendly offense. We all expect D.J. Moore to take that next step to full-fledged fantasy WR1 status, but can Teddy help get him there? The only thing for sure is that Robby Anderson, Curtis Samuel and Ian Thomas shouldn't be relied on for consistent, weekly fantasy relevance. Each is slated to be a better DFS play than season-long option.

Defensive Outlook: The defense is starkly young and will likely not be good in 2020. In 2019, they were near the bottom of the league in total defense. Having lost its top CB and relying on too much youth, the Panthers' D doesn't look to have many positives in store for stopping the opponent.

2020 Outlook: The Panthers seem to be the best wager to finish last in a loaded NFC South, considering they have to face Drew Brees, Matt Ryan and Tom Brady twice. The Saints, Falcons and Buccaneers have all improved their defenses. Carolina is also the only team in the division with a 1st-year head coach. It doesn't help matters that the COVID-19 pandemic has kept the Panthers from gathering at team facilities and getting in those ever-important workouts and practices, with everyone learning a new offensive system. For most of the year, I'd expect this to be a competitive team in totality, though, which should give the fantasy owners rostering their players some success -- and Panthers fans a silver lining for the future, if nothing else.

NEW ORLEANS SAINTS

Key Losses: LB A.J. Klein, QB Teddy Bridgewater

Key Additions: WR Emmanuel Sanders, QB Jameis Winston, DB Malcolm Jenkins

Bridgewater headlines the offseason losses as he heads to the division rival Panthers to replace Cam Newton at QB. merely helped in multiple areas of the LB corps and won't be difficult to replace; Klein's snaps totals were all over the place over his 3 years in New Orleans.

Jameis Winston comes to town to replace Bridgewater. After finding zero interest on the open market as a starter and little as a backup, Jameis signed on for only $1.1M on a one-year deal. If Drew Brees were to go down, the difference in pay might tell you Taysom Hill (on a new 2-year, $21 million pact) will slide in as the starter, but Winston would still likely be the favorite to lead both QBs in snaps under center.

Sanders comes over from the 49ers to give Brees and Co. another quality weapon on offense. Sanders figures to slide right into the slot role and take over second place on the targets totem pole ahead of Jared Cook and Tre'Quan Smith.

Jenkins returns to New Orleans and will replace elite run-stopper Von Bell, now with the Bengals.

Drafted Players of Fantasy Note: LB Zack Baun, TE Adam Trautman

The Saints were able to steal a 1st-round talent in Wisconsin alum Baun, who figures to pay immediate dividends on a defense looking to replace the departed A.J. Klein. He'll be a popular pick in rookie IDP drafts.

Trautman likely won't see much valuable playing time in 2020 a 3rd-round pick competing for scraps behind starter Cook. But he does profile as a player to draft and stash on dynasty taxi squads in hopes of an impact in 2021 and beyond.

Offensive Outlook: The Saints finished 9th in total yards and YPG in 2019. Brees threw the ball only 378 times, low for his standards, and for under 3,000 passing yards for the first time since 2003. I fully expect a bit of an uptick in passing attempts this year with Sanders in tow. I'd also expect a better fantasy finish for Brees than last year's QB21

New Orleans' biggest fantasy water-cooler talk will go to Sanders. Coming over from the 49ers, Sanders is already looking like a better 2020 option after his up-and-down 2019 with Denver and San Francisco. With Thomas and Cook around to help open things up, Sanders should have a ton of free releases and see plenty of targets this year. He makes for a solid WR3 fantasy option with WR2 upside in PPR leagues.

Thomas should once again be among the elite WR1 options in fantasy, if not *the* top name. Alvin Kamara's star may not be *as* shiny as it once was, but he'll be a 2nd-round pick at worst and should have no problem once again churning out RB1/high-end RB2 production.

Cook could disappoint now that Sanders is in the fold. Don't expect TE1 production this season from last year's TE7. And yeah, lock in Brees for another stellar campaign and a rebound in aerial attempts.

Defensive Outlook: A 2019 top-11 defense suffers a big loss in Bell but replaces him with 32-year-old Jenkins. 2018 1st-round pick Marcus Davenport was lost for the season with a bad foot injury but should be ready in plenty of time for the 2020 season. The DE will be relied upon heavily after having 6 sacks and 31 tackles in 13 games last year. The defense should once again be solid, but if New Orleans can elevate higher into the top 10, this is going to be a tough team to beat overall.

2020 Outlook: The Saints will likely be the favorites once again to take the NFC South crown, even with Tom Brady joining a Bucs team with a ton of hype. New Orleans' offense will continue to be the story, and the Saints will need to keep it going in a loaded division with Brady and Matt Ryan nipping at their heels. Regardless, it's almost impossible to think of the Saints as anything other than a playoff team with strong Super Bowl aspirations, and they are set up well to once again be in that mix.

TAMPA BAY BUCCANEERS

Key Losses: QB Jameis Winston, WR Breshad Perriman

Key Additions: QB Tom Brady, TE Rob Gronkowski

Okay, so they may not be "key" losses, but nonetheless Winston and Perriman are the two biggest names leaving the roster. Winston arguably did more harm than good for an offense that was always just waiting for that last piece to the puzzle (more on that in a minute). Without him, the offense should now be in much better shape to compete in the NFC, with significantly fewer turnovers. Speaking of waiting, we've been waiting on Perriman to have more than 600 receiving yards in a season since he was drafted by the Ravens in 2016. That happened with the Bucs last season, and he ended on a 5-game tear where he likely helped a lot of owners win their fantasy title.

Remember that final piece to the puzzle I mentioned? Yeah, Brady could be it. That's not all: Gronk is back. The Bucs signed Brady to a 2-year, $50M deal, and he should provide much more stability under center than Winston ever did. While Gronk seemed happy with retirement, it seemed all he REALLY wanted was to play with Brady outside of New England. He'll get his wish, and it will be another Tampa Bay upgrade; as long as he stays active, Gronk should pay much bigger dividends than O.J. Howard ever did, considering his chemistry with Brady.

Drafted Players of Fantasy Note: RB Ke'Shawn Vaughn, OT Tristan Wirfs, WR Tyler Johnson, RB Raymond Calais

While Wirfs won't have a fantasy impact himself, he will have the task of helping with Brady's protection. He could directly help give Brady more time to throw, on average.

Vaughn adds pressure to Ronald Jones' job and could be thrust into the starting role if Jones doesn't show quick, vast improvement in this revamped offense.

The talented Johnson should help fill the slight void left by Perriman but likely won't have much fantasy relevance in his rookie season barring injuries ahead of him. Calais is a space player who will need to get more experience with receiving to have much value; right now, he's a deep dynasty stash.

Offensive Outlook: The addition of Brady shouldn't go understated. Fewer turnovers means more offensive opportunities. Brady finished 2019 as a QB1 in fantasy (QB12) with 24 TDs and 8 INTs. The TDs should easily go up in a more aggressive, downfield offense than what he played under in New England. It's hard to ask Chris Godwin to be better than he was last year (fantasy WR2 overall), and everyone should expect regression there, though WR1 status is still easily within reach. Mike Evans was WR4 last year in PPG but overall finished as WR15, so don't be surprised if Evans has one of his best seasons of his career now that he finally has some competence under center.

Gronkowski is a big question mark for a couple of reasons: Does he still have it? How will the offense utilize him? Bruce Arians' offenses have not been kind to tight ends since Heath Miller, and what will happen with Howard? If Howard doesn't get traded (he was rumored pre-draft to be on the block), then the waters are bit murkier for Gronk to have a huge fantasy season. (You still have to factor in Cameron Brate's presence, as well.) A rotation at TE is also likely given that they'd like to keep Gronk as healthy as possible. On the other hand, they could also want to squeeze as much out of him while he's still playing. The TE position is not likely to produce a great TE1 season unless Howard is dealt, which now looks unlikely. Gronk should be treated as a solid TE2 candidate, however.

The run game with incumbent starter Jones and draftee Vaughn could hold a lot of fantasy relevance. Both should be owned, but while the hype around Vaughn's landing spot is driving up his price in both rookie and startup drafts, people need to keep in mind that "RoJo" is likely to start the season as head of the backfield and get the first crack at lead duties, though he undoubtedly has a short leash. Neither Jones nor Vaughn should be considered a reliable week-to-week fantasy starter.

With Brady, Gronkowski, a revamped OL, and RB help added to the Godwin-Evans WR combo -- arguably the league's best -- this offense should be among the NFL's best. They will not struggle to score points and could repeat last year's finish as 3rd in the NFL in total offense. However, we should keep in mind that they are likelier to face fewer deficits than they did last season. That means a tad less throwing and a bit more rushing. Nonetheless, Brady and the Bucs should easily have a top-10 NFL offense.

Defensive Outlook: The defense is in great shape to improve from last year. 2019 saw this unit give up the 4th-most points in the entire league. That should change rapidly this year with what is regarded as one of the best front-7 groups, including sack machine Shaquil Barrett and linebackers Devin White and Lavonte David. It's not going to be easy getting the best of this defense, if key players are healthy.

2020 Outlook: The Bucs, like the other 3 division teams, will be slugging it out in what should be the toughest division. This team is suddenly injected with a ton of experience and a winning mentality. The defense should pace the division, and the offense could do the same. There's not a lot to dislike about this team, and as long as Brady is healthy and the O-line can protect him, the sky really is the limit. Making the playoffs won't be easy, but with an expanded postseason field and after an offseason spent reloading, the Bucs should be playing meaningful football deep into December -- including Super Bowl aspirations, even in a strong division.

NFC WEST

Matt Franciscovich

ARIZONA CARDINALS

Key Losses: RB David Johnson

Key Additions: WR DeAndre Hopkins

In arguably the biggest blockbuster transaction of the entire offseason, the Cardinals made waves when they swapped Johnson to the Texans for the All-Pro Hopkins (with picks involved.) Johnson was all but phased out of the Arizona backfield last year with the arrival (and statistical explosion) of Kenyan Drake. Hopkins comes to an Arizona offense on the rise with second-year QB Kyler Murray looking to take another step forward after a big rookie campaign. Hopkins should benefit from the fast-paced offense the Cardinals run and should dominate targets from Murray all year.

Drafted Players of Fantasy Note: LB/S Isaiah Simmons, RB Eno Benjamin

Arizona didn't add much in terms of skill-position (or fantasy-relevant) players in the draft, save for this 7th-rounder. Benjamin, a small-ish and elusive running back from Arizona State, should start the season as the RB3 behind Drake and Chase Edmonds, and he isn't likely to play more than a low-volume change-of-pace role.

Simmons won't single-handedly make Arizona's defense more trustworthy for fantasy purposes, but the versatile Clemson alum should at least give them more potential to register takeaways. Fantasy streamers could have a smidge more confidence in the right matchup.

Offensive Outlook: With one full season under his belt, Murray is positioned for an incredible fantasy season. He posted a 20:12 TD:INT as a rookie, so he has a ton of room to improve. He also rushed for 544 yards (2nd-most among QBs) and 4 TDs. The arrival of Hopkins only adds fuel to the fire that Murray's value is going to skyrocket. Veteran Larry Fitzgerald led the Cardinals in receiving last season with 109 targets (75-804-4), and Christian Kirk saw 107 looks that he converted into 68-709-3. Hopkins is sure to soak up at least 100 targets of his own, and Fitzgerald could be the odd man out given his age.

In the backfield, Kenyan Drake averaged 18.9 touches per game as the overall QB4 in the Cardinals final eight contests to end last season. He'll kick off the year as an RB1 in fantasy and his versatility should keep him on the field for all three downs, which only pads his fantasy value.

Defensive Outlook: Considering the Cardinals had one of the worst defenses in 2019, there's nowhere to go but up. Simmons brings versatility and speed to a defense that allowed more yards to opposing teams than any other unit in the league last season. Arizona still has a pair of veteran All-pros in cornerback Patrick Peterson and EDGE rusher Chandler Jones. The Cardinals defense isn't as good as the 49ers', but it could definitely be better than the Rams' and Seahawks'. After a tough Week 1 clash with San Francisco, Arizona has a favorable draw of the Redskins, Lions, Panthers and Jets in Weeks 2-5.

2020 Outlook: The Cardinals didn't rank highly in any significant offensive category a season ago, but it was Kliff Kingsbury's first year as an NFL head coach, and he delivered the team's best record (5-9-1) since 2017. Murray also set franchise rookie records for the most pass yards and pass TDs.

By all accounts, you're going to want a piece -- or multiple pieces -- of this rising squad on your fantasy roster this season. Early ADP data shows Hopkins coming off draft boards as the WR2 overall, Murray slated as QB6, and Drake at RB23; Drake is criminally undervalued, though his value is creeping up. The hype is real, and it'll be exciting to see how Arizona fits into the NFC West pecking order.

LOS ANGELES RAMS

Key Losses: RB Todd Gurley, WR Brandin Cooks, LB Cory Littleton, DC Wade Phillips, S Eric Weddle, EDGE Dante Fowler Jr., LB Clay Matthews

Key Additions: None

After a season marred by mysterious low usage attributed to an alleged arthritic condition in his knee, Los Angeles parted ways with former fantasy superstar Gurley (now with the Falcons). Gurley single-handedly won fantasy championships for his owners back in 2017, but his heavy volume over the years has taken its toll, and though he still managed 14 total touchdowns last season, he's coming off a 3.8 yards-per-carry average and the lowest rushing total of his career (223 att., 857 yards). That's still a huge amount of rush attempts, but it was obvious the Rams were closely managing his workload on a weekly basis. His departure creates a potential committee approach for 2020.

The team also traded Cooks to the Texans, opening up additional receiving opportunities for Cooper Kupp, Robert Woods and perhaps Tyler Higbee and Josh Reynolds. Cooks' fantasy value faded last season as he dealt with more concussion issues (started 11 games with a 72/583/2 line).

Drafted Players of Fantasy Note: RB Cam Akers, WR Van Jefferson

Akers is an elite athlete and an all-around versatile back who can play all three downs if called upon. He'll have to beat out Darrell Henderson and Malcolm Brown for the lead role, but he's perfectly capable.

Jefferson will have to fight for playing time with Kupp, Woods and Reynolds all ahead of him in the WR pecking order. For redraft leagues, he's nothing more than waiver-wire fodder to start the year.

Offensive Outlook: Jared Goff suffered through an extremely rough midseason rough patch for fantasy production in 2019 (4 single-digit fantasy point totals between Weeks 6-12) but came on strong to close out the year. He finished the season as the QB13 overall with a 22:16 TD:INT, and Goff threw for 4,638 yards on the 2nd-most pass attempts in the NFL (626).

Because the fantasy position is so deep, Goff is QB16 in early ADP data, and outside of 2-QB leagues, he's not worth a look until you need a streamer. At that point, he's only viable in favorable matchups (preferably at home).

Kupp (94-1,161-10) is coming off a 134-target season as fantasy's WR4 overall, though he went through a bit of a drought statistically that coincided with Goff's aforementioned struggles. Kupp should again be a top-10 fantasy WR at worst and should repeat his 10-touchdown campaign. Woods (90/1,134/2) posted his 2nd-straight 1,000-yard season but found the end zone just twice in 2019. He still put up top-25 numbers at his position, and believe it or not, he still has room to grow with Cooks out of the picture.

The Rams backfield could be a bit muddled until we see a leader emerge in camp or during the preseason. As mentioned above, Akers could easily bring the most value to fantasy owners from this backfield as his versatile 3-down upside could keep him on the field. But Brown and Henderson are sure to chip away at some of Akers' potential touches. Don't expect any of these backs to see the 200+ rush attempts that Gurley provided in past seasons.

TE Tyler Higbee also blossomed ahead of Gerald Everett last year, leading the NFL with 522 receiving yards over the final 5 weeks of the regular season.

Defensive Outlook: The Rams defense wasn't very good last year, but they have game-wrecker Aaron Donald on the defensive line. Phillips is no longer coordinator and is replaced by the unproven Brandon Staley, Denver's linebackers coach last year. The departure of Weddle, Littleton, Fowler and Matthews makes way for opportunity for younger players, which could result in some defensive growing pains.

2020 Outlook: The Rams hired new coordinators on both sides of the ball, including the aforementioned Staley on defense and Kevin O'Connell on offense. O'Connell spent last season as the Redskins offensive coordinator and has a lot more to work with in 2020 than he did last year.

If the team wants to bounce back after a disappointing season, Goff will need to carry over his momentum from late last year. The team needs to be smarter with the run game; it was almost like LA played scared with Gurley. The defense definitely has some question marks following a veteran exodus, but the Rams' schedule for the 1st half of the season isn't too intimidating on paper. They have matchups against the Giants, Redskins, Bears and Dolphins in the first 8 weeks.

You'll still want to roster the Rams receivers. Higbee squarely deserves consideration as a top-10 fantasy tight end. Akers will be a hot commodity as a rookie sleeper.

SAN FRANCISCO 49ERS

Key Losses: WR Emmanuel Sanders, RB Matt Breida, WR Marquise Goodwin, T Joe Staley

Key Additions: LT Trent Williams, WR Travis Benjamin

Sanders (66-869-5) leaves behind a San Francisco WR-leading 97 targets, most of which will fall into Deebo Samuel's lap. Samuel is looking to take a leap in his second pro season after a hugely successful rookie year.

Breida was traded to Miami during the NFL Draft. Breida, who led the 49ers in rushing in 2018, was part of a backfield committee last season. He popped early in the year but fell off late due to ankle injuries and the emergence of Raheem Mostert. Breida (123-623-1) was one of 3 San Francisco backs to pile up 500+ rushing yards last season, and his departure releases 123 carries to the backs who remain.

The team also replaced speedster Goodwin with deep-threat Travis Benjamin, but he's unlikely to have reliable fantasy value outside of a 1- or 2-game spike.

Washington finally found a suitor for Williams, who replaces Joe Staley and fortifies an already great O-line.

Drafted Players of Fantasy Note: WR Brandon Aiyuk

The Arizona State product was the 25th overall pick in the 2020 draft, and he could immediately step into a starting role in the 49ers receiving corps. Aiyuk (5'11", 205 lbs.) piled up 1,192 receiving yards and 8 touchdowns as a senior and averaged a ridiculous 11.1 yards after the catch. He could slot in as SF's WR2 behind Samuel if he can prove he's capable of expanding his route tree. He's likely not a player you should be targeting in redraft leagues but is a name to monitor on the inseason waiver wire.

Offensive Outlook: The San Francisco run game is where the most fantasy value lies. The 49ers boasted the No. 2 overall rushing offense last season, averaging 31.1 attempts per game, 144 rush yards per game, and totaling 23 rushing scores as a unit. Unfortunately for fantasy owners, the RBBC was a bit of a headache last year. Between Mostert, Breida, Tevin Coleman and goal-line vulture Jeff Wilson, it was difficult to predict which back would be most productive week-to-week. But Mostert emerged late in the season as the go-to, and he proved his value during the postseason posing a combined 41-carry, 278-yard, 5-TD line in the NFC Championship and Super Bowl. He's extremely undervalued as the RB36, according to FantasyFootballCaluclator.com's ADP data, though that value is increasing by the day. Coleman is still lurking, too, and knowing how coach Kyle Shanahan rolls, the former Falcon will probably get significant playing time of his own.

The team's passing attack obviously relies on Jimmy Garoppolo's ability to connect with his weapons downfield, the most valuable being George Kittle. The tight end became the 4th player in 49ers history to have back-to-back seasons with 1,000+ receiving yards (Jerry Rice, Terrell Owens, Anquan Boldin) and set the single-season record for receiving yards by a tight end in 2018 with 1,377. He's bound to be the first TE off most draft boards this season (it's a coin flip between Kittle and Travis Kelce).

The aforementioned Samuel enters his 2nd season as a pro, where he'll look to take a significant leap forward from his already successful rookie campaign. Samuel posted a 57-802-3 line on 81 targets in 2019 and proved himself as a key playmaker in this offense. Sanders' departure leaves 97 targets up for grabs, so Samuel is primed for a big year.

Defensive Outlook: Last season, the 49ers ranked 1st in passing defense and 2nd overall in yards allowed per play, total defense and 3rd-down defense. The San Francisco defensive line was arguably the NFL's best for 2019, and the unit absolutely wreaked havoc on opponents. San Fran traded away DeForest Buckner. Still, the team immediately filled the gap in the draft, picking up defensive tackle Javon Kinlaw with the 14th overall pick and adding explosiveness to an already dominant defensive line. This defense should remain the best -- not only in the NFC west, but in the NFL.

2020 Outlook: The 49ers are moving forward with 2 young wideouts in Samuel and Aiyuk to support the passing game, along with Kittle at tight end. With Mostert and Coleman in the backfield, this offense has more than enough firepower to make another postseason run. Add to it an already dominant defense and what looks to be a pretty easy schedule early on, and you can see why it's a good idea to target 49ers players on both sides of the ball in fantasy drafts.

SEATTLE SEAHAWKS

Key Losses: WR Josh Gordon (indefinite suspension)

Key Additions: RB Carlos Hyde, WR Phillip Dorsett, TE Greg Olsen

Despite teases of them bringing Marshawn Lynch back, the Seahawks instead grabbed Hyde from the free-agent pile as a complement to Chris Carson and a fill-in for Rashaad Penny, who's likely starting the season on IR. Hyde relies heavily on volume and won't eat much into Carson's lead. Plus, he'll have someone else with whom he'll share secondary touches. (More below.)

Dorsett brings elite speed. When combining his deep abilities with QB Russell Wilson's deep-ball accuracy and ability to keep plays alive with his feet, the Dorsett pickup makes a ton of sense. (Wilson had the highest deep-ball percentage last year, according to NextGenStats, with 16.8%.) Dorsett should take some pressure off Tyler Lockett to do it all and should complement D.K. Metcalf nicely.

Though given Seattle's run-first tendencies, opportunities could be limited. Though Olsen could emerge as a weekly fantasy option at a position that lacks certainty beyond the top tier, his best days are behind him. Wilson targeted his tight ends 97 times last year, so opportunity could tilt Olsen's way, depending on the health of Will Dissly (Achilles') to start the year.

Drafted Players of Fantasy Note: RB DeeJay Dallas

The 144th overall pick, Dallas enters a crowded, but injury-prone RB room. Dallas is a versatile back who projects a dynamic 3rd-down pass catcher. Seattle wanted to replace the skill set of C.J. Prosise, who has seemingly been injured since he entered the league.

Offensive Outlook: Wilson is coming off draft boards as a top-5 QB and has finished as a top-3 QB in 2 of the past 3 seasons (QB1, QB9 and QB3, respectively). He's once again blessed with talented receivers in Metcalf (WR22 ADP), Lockett (WR15 ADP), Dorsett and Olsen. Chris Carson should be healthy and will be complemented by Hyde and Dallas.

Carson (hip) and Rashaad Penny (knee) both landed on IR late last season. Carson is expected to be ready for Week 1, while Penny is set to start the year on the PUP list. Lynch's status with the team remains unknown, but he could add some much-needed experience and depth to the backfield in a pinch. The 34-year-old is not the same Beast Mode he once was, but he can still push a pile forward.

Even if this backfield again offers fantasy headaches, it should again be productive; Seattle was a top-5 rushing offense last season that averaged 30.1 rush attempts per game and combined for 15 rushing touchdowns (3 by QB Russell Wilson).

Defensive Outlook: Seattle boasted a top-5 turnover differential last year but struggled on defense otherwise. They allowed 381.6 yards per game, a bottom-10 rank. The unit also averaged 24.9 points against per game, ranking 11th-worst in the league.

As of publication, the team has left defensive end Jadeveon Clowney available in free agency. Linebacker Bobby Wagner, one of the best tacklers in the entire league, reunites with defensive end Bruce Irvin, who left Seattle after the 2015 season. This duo could shake things up, but the jury is still out on just how improved the Seattle defense will be.

2020 Outlook: Wilson is a top-5 QB, and early ADP data has him coming off the board late in Round 5. Given the depth at WR, Lockett feels overvalued at his current Round 3 ADP, while Metcalf feels about right at his late-Round 4 ADP. If healthy, Carson (RB13 ADP) should be the primary back in a RBBC that will likely see Hyde and Dallas split complementary assignments. (Neither is an exciting draft-day target, though.) Though the Seahawks have the offensive pieces to contend in the NFC West, the division is one of the most competitive in the entire league.

Chapter 14

Primer for Daily Fantasy Sports (DFS)

Eliot Crist

"Gone are the days when your goal is
to just play the best players and let the chips fall where they may."

WHAT IS DFS?

Daily Fantasy Sports, or DFS, is a fantasy sports game hosted on different sites such as DraftKings, FanDuel, FantasyDraft, SuperDraft, and more. You are assigned roster spots to fill out with a team salary cap, and it is your job to assemble the best team possible within your constraints.

DFS has evolved over the years. Gone are the days when your goal is to just play the best players and let the chips fall where they may. Now, we focus on contest selection, ownership percentages, leverage plays, and advanced algorithms. The competition improves every year as millions of dollars are won each week.

Each site has its own rules and twists on the action in the form of unique contests, payout structures, rake (fee taken by the host site to run a contest), and prize pools. DraftKings rewards a point for each reception (PPR), while FanDuel is half-point PPR. FantasyDraft gives you two flex spots. SuperDraft has multipliers. (In SuperDraft, you can decide whether it's better to use the top running backs, at their actual point values, instead of lower-tiered backs, who'll have their output multiplied by 1.6).

This can all be intimidating to a new player, but that does not mean all hope is lost. There are places who can help like at fadethenoise.com, where you can find my work, alongside advice from people who have won millions! Before you get the help, let's learn some basics.

CONTEST SELECTION

Cash Games

Cash games are considered safer games: A higher percentage of the field wins money, but the prize pool is flat. These game types include 50/50s, double-ups, head-to-heads, and three-man games.

50/50 games are where half the people win money, half the people lose. In double-ups, 45% of people double their money, while 55% lose. Head-to-head is where your team must beat a single team, while in three-mans, you compete with two other people to come out with a bigger prize.

The goal of cash games is to slowly build your bankroll over the course of the season. You can compete in 10-person double-ups or 500-person double-ups and study which contests fare better for you. I personally have found the most success in three-man games. The win rate needed for profit is much lower, but the scores don't tend to be much higher. The complaint with cash games is how good the field has gotten and how similar teams now are, so while a lineup might contain nine players, one or two players can make or break your entire week.

Cash Game Strategy

Typically, you can ignore a player's ownership rate (percentage of teams picking him in a contest) in cash games. Though you look for the ceiling in GPP/tournament formats (more on this shortly), you look for a high floor in cash games. Your goal is not to finish first, but to finish in the green, so taking that highly volatile receiver is best left for tournaments.

In cash, focus on who is getting the most volume. What follows is opportunity is fantasy points. Build a nice blend of floor and ceiling around workhorse backs, high-volume receivers, and quarterbacks with rushing upside.

I mentioned at the start that you can typically throw out player ownership in cash games, but I'll offer two exceptions. One is the cash-game block. This is when a late-week injury has left a player completely mispriced as a backup, now set to see 20 touches at near minimum price. He will be heavily rostered, and even if you don't like him, you play him just to see if he does anything to completely destroy you. Remember, we don't win more for coming in first, our goal is just to "cash."

The other example is the late-game pivot, likely the least utilized tool in a DFS game. On both major sites, DraftKings and FanDuel, a player is locked into your lineup when his game starts. While most games start at 1 p.m. ET, the few games at 4 p.m. leave opportunities to change your lineup. Maybe the Cowboys play the Packers and everyone is playing Ezekiel Elliott, including you. However, one of your studs had a horrible game, and you are behind the field. You know people ahead of you are playing Elliott, so why leave him in the lineup? Instead, pivot from Elliott to his opponent, Aaron Jones. While Jones might be the lower-projected player, this swap keeps your lineup "alive" (raising your ceiling by separating yourself from the majority).

Tournaments/GPPs

You will often hear tournaments called GPPs (guaranteed prize pools). This means that the tournament does not have to fill in order for the prize pool to be paid out. When a GPP doesn't fill, that is called overlay, which while rare is worth hunting late on Sunday mornings. Why is an overlay worth the hunt? Unlike cash games, these contests are more difficult to win money: About 17-20% of the field finishes in the green. Therefore, if only 90% of the tournament is filled, a higher percentage of people finish in the money.

Contest selection for your strategy type is key when determining tournaments to play. Single-entry? 3-max? 20-max? 150-max? Each number is reflective on how many teams you can enter in that contest. If you just want to play a few lineups, stick to single entry and three-max tournaments. You don't want your single team to compete with players creating 150 total lineups. That is a losing strategy. People too often chase the top prize; looking at the payout structure is just as important. You don't want to finish 5th and win scraps. Target a well-balanced payout structure before entering a tournament.

GPP Strategy

A couple paragraphs on GPP strategy will not be enough, but they're a good start. Your goal in a tournament is not to cash, but to finish top-10 and ultimately win. This is how you turn your $100 into $10,000 in a matter of just a few hours. Be different. Correlate your lineup. Understand how many people you're trying to defeat. Ownership rate plays a big role in tournament-lineup construction. Identify which players will be "chalk": likely popular selections. Even if he is a good player, sometimes it's smart to pivot to the guy who'll be owned at only, say, 5% in the same price range as the chalk. Even if the largely owned player has higher upside and a higher projection, if the lower-owned guy has a better output, you might've just moved ahead of 25% of the field.

Just because someone is largely owned, doesn't mean you can't play them; there are other ways to be different. this is where correlation comes in. If Patrick Mahomes is the chalk, adding Tyreek Hill to your lineup makes you different. However, a quarterback-receiver stack is one of the most popular DFS strategies, for good reason, so it will be more complex than that. Maybe Mahomes and Hill are chalk because they are playing the Panthers' horrendous secondary. Moving off Hill to Travis Kelce and running it back with Carolina wideout D.J. Moore has turned your "chalk Mahomes and Hill stack" into a more unique build in a popular game.

In fact, running back your offensive stack with a player on the other team gives you even more correlation. Often, for one team to hit their offensive ceiling, someone on the other team has to have a big enough game to push them. The more people in your tournament, the more creative you should try and be with each lineup. For example, if you are trying to beat 100 people, go ahead and play Mahomes and Hill, but if you are trying to beat 100,000 people, you may want to go Mahomes, Kelce, Mecole Hardman, and Moore. You need to be different to even have a shot at the top prize.

POSITION STRATEGY

Quarterback

The quarterback pricing has become flatter as the years have gone on. Gone are the days where you can save $2,500 off the top option for a player in just a tier lower. When I look for quarterbacks, I am looking for (1) the highest projected game totals from betting lines, (2) the worst secondaries, (3) opposing offenses who can push the pace of the game, and, most importantly, (4) rushing upside. Rushing upside is gold for quarterbacks, yet people are still fighting this strategy. Adding 40 rushing yards and a ground touchdown is the equivalent to 250 passing yards. Despite having never thrown for 300 yards (you get a 3-point bonus on DK for that), Josh Allen averages 18.9 DraftKings points per game, due to his rushing upside. Give me quarterbacks with rushing upside or give me death in DFS.

Running Back

Running back is the most volume-dependent position. Snaps and weighted opportunity are king. In PPR scoring, a target is worth 2.8 times as much as a carry, so we don't want to just talk about total touches. We must weight adjusted value to the touches, which gives us weighted opportunity. It is hard for a guy who touches the ball 25 times to have a bad fantasy day, and while every once in a while, the guy with five carries will have multiple touchdowns, chasing that is a fool's errand. Find guys who will stay on the field regardless of down and distance or game script while commanding work near the goal line.

Wide Receiver

Embrace variance. A wide receiver's volume is so much less predictable, and a 20% owned receiver is much more likely to bust than a 20% owned back. The receiver position is often the best way to stack games when you are trying to catch lightning in a bottle and have multiple pieces in a shootout. While getting the game wrong can kill a lineup, getting a game right can lead to a GPP takedown. When figuring out the best way to attack the position on a weekly basis, I am looking for air yards (yards downfield from the line of scrimmage on a receiving target), market share, matchups, and expected ownership.

Tight End

This position rarely kills you. While there are plenty of receivers who will score 20-plus points on any given week, the tight end position has maybe three guys with that kind of upside. If all three fail to reach their ceilings that week and you play Darren Fells, who caught three passes for 30 yards on a minimum salary, you are well ahead of the curve. The flow chart gets smashed but works well for tight ends. Find the cheapest plays in the best matchups with any kind of volume floor.

Defense/Special Teams

I am looking to target cheap defenses who can get pressure on quarterbacks. Pressure leads to sacks and, even better, turnovers, which leads to defensive scoring opportunities. A defense's entire day can be flipped on a defensive touchdown, and while they are the most random event in fantasy, playing defenses who get pressure is the best way to chase them. I like to target D/STs facing bad quarterbacks and, just as importantly, bad offensive lines. I typically look to pay down at the position; the pricier defenses often are prone to busting. The "points allowed" stat rarely moves the needle outside of a shutout, so without a defensive touchdown, the top D/ST can outscore a middle-of-the-pack defense by just a few points. The often significant salary saved by choosing a midrange-or-lower defense can often be put to better use at running back or receiver. D/ST is almost always my last piece of lineup-building.

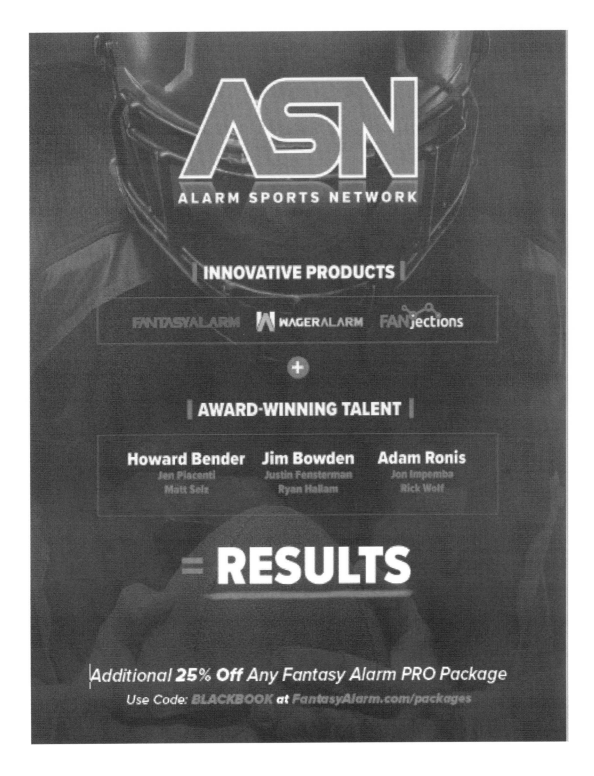

Made in the USA
Coppell, TX
16 June 2020